LIVING BEYOND

Making Sense of Near Death Experiences

IVAN RUDOLPH

Foreword by Captain Dale Black

Copyright © 2015 Ivan Rudolph.

All rights reserved. No part of this book may be used or reproduced by any means, graphic, electronic, or mechanical, including photocopying, recording, taping or by any information storage retrieval system without the written permission of the author except in the case of brief quotations embodied in critical articles and reviews.

Author photo credit for Cornelis.

This book is a work of non-fiction. Unless otherwise noted, the author and the publisher make no explicit guarantees as to the accuracy of the information contained in this book and in some cases, names of people and places have been altered to protect their privacy.

Scripture taken from the Holy Bible, NEW INTERNATIONAL VERSION®. Copyright © 1973, 1978, 1984 by Biblica, Inc. All rights reserved worldwide. Used by permission. NEW INTERNATIONAL VERSION® and NIV® are registered trademarks of Biblica, Inc. Use of either trademark for the offering of goods or services requires the prior written consent of Biblica US, Inc.

WestBow Press books may be ordered through booksellers or by contacting:

WestBow Press
A Division of Thomas Nelson & Zondervan
1663 Liberty Drive
Bloomington, IN 47403
www.westbowpress.com
1 (866) 928-1240

Because of the dynamic nature of the Internet, any web addresses or links contained in this book may have changed since publication and may no longer be valid. The views expressed in this work are solely those of the author and do not necessarily reflect the views of the publisher, and the publisher hereby disclaims any responsibility for them.

Any people depicted in stock imagery provided by Thinkstock are models, and such images are being used for illustrative purposes only. Certain stock imagery © Thinkstock.

ISBN: 978-1-5127-1696-2 (sc)
ISBN: 978-1-5127-1697-9 (hc)
ISBN: 978-1-5127-1695-5 (e)

Library of Congress Control Number: 2015917382

Print information available on the last page.

WestBow Press rev. date: 12/03/2015

Contents

Foreword by Captain Dale Black PhD vii
Author's Introduction ix

1 – Surviving A Near-Death Experience (NDE) 1
2 – What Happens at Death 29
3 – Pre-NDEs 48
4 – Blast-Off! The NDE Begins 62
5 – Entering the Spirit World 92
6 – Paradise and God 105
7 – The Life Review 126
8 – Society in Paradise 145
9 – The Void 167
10 – Other Prison Sections of Hades 180
11 – Suicides: A Special Case? 212
12 – Tours: Heaven, Hell and the Cosmos 235
13 – The Return and Its Challenges 255
14 – Succeeding as a Returnee 283
15 – The Global NDE 301

Website 335
Appendix 337
    Statistics, Research and Support
Acknowledgements 347
Endnotes 349

Foreword by Captain Dale Black PhD

Dale is author of the bestseller
Flight To Heaven.

Ivan Rudolph is a much-respected writer in Australia who is known for his painstaking research and comprehensive writing style. The majority of his books are historical and factual, winning critical acclaim and making him an excellent choice for authoring the book you hold in your hands. I'm honored to be asked to write this Foreword.

In *Living Beyond* the author addresses vital questions that persons who have returned from a near-death experience (NDE) invariably struggle with when adjusting back to life on earth. Ivan does so in a fresh, frank and meaningful way that is both helpful and insightful.

This book is fluent and easy to read and will elevate your understanding of NDEs.

My own near-death experience occurred when I was a young, aspiring airline pilot in training. The horrific airplane crash and aftermath changed my life forever. Throughout the 43 years since my journey to heaven and back, the effects have not lessened, but have continued to shape the choices I make. Upon waking from a coma I knew that earth was not my home. I am temporarily assigned here for the divine purpose of helping others learn about the One True God. I am also preparing myself for a permanent heavenly home.

Near-death experiences often result in returnees struggling to readjust to their former life. An experience outside of the body brings the stark realization that life does not end at physical death. In fact, life outside of the body is far more pure and the individual may discover they feel profoundly more "alive" than ever before.

This near-death journey often causes great difficulty in adjusting to one's former life. Careers may be upended as returnees embrace a vibrant new purpose for their lives. This is certainly what happened in my case.

Much confusion surrounds the basic nature of near-death experiences and Ivan meets the varied accounts head-on masterfully. He also supplies a solid Christian interpretation of these events, thus helping readers unlock much of their mystery.

Now fasten your seat belt and get ready for an amazing ride with author Ivan Rudolph in *Living Beyond.*

Author's Introduction

I was eleven years old, growing up in Africa in the late 1950s, when my father died of a heart attack. On recovery, he told us very little about what had happened, except that his spirit had left his body and that the experience had been wonderful. He spoke about 'floating' and a dark corridor and a bright light. What remains indelibly imprinted in my memory is his happy smile when he spoke regarding his near-death experience (NDE). He told us emphatically that death was nothing to be feared.

My interest was piqued and as I grew older I began speaking to others who had had similar experiences to that of my father. A pattern emerged that was similar to the one proposed later in 1975 by Dr Raymond Moody, in an influential book *Life After Life*.

I read in addition the teachings of different religions about what happened in the afterlife, including Christian viewpoints. My family did not attend church and I had no relevant teaching on spiritual matters.

In my reading, I discovered that some religions taught several points of similarity to the NDE pattern that I had noticed emerging in people's accounts. Nonetheless, they all differed from this pattern in significant ways.

An exciting development was that some doctors and scientists began to investigate NDEs. Unfortunately, most researchers concentrated on the brain or psychological issues in their search for explanations. I found this perplexing. It seemed to me that anything less than a spiritual explanation must be incorrect because the NDE began in earnest only once the spirit left the body and found itself experiencing consciousness outside the brain. Soon there were hundreds of reports of NDErs looking down on their physical bodies from above – describing activities that they could not possibly have seen unless they were observers who had been separated from their bodies and brains. People who had been at the scene confirmed the accuracy of a significant number of these observations.

I studied chemistry, geology and physics at university and became a science and mathematics teacher, all without delving any deeper into the nature of NDEs.

When I developed a strong Christian faith in my late 20s, I began to seek insights from the Bible to help explain the NDE phenomenon. I discovered that the majority of descriptions given by those who had had the experience were consistent with biblical writings, particularly those relating to the topic of death. This I found to be the case irrespective of the faith stance of the returnees.

In this book, *Living Beyond*, I will present fresh perceptions regarding life after death that I have developed over the years. There are thousands of NDE accounts that I have read and I quote widely from them. While they are from many different sources, in which the experiences are interpreted in various ways, the analysis that accompanies the accounts in this book is my own, and is therefore unique. My selection of material is also a little different. Many NDE accounts provide information from friends, medical personnel and witnesses of the events surrounding that episode. This is interesting and gives credibility to that particular NDE. My purpose, however, is to focus on the NDE itself, leaving out much accompanying detail.

I had no intention of writing a book on afterlife experiences until I spoke to and read about many NDErs who were perplexed and disturbed. Consequently, a significant number were struggling with life after their return. I believe I am the first to set out in this way to provide a solidly biblical Christian overview and interpretation of NDEs aimed at addressing confusion in both returnees and those interested in life after death.

Our only knowledge of NDEs comes from those who have had them, or have studied them. So I have used a large number of quotes in this book. The use of italics for emphasis within quotes is mine.

Bible quotes are from the NIV Bible unless another version has provided more clarity in certain circumstances, in which case I have designated the version I have used.

You may notice that there are some popular books or articles about NDEs that I have not mentioned; this is because I consider them to be internally inconsistent or externally inaccurate – or if one of the compilers has subsequently thrown doubt on the account.

While gathering information from books, I also checked other sources; for example, I supplemented the information from Dr George Ritchie's 1978 book by facts taken from an earlier *Guideposts Magazine* article of 1963 about him.

Many websites on the Internet are full of information. That of Dr Richard Kent, a retired British doctor, is good to visit, as is that of the more sensational Sid Roth.

Thus, this book presents the conclusions that I have derived from over 40 years of interest in the subject, including personal interviews, religious studies and a wide analysis of NDE research. It is structured to develop its more mysterious topics slowly, such that insights not explained fully when first mentioned are revisited later.

Much of today's NDE confusion is with regard to the 'venue' in which a person has found themselves when temporarily out of their body. Consequently I have capitalised the different venues I write about, to emphasise where the activity is taking place – Earth, Heaven, Paradise and others. Venue is vital!

I hope you will accompany me as I describe my own exciting journey of discovery regarding the deeper nature of NDEs.

1

Surviving A Near-Death Experience (NDE)

My last memories were when I had been in hospital, seeing myself in the operating room from a vantage point near the ceiling. I remember feeling lighter and lighter, being drawn down the hallway and swept out of the door of the hospital, and then suddenly I was gone.
—Captain Dale Black[1] (2010), describing entering the afterlife.

Have you ever had a near-death experience? The sort where you actually physically died, and found yourself 'somewhere else', no longer inhabiting your dead body?

If you did, you may have had a taste of the afterlife – and may have been fortunate enough to recall this fact! You can probably also still vividly recall details of your experience, and it may well have changed for the better your whole approach to life, people and priorities.

On the other hand, you may have returned from this experience confused, disorientated, and even disbelieved by family and friends. Your life afterwards may have crashed around you.

Either way, it is really important for you to know what happened to you, not just what happened to your body while you were absent from it, but to the *real you* that left it during your NDE.

As for those of us who have never had such an experience – by listening and analysing the accounts of NDErs, we can benefit from knowing what we might anticipate when we die, which for most people is a one-time experience!

This book is therefore intended to be helpful to both NDErs and anyone simply interested in the phenomenon. NDE books and reports have been shown to change the way in which the population as a whole views dying. In these perilous times, I believe an accurate comprehension of what to expect at death is vital. What a society believes about death decides how it approaches life and living it, and has done so throughout history. An individual's personal belief about death and the afterlife fires up the destructive actions of suicide bombers, and at the other end of the scale it motivates the compassionate work of people such as Mother Teresa.

Because of my concern for returnees, I will at times speak as if addressing them directly. For example: 'You may have been given an option to return…' If you are not a returnee, and of course most of us are not, please simply translate this as something that can happen to NDErs. Hopefully, context will make it clear who is being addressed.

However, if you have had an NDE, be aware that you are part of a very large group. There are *millions* of others like you! Based on an earlier respected Gallup Poll[2] and other investigations, there are likely to be at least 16 million adult NDErs in America alone, and 350 million worldwide! (These are conservative estimates based on a number of researches – see Statistics section in Appendix).

Only a small proportion (around 18%[3]) of those who have revived from death have had NDEs; nevertheless the total number of NDE returnees grows daily at a staggering rate. It is beyond reasonable doubt nowadays (though there are still sceptics!) that NDEs demonstrate that a person's consciousness and spirit survive after physical death – the evidence of 16 million adult American witnesses is overwhelming. Many of these witnesses are regarded as being of the highest integrity, and include a significant number who are medically or scientifically trained to evaluate evidence objectively. Others have no reason to claim an NDE, such as celebrities who are already rich and famous and who risked being scorned. Elizabeth Taylor, Sharon Stone, Peter Sellers, Burt Reynolds, Chevy Chase, Goldie Hawn, Eric Estrada, Larry Hagman, Jane Seymour, Donald Sutherland, Tony Bennett, Nikki Sixx and others are in this category.

If you are part of the greater proportion of NDErs who enjoyed profoundly pleasant experiences, yours have been sublime, but probably also confusing, which may have made a return to your previous life and lifestyle challenging.

If you are part of the lesser proportion of NDErs who have had unpleasant experiences, these too may be confusing. Be encouraged, most returnees who have had frightening NDEs say they have found positive consequences developing in their lives over time.

Whether your experience was sublime or terrifying, your life will never be the same again.

Even at an early stage of my searching for truth, it struck me that more folk had had this kind of experience than was realised. But in those days people were very hesitant to talk about what had happened to them, and the experience was often kept under wraps. Here is a quote from my cousin about her mother, my aunt:

> My mother told me of her own experience – she was under general anaesthetic to sort out cataracts and she found herself floating up by the ceiling looking down. She was desperate to leave and move to the voices that were calling her away – but a much bigger voice interposed and told her it was not her time. She woke up back in her body feeling hugely disappointed and thwarted. I don't think

she ever told Dad – he would have been very hurt that she was so eager to pop off and leave this vale of tears.

Some folk of that era were concerned they might be considered strange, perhaps even mad, were they to tell others, so they tried to deal with their experiences largely alone. In *Life after Life*, Raymond Moody[4] described NDEs as 'very widespread, and very well-hidden'. Even today, Dr Mary Neal[5] states that she has had the opportunity of listening to many other people describe their own near-death experiences, and that their stories usually begin with their saying, 'I never told anyone about it, because I didn't think anyone would believe me.' And this hesitation is despite NDEs becoming part of our modern psyche. For example, there are many interviews with returnees on YouTube.

My own experience is that most returnees say little unless asked because of embarrassment, personal confusion or fear of being labelled 'strange'. However, if prompted, their words flow freely and often with apparent relief. Dr Cherie Sutherland[6], a researcher and an NDEr herself, discovered that 'when people tried to discuss the NDE, 50% of the relatives and 25% of friends rejected the NDE, and 30% of nursing staff, 85% of doctors and 50% of psychiatrists reacted negatively.' No wonder returnees prefer not to tell others!

My father was only in his late 40s when he had his heart attack and died. Dad was an intensely practical man who did not attend church and had *never* spoken to us about spiritual things, and so for him to tell us about life after death as a definite reality carried weight with me.

Later on I discovered that there was a real and indisputable spiritual dimension to life. My training in the sciences at university had not prepared me at all for some rather nasty spiritual events that I had, but ultimately these, along with some positive spiritual experiences, convinced me to become a Christian.

A variety of new and unexpected experiences then invaded my life, including meeting with people of the highest integrity who had had NDEs. These were not dreamers or people who had been on a drug trip or had had hallucinations, but they were utterly reliable witnesses who while dead had visited somewhere else, and whose lives had been changed and enhanced as a consequence. The fruit of their changed lives was a loving and practical contribution made into the lives of others – which I have now come to appreciate to be the most reliable test of a 'successful' return to life on Earth.

I'll recount a few of their experiences, along with other similar ones gathered more recently. But first, I'd like to give readers a reassurance won from considering thousands of NDEs – an NDEr enjoys a freedom from pain and a wonderful feeling of peace at the moment of separation from the physical body. Comments abound such as: 'No choking or smothering', 'A great release into peace', 'Just like fainting', 'Like a lost breath', 'So quick, and painless' and 'Quicker and less of an issue than an anaesthetic'.

Chuck,[7] who died during a motorcycle collision with a truck, gives a typical description:

> Then all of a sudden I have this warm, very comfortable, wonderful feeling – and it seemed like all the worldly worries just disappeared, and nothing was important anymore. It felt like I slid into this Jacuzzi that was just a perfect temperature and everything felt as wonderful as it could feel to the physical body. And I believe that at that moment I was dead.

He felt so good! His subsequent experiences in the spirit world were so positive, that when he hears nowadays of someone dying, his immediate response is that he is happy for them, because they are now going home to God.

Denis Cooper and his wife Joan ran a Christian Centre 'on the smell of an oil rag' on their farm in Rhodesia (now Zimbabwe) in the 1970s. They helped a number of desperate young people, rescuing some who had been on the verge of suicide. Denis's upright life and good works plus a freedom from addictions stamp him as an impeccable witness. That he provided me with details of his NDE before the term had been popularised makes his recollections 'untainted' by modern expectations.

During the Second World War, Denis had the experience of an artillery shell landing nearby and finding himself as a spirit floating high above the devastated trench, thinking to himself as he looked down on the scene, *Those men are in a bad way* – that is, before making out that one of them was himself, lying in a pool of blood with a chunk blown out of the side of his helmet! An NDEr not recognising his or her corpse lying below is more common than one might suppose. A similar but more recent example happened in the Sunni Triangle, during the Iraqi war that toppled Saddam Hussein. Marcus[7] was in a Humvee blown up by a roadside bomb. He too did not at first identify his broken body lying in the road. Floating above the scene and looking at his shattered body below, he thought, 'I don't want to go through what that man is going to go through during rehabilitation'. In one sense he was correct, he found his rehab painful and challenging, but he was successful and today is a happy man, enjoying each day of a restored life.

Denis Cooper supplied me with another fascinating example of an NDE. He had recently found their granddaughter, three-year-old Amy, floating face down in the swimming pool, apparently drowned. He and her mother Vicky, a trained nurse, applied mouth-to-mouth and CPR until Amy revived. Later on, the little girl told him, 'Grandpa, you looked funny jumping into the pool with your watch still on', which she could not have seen while floating unconscious face down! She also asked him, 'Where is that doll that was lying in the pool?' On further questioning, she described what could only have been a view of herself floating there – seen from above. I was impressed. Certainly Amy had no pre-existing concepts of what might have happened to her at death, nor did she, being a child, identify herself as the doll afloat face down below.

Children's Testimonies.

Amy's account impressed me because young children call it as they see it, without bluffing, and I have ever since paid particular attention to what they report, unless it is obvious they are being coaxed or coached in their accounts. Of particular interest to me are the reports of the very young who would not have had time to be enculturated by adult beliefs about NDEs.

Separate studies on children have shown that they describe what they have seen and experienced without embellishment or subterfuge when compared with a similar group of adults recounting experiences. It is therefore fascinating that young children have a startling consistency when relating NDEs, while massive deviations occur when they relate fantasies or dreams. NDEs are not their fantasies nor dreams. In addition, they recount afterlife experiences by describing a similar sequence of events to adult NDEs. Furthermore, most children on return seem to progress with a sense of purpose and direction as they mature, without developing a fear of dying.

Here are a few accounts given by children.

Colton Burpo, as remembered and recorded by his parents Todd[8] and Sonja, gave a description of looking down at his body on an operating table. Colton had been three-years-old at the time of the operation, but had turned four by the time this conversation took place. He moved from looking at his body to watching what his parents were doing:

> 'But you were in the operating room, Colton,' I (Todd) said. 'How could you know what we were doing?'
> 'Cause I could see you,' Colton said matter-of-factly. 'I went up out of my body and I was looking down and I could see the doctor working on my body. And I saw you and Mommy. You were in a little room by yourself, praying, and Mommy was in a different room, and she was praying and talking on the phone.'

Todd and Sonja Burpo were astounded. How could Todd have possibly known these details, unless he had been looking from above as he claimed?

It is amazing that the youngest of children, even babies, can have an NDE. PMH Atwater[9] is a brilliant and bold researcher of NDEs: consequently, I quote her work often, despite her not sharing my Christian worldview. She describes the case of Robin Michelle Halberdier of Texas City, whose near-death episode took place in a hospital when she was between one and two months of age. Born prematurely, and with Hyaline Membrane disease, Robin was not expected to live. Her recollections years later are given below, but with her adult perspectives and language.

> My first visual memory was looking forward and seeing a brilliant bright light, almost like looking directly at the sun. The strange thing was that I could see my feet in front of me, as if I were floating upward in a vertical

position. I do not remember passing through a tunnel or anything like that, just floating in the beautiful light. A tremendous amount of warmth and love came from the light.

There was a standing figure in the light, shaped like a normal human being, but with no distinct facial features. It had a masculine presence. The light I have described seemed like it emanated from that figure. Light rays shone all around him. I felt very protected and safe and loved.

The figure in the light told me through what I now know to be mental telepathy that I must go back, that it was not time for me to come here. I wanted to stay because I felt so full of joy and so peaceful. The voice repeated that it wasn't my time; I had a purpose to fulfil and I could come back after I completed it.

The first time I told my parents about my experience was right after I began to talk. At the time, I believed that what happened to me was something everyone experienced. I told my mom and dad about the big glass case I was in after I was born, and the figure in the light and what he said to me. They took my reference to the glass case to mean the incubator. My father was a medical student at the time, and he had read a book about near-death experiences. From comparing the information in the book with what I told them, they decided that's what I was describing. My mom told me all of this some years later when I brought the subject up again.

I began attending church at the age of five, and I would look at the picture of Jesus in the Bible and tell my mom 'that's who it was in the light'.

I still have many physical difficulties with my health because of being premature. But there is a strong need inside me that I should help others with what death is, and talk to terminally ill patients. I was in the other world and I know there is nothing to be afraid of after death.

Such coherent memories when Robin's brain was not yet sufficiently formed to record them in this detail are a conundrum for researchers. Some NDEs experienced by babies still in the womb, and only recounted by the returnee years later, pose an even greater puzzle, because the brain should have been far too immature to form memories in such graphic detail. Nonetheless, where medical and other details have been investigated, they have checked out precisely. Personally, I believe that a myriad of NDEs illustrate that consciousness survives death – that the spirit and soul separate from the body and brain at death and receive information directly in the spirit world. Thus this particular difficulty disappears.

Consciousness is therefore the ultimate survivor – beyond atoms and molecules that are left behind at death – beyond our energy cycles – beyond our time and space – in new afterlife venues with their own time, space and elegant physical laws.

Returning now to my personal journey delving into NDEs.

The account that Rhoda Fryer told me in the 1970s helped to expand my growing understanding. Rhoda was a no-nonsense colleague of mine at Marlborough High School in Salisbury, Rhodesia (now Harare, Zimbabwe). She was a respected and dedicated teacher as well as a faithful member of her church – and is still helping to set up and run women's fellowship groups. Rhoda and I had not been in communication for almost 40 years and I found myself wishing I could freshen up my information about her NDE when preparing material for this book.

Out of the blue, I received an email – Rhoda was visiting Australia from Zimbabwe and would like to catch up with a phone call! After our conversation, she kindly wrote out what had happened to her in more detail than I had known previously – and the salient points follow.

Rhoda believes she died during childbirth on the operating table on 27 July 1961 at St Joseph's hospital in Mowbray, Cape Town, South Africa, with nuns in attendance. Her spirit had floated out of her body, while her doctor and surgeon were scrubbing up in a separate room down the corridor. Here is her account, written out for me in 2014:

> I looked down and saw my body on the operating table with the nuns busy around me. One was monitoring my heart, another the baby's heart, and they were concerned that they were not hearing heartbeats.

Then her consciousness somehow allowed her to see and hear the surgeon and doctor in the scrub room down the corridor.

> I saw the surgeon and my doctor scrubbing up and imagine my surprise when I heard them discussing fishing they had done together that day. I was outraged! Time was critical and they seemed to be quite unconcerned!
>
> The surgeon and doctor moved into the theatre and the next thing was an incision made vertically on my abdomen. The baby was removed and I heard it cry. One of the nuns said, 'It's a girl'. I looked at the clock; it was 8pm.
>
> They worked on the womb, and then the surgeon took out a machine and 'zipped' up the incision. It was a new and innovative device and the surgeon was inviting comments from the doctor and nuns. It seemed they were more interested in this machine than my welfare.
>
> I heard someone saying, 'Mrs Fryer, you can wake up now. Your baby is a 10 pound girl'. I regained consciousness in the bed in the ward.

> The next morning I woke to find both surgeon and doctor standing by my bed. I sat up and demanded to know why they had been discussing their fishing trip when I was in a critical state!
>
> They were dumbfounded. 'You couldn't possibly have heard us. We were in another room down the passage. We were fully aware of the urgency and did not delay', they said.
>
> 'I saw you', I said. 'You were laughing and joking; meanwhile, I was dying!'
>
> The doctors told me afterwards that my heart had stopped, but that they wanted to remove the baby before they got it going again. I insisted that I had seen and heard them.

Having some knowledge of medical procedures, Rhoda had taken great interest in what the surgeons were doing and had felt no fear, but rather a strange sense of wellbeing. She surmised years later that her spirit had left her body in an out-of-body-experience (OBE), which is usually the first stage in an NDE. She deduced this only years later because at the time she knew nothing about NDEs and OBEs.

What struck me in particular about Rhoda's account was that the surgeon and doctor knew that Rhoda, her body and brain lying on the operating table, could not possibly have heard what they were talking about in that separate room down the corridor! She also described how the one had removed his wristwatch and placed it on a glass shelf above where they were cleaning their hands. Rhoda told me later that this tiny observation of hers had convinced them that she had been watching them as well as listening.

Initially, my scientific mind suggested to me that a dying brain might be generating hallucinations, there being so much about brain function still unknown. However, Rhoda's case could *not* have been that of a dying brain alone, because her brain clearly remained on the operating table while her consciousness somehow had access to the scrub room down the passage.

The doctor and the surgeon at Rhoda's bedside had been dumbfounded when she told them details of their conversation in the scrub room. Because of their close proximity to the dying, those in the medical profession can be startled by NDEs, especially by examples of observations made by a comatose patient. Here is an example given to Dr Pim van Lommel[3] by a Dutch cardiac nurse in the late 1980s and reported in the influential *Lancet*:

> During night shift an ambulance brings in a 44-year old cyanotic, comatose man into the coronary care unit... When we go to intubate the patient, he turns out to have dentures in his mouth. I remove these upper dentures and put them onto the 'crash cart'...
>
> Only after more than a week do I meet again with the patient, who is by now back on the cardiac ward. The moment he sees me he says: 'O, that nurse knows where my dentures are.' I am very surprised. Then he elucidates: 'You were there when I was brought into hospital and you took my dentures out of my mouth and put them onto that cart, it had all these bottles on it and there was this sliding drawer underneath, and there you put my teeth.' I was especially amazed because I remembered this happening while the man was in deep coma and in the process of CPR.
>
> When I asked further, it appeared the man had seen himself lying in bed, that he had perceived from above how nurses and doctors had been busy with CPR. He was also able to describe correctly and in detail the small room in which he had been resuscitated as well as the appearance of those present like myself...

He is deeply impressed by his experience and says he is no longer afraid of death. Four weeks later he left hospital as a healthy man.

His interest piqued by this and other corroborated NDE reports, Dr Pim van Lommel[3] gathered a team in Holland to do an extensive study of NDEs, the details of which were reported in the Dec 15th 2001 edition of *The Lancet*, which is peer-reviewed and one of the most prestigious medical journals in the world.

The study concluded that the afterlife experiences were unrelated to processes in the dying brain!!

In addition, most patients had excellent recall of the events, which undermined the theory that the memories were dreams or false. Bruce Greyson[10] quotes longitudinal research that illustrated the accuracy and durability of NDE memories over twenty years, which makes them extraordinary when compared to other memories.

Independent research shows that the majority of people in Holland do not believe in life after death, so expectations of an afterlife hardly played a role, and the fact that the experiences parallelled thousands already reported in America and England could hardly be co-incidental. Furthermore, the NDErs reported marked changes in their personalities and lifestyles – having become more compassionate, loving and giving when compared with those patients who survived cardiac arrest without NDEs. They had in addition lost their fear of death, were non-materialistic, and gravitated towards professions that helped and served others. Van Lommel[11] did follow-up longitudinal studies that demonstrated these changes were enduring over the years.

Of course some returnees in the study may have kept their afterlife experiences to themselves. There are always some, such as my own father, who prefer not to discuss their NDEs for social or personal reasons. Others for whatever reasons will not

Living Beyond

readily at the time admit to such unusual experiences, although they may do so later. For example, Pim van Lommel[12] in 2004 reported the extensive NDE of a Dutch man who, during a cardiac arrest, saw his deceased grandmother and a man who looked at him lovingly, but whom he did not know. More than a decade after his NDE, his mother, on her deathbed, confessed to him that he had been born from an extramarital relationship, and that her husband was not his biological father. His biological father was in fact a Jewish man who had been deported and killed during World War II. She showed her son a photograph of his biological father, whom he immediately recognized as the man he had seen in his NDE a decade earlier.

Reflecting on the researches above, we perhaps wonder why only around one in five of those revived recalled having an NDE? Whatever the reason, I believe it to be a seminal principle governing NDEs, and one that will be developed progressively during this book, that:

> ***An NDE is a spiritual gift from God to act as a personal course correction; it is a learning experience during a brush with death.***

Most spiritual gifts and course corrections in people's lives, whether or not they ever experience an NDE, occur during life here on Earth. But I believe that reflecting on NDEs has a lot to teach us.

A point needs to be emphasised here – to learn about NDEs, we can only turn to those who can personally recall them, regardless of what percentage they are of the people who die and revive.

OBEs and NDEs

From interviewing returnees and from other sources, I have deduced that an out-of-body experience (OBE) marks the beginning of genuine afterlife experiences. Thousands of examples have convinced me that the first stage of an NDE is the consciousness leaving the body in an OBE. The spirit and soul float upwards and can usually see lying below the physical body that has been left behind. When the spirit or consciousness exits the body, it is logical that the body, people and real events below may be observed, at least in the majority of cases.

In fact, an OBE can occur whether the person is dead, or simply alive and very stressed or fearful; an OBE can even be induced. Therefore, an OBE may occur not linked to an NDE. However, the converse is not true, and leads to an important principle, based on a spirit having to depart from a body before an NDE can begin. The principle is:

A genuine NDE always begins with an OBE.

The OBE launches the NDE, which may then proceed to a number of further afterlife experiences. Let's look at these.

Defining a Classic NDE

This is by way of a brief generalisation.

Detailed afterlife experiences during NDEs will be fleshed out in the pages that follow.

Raymond Moody[4] in the mid-seventies noted that there was no strict sequence or nature for these experiences, but that many followed a remarkably similar pattern – one which later researchers in the West verified on the whole.

Early research suggested the NDE was not related to a person's gender, race, education, occupation, or previous knowledge of these experiences.

NDEs have been around since ancient times. In a very broad sense, we see the kernels of common afterlife features in the NDE of Emmanuel Swedenborg[13] in Sweden in the early 1700s. He first met angels, who communicated telepathically, 'the speech of an angel or spirit flows first into the man's thought.' His spirit body was readily recognised by those friends who had pre-deceased him, and he recognised them in similar fashion. While in Paradise, he experienced a stunning Life Review. All of the things he had 'spoken and done were made manifest before the angels, in a light that is clear as day, and there is nothing so concealed in the world that is not made manifest after death.'

The angels mentioned by Swedenborg are spirit beings that act as messengers and servants of God. They can take on a variety of physical forms. They are described in more detail later.

Working from hundreds of descriptions, both ancient and modern, here is my updated sequence for a 'classic' NDE, which commonly includes some or all of the adventures below – although a variety of others may also occur:

1. The spirit may leave the body when near-death occurs and the body can be observed lying below – termed an out-of-body experience or OBE. Pain and fear cease immediately.
2. The spirit may wander about the Earth – temporarily Earth-bound. Most, however, leave quickly to enter nearby spirit dimensions.
3. The closest spirit dimension would appear to be the Void. Some step into the Void without experiencing a tunnel, but a short tunnel may deliver the NDEr to a particular section of the Void – for example to where a specific experience awaits them.

4. Most spirits travel across the Void through a variety of long tunnels that lead to a diversity of afterlife venues. Guides, such as angels or dead relatives, may accompany and guide them along the tunnel, or even 'fly' them more directly outside of it to their destinations.
5. There is usually a 'dazzlingly bright light at the end of the tunnel', or in the distance, towards which the NDEr is strongly attracted.
6. The NDEr finds himself/herself in a pastoral or garden idyll – termed in scripture Paradise. An unfortunate smaller number of NDErs find themselves in an unpleasant Prison environment instead.
7. A welcoming committee in Paradise, generally comprising pre-deceased family members also in spirit bodies, including ancestors, greets the newcomer. Besides family members, deceased friends may also be present, and/or other spirit beings such as angels. Some ancestors may only be identified later when searching old family photograph albums.
8. At some stage, the NDEr meets a Being of Light who emanates Love, Peace and Security – in which they bask. The vast majority of NDErs (even those previously atheists) identify this impressive Being as Creator, God, God the Father, or Jesus Christ. An interview, interaction and familiarisation process takes place.
9. The NDEr is often shown a Life Review for personal assessment, and to help guide their future priorities on return to Earth.
10. The NDEr is told that he or she will have to return to Earth, as there is more for them to do there.
11. The return is usually quick and returnees suddenly find themselves back in their own bodies.
12. Many returnees believe they need to love others in a new way, and to tell others of their experiences, as typified

by an example described by Professor Bruce Greyson[14] where, after his NDE, a truck driver 'awoke with an intense passion for helping others, and a desire to talk about his experience, much to the dismay of his embarrassed wife'!

While this classic NDE sequence has been established mainly by investigations in the Western world, it appears to hold true worldwide with some cultural variations, as discussed in a later chapter. Because most reports derive from the West, most of the experiences I quote do too.

Despite the widespread reporting of NDEs, most returnees still express surprise at what they have experienced with descriptors such as 'unexpected' 'amazing',,' astonished' and 'astounded' being commonplace. Their NDE was in no way driven by their expectations! In fact, to quote J. Steve Miller[15], 'Experiences often run sharply counter to the individual's specific religious or personal beliefs and expectations.'

The steps above appear to be purpose driven rather than programme driven, as if planned for personal benefit. This sublime truth will become abundantly apparent in these pages – that each NDE, while it shares commonalities with others, nevertheless appears to be designed to benefit that one particular NDEr. Thereby, the steps may take place in any order, tailored to the individual, and certain steps may not occur. Other adventures, such as tours of Heaven or the Cosmos, may be included.

Perhaps the most impacting step is the Life Review, during which many NDErs describe being shown their lives in great detail. I remember questioning Bob Bosworth about his NDE following a car accident in the 1970s. Bob, the son of the famous evangelist Fred Francis 'FF' Bosworth, had spent his life as a Christian missionary dedicated to serving the needs of others, working mainly with the poor in Africa. He died in the accident and experienced a classic NDE. He told me that his Life Review had made him uncomfortable. 'Details of my ministry passed before my eyes, and I saw weaknesses and things I should have done differently. I was not being judged,' he quickly assured me, 'I was being led into self-evaluation. God's Judgement Day is not yet.' Bob assured me his life and ministry had been impacted positively by his NDE. He died in 2009, serving God and his fellow man to the last through World Outreach and other ministries.

Others who have returned have repeated Bob's assertion, 'God's Judgement Day is not yet.' For example, Howard Storm[16], as a confused erstwhile atheist whose NDE began with unpleasant experiences, had many questions he asked of spirit beings he encountered during it. Afterwards he concluded:

> God will *ultimately* judge every individual.
> And God will allow people to be dragged into darkness with like-minded creatures. I have told you, from my personal experience, what goes on in there.

Scripture confirms in several places that Judgement lies ahead on a particular day that God has appointed, as yet unknown to us. One verse, Acts 17:31, reads: 'For he has *set a day* when he will judge the world with justice'.

Investigation of One Classic NDE

Of many possible examples, one that caught my attention in particular was that of Pam Reynolds (a pseudonym). Her case is written up well by IANDS (the International Association for Near-Death Studies) and also appears in a variety of easily accessed articles on the web, so I will keep my account brief.

In order to perform surgery deep in her brain, Pam underwent a rare surgical procedure called 'Operation Standstill'. The blood was drained from the body like oil from a car, stopping all brain, heart and organ activity – such that the brain waves flatlined. Her body temperature was lowered to 50 °F (10 °C). While fully anesthetized, she was fitted with sound-emitting earplugs that clicked at 90 decibels, louder than a lawnmower, 11 to 33 times per second. This clicking prevented all external sound from being heard, but did not register at all in her brainwaves, which still flatlined. Her brainstem potentials had ceased and blood was completely absent from her brain. Her eyes were also taped over to prevent vision. To all intents and purposes, she was totally isolated from the world, and by all conventional criteria was 'dead' without brain function during the main part of this procedure – and even if her brain had been still active, vision and hearing of events in the theatre had been made impossible.

Dr Spetzler, the surgeon, was sawing into her skull when Pam suddenly heard the saw and began to observe the surgical procedures (despite taped-over eyes) from a vantage point over his shoulder. She also heard what the nurses said to the doctors (despite the ear plugs). Upon returning to consciousness, she was able to describe with accuracy the distinctive surgical instruments used and she was able to report the statements made by the nurses. These details were corroborated independently.

The surgical equipment that she saw and described on return to her body was unique. She could not have seen this specialist equipment beforehand, though confidently described 'what looked like an electric toothbrush with a dent in it', and she said that 'the tool had interchangeable blades that were kept in a tool box that looked like a socket wrench case' – extraordinarily good descriptions for a person not specialised or knowledgeable in brain surgery. In fact she managed to describe the operation itself and the equipment in great detail even some years later when interviewed, confusing only minor details despite the passage of time, which makes her an extraordinarily convincing witness. The cardiologist Michael Sabom[17] comments further on her case:

> Pam was monitored extensively during this ultra-tricky procedure. No brainwave activity. No brain stem activity. So this eliminates the possibility that her NDE was a seizure phenomenon because during the experience she had no seizure activity recorded on the EEG... Could there have somehow been brain activity e.g. memories, dreams, hallucinations, oxygen deprivation etc? NO! There was NO brainwave activity such as characterises these during the operation.

Wherever Pam's memories were forming, it could not have been in the brain!

Many Christians believe Pam's memories were forming in her soul, which is the true seat of intellectual activity into which the brain feeds while alive, but which departs together with the spirit at death. Some research on mice suggests that the brain may remain conscious for some time after the heart stops beating, according to University of Michigan researchers. It may even function more acutely in the moments immediately following a cardiac arrest compared with when the body is in a normal state. Pam's brain waves, however, were constantly being monitored and she flatlined much of the time, so these findings could not explain her observations.

The accuracy with which Pam and thousands of others have described conversations and procedures while supposedly dead can give us great confidence in their descriptions of what happened next to them as they entered into the spirit world. They are demonstrably accurate witnesses. Here are some of Pam's brief descriptions of her experiences as she entered that 'parallel' world[17]:

> There was a sensation like being pulled, but not against your will. I was going on my own accord because I wanted to go.
>
> It was like a tunnel but it wasn't a tunnel. At some point very early in the tunnel vortex I became aware of my grandmother calling me. The feeling was that she wanted me to come to her, so I continued with no fear down the shaft.
>
> It's a dark shaft that I went through, and at the very end there was this very little tiny pinpoint of light that kept getting bigger and bigger and bigger. The light was incredibly bright, like sitting in the middle of a light bulb...
>
> I began to discern different figures in the light — and they were all covered with light, they were light, and had light permeating all around them. They began to form shapes I could recognize and understand. They would not permit me to go further. I wanted to go into the light, but I also wanted to come back. I had children to be reared.

Still in her NDE, Pam recalls being led down the tunnel by her deceased uncle and re-entering her chilled physical body as her heart was shocked back to normal rhythm.

I have read attempts by sceptics to explain away the Pam Reynolds case. Writers locked into a material Universe cannot conceptualise a spirit, or that spirit leaving a body and making observations. Multiple accounts confirm this phenomenon, however. Dr Michael Sabom[18] published his astonishing research on the accuracy with which comatose and clinically dead patients were able to describe medical procedures. He took special care to examine independent corroborative evidence such as medical records for the visual and auditory observations reported during OBEs. His research data strongly supports the claims made by his subjects, that though they were in a coma or had even been declared medically dead, they were nevertheless conscious outside of their bodies! His data illustrates that those who reported seeing the resuscitation process were astonishingly accurate in what they say they observed. Sceptical at the start of his investigations, which began in 1976, Sabom became convinced by the evidence of the reality of NDEs.

Dr Penny Sartori[19], an investigator in Wales, carried out a study on NDEs in cardiac arrest and asked those who had such an experience to describe what they saw. She also asked patients who did not have an NDE during their cardiac arrest to describe what they thought had happened during the resuscitation. She was able to support Sabom's observation that those who said they saw their resuscitation procedures were much more accurate than those who were asked to describe what they thought had happened. NDEs are not simply 'good guesses' of what had happened.

Dr Kenneth Ring[20] reported an interesting example in 1985 of an extremely short-sighted patient on an operating table with an anaesthesia machine behind her head. When her spirit floated to the ceiling, she remembered the identification numbers on the machine that she could not have possibly seen from her position on the operating table. She noticed too that the light fittings were dirty. On return to her body, her memory of the numbers was found to be correct, as was the need to clean the tops of the light fittings!

Consequently, there is nothing unique in the experiences that Denis Cooper, Rhoda Fryer, Bob Bosworth and others described to me in the 1970s; in fact millions can testify to similar experiences.

Imagine sitting on a jury where just one million NDErs, many of them with impeccable credentials for reliability and honesty, step up to the witness box to give reports of their NDE before being cross-examined. Suppose you could hear a hundred witnesses a day, a gargantuan task – to hear only a million would keep you on the jury for more than 27 years, and that would be only the first million. Any objective juror would declare the case proven long before listening to all one million testimonies! And there would be millions more NDErs waiting in the wings to testify in order to convince hard-nut jurors...

I am forced to conclude that critics of the reality of NDEs are simply not realists, or perhaps have not looked yet at the wealth of evidence available.

Most of the prominent researchers of NDEs began their interest believing there must be a naturalistic earthly explanation for them – including Raymond Moody, Bruce Greyson, Penny Sartori, Michael Sabom, Maurice Rawlings, Pim van Lommel and other distinguished members of the medical profession. Each became convinced otherwise. Professor Bruce Greyson[21] explains their change of heart: 'Most near-death researchers did not go into their investigations with a belief in mind-body separation, but came to that hypothesis based on what their research found.'

Blind People and NDEs

I learned in the 1970s that patients during operations could see events during their OBEs when their physical eyes remained closed, and could describe occurrences at a distance even in another room, such as Rhoda Fryer had been able to. But could this ability to see in the afterlife apply even to blind people, I wondered more recently? A number of convincing reports indicate that this can indeed happen.

Researchers Kenneth Ring[22] and Sharon Cooper became interested in the extraordinary phenomenon of sight in the afterlife. They conducted a study on blind people who had had NDEs. These people reported experiences that included similar aspects to the traditional NDE, such as watching doctors operate on them as well as otherworldly perceptions such as radiant light, angels, deceased relatives etc. That their reports included watching occurrences on Earth was the most startling fact to emerge. Reliable eyewitnesses at the time corroborated their testimony. In fact, 80% of the blind NDErs interviewed recorded things they saw during their NDEs that they could not possibly have seen through their sightless physical eyes.

To give you a 'feel' of what their NDEs were like, I will briefly quote Vicki Umipeg's[20] account. She was blind because her optic nerves had been completely destroyed at birth because of excess of oxygen delivered to her in an incubator. Vicki said she had a hard time relating to sight, as it was entirely novel to her.

> I've never seen anything: no light, no shadows, no nothing... And in my dreams I don't see any visual impressions. It's just taste, touch, sound, and smell, but no visual impressions of anything.

After dying, she found herself floating upwards and viewing with perfect clarity the scene in the emergency room below, where a frantic medical team worked feverishly to revive her. They were the first people she had ever seen.

Nor had she seen herself previously!

> I was quite tall and thin at that time. And I recognised at first that it was a body, but I didn't even know that the body was mine initially. Then I perceived that I was up on the ceiling, and I thought, 'Well, that's kind of weird. What am I doing up here?' I thought, 'Well, this must be me. Am I dead?... I just briefly saw this body, and I knew that it was mine because I was not in my body.

Vicki also recognised the ring that she wore on her finger, which was of unusual design, having orange blossoms on the corners of it. That ring confirmed her identification of herself!

She then found herself going up through the ceilings of the hospital until she was above the roof of the building itself. During this time she had a brief panoramic view of her surroundings. She felt exhilarated, and enjoyed tremendously the freedom of movement she was experiencing, unfamiliar to one congenitally blind.

Vicki then experienced seeing the beautiful flowers and trees of Paradise. She also met again dead friends who had preceded her, including two children aged 11 and 6 who had both been blind. She was delighted to find they could also see now! They were no longer children, but in their prime: happy, healthy and bright.

Vicki's NDE was truly extraordinary. She has returned to being blind on Earth, but recalls with joy the beautiful people and places that await her.

I have read of similar cases to Vicki's; an unusual one was featured on national TV[7]. It involved a young rap artist, Jason, shot twice in the face in a random shooting at a gas station by a man on drugs. The gunman was subsequently arrested and sentenced to six years in jail. Tragically, the bullets permanently destroyed Jason's sight: 'My retinas have been separated, both of them. The bullet burned out my pupils.' However, his spirit hovering above the car which was rushing him to hospital could see all the details. Here are his words, with my emphasis on words that illustrate his ability to see:

> I was levitating above the car, and *looking down* at myself. And the car was moving, and I was moving with the car. I could *see* my head leant against the window – I *see* the blood. There was an incredible amount of blood dripping down my face. (Doctors did CPR at the hospital while family and concerned friends gathered.)
>
> I was still floating. I was still levitating, *looking down* at myself. I knew that was me, but at the same time I knew that this was me too!

> All of a sudden, my thought patterns picked back up, my head 'popped back'. I returned to normal. Coming back into my body, I felt – total pain. I can feel the blood dripping down my face, and I kept trying to adjust my eyesight to see what was going wrong. It wasn't happening.

He did not realise yet that he had been blinded. He then died a second time in hospital and experienced a second NDE.

> I was outside myself – definitely. Standing there, *looking* at myself on this stretcher, I had no fear. I had no feeling of hurt anymore – no pain – I felt happy!

Soon afterwards, a voice told Jason it was not yet his time and that he must return. At once, he found himself in his body again. Two difficult years learning to live as a blind man followed. He went back to school, and is now a teacher. Wow!

These adventures all began with death, but what precisely is death?

2

What Happens at Death

Pre-NDE → spirit leaving body (OBE) →'deep' NDE

Armed with just a small number of NDE accounts in the 1970s, but completely convinced of the integrity of those who had kindly told me their experiences, I set about trying to understand what was going on. I soon discovered that Christian ministers and other believers had little interest and no convincing explanations for NDEs.

How could I find the truth? For a number of reasons, some experiential, I had come to look at the Bible as a unique window into God, but one having to be illuminated by God's Spirit. Of interest, this understanding has been given to a few NDErs who asked about the Bible while visiting the afterlife, the atheist Howard Storm[1] being one.

> I asked if it was true, and they (spirit beings) said it was. Asking them why it was that when I tried to read it, all I saw were contradictions, they took me back to my Life Review again – something that I had overlooked. They showed me, for the few times I had opened the Bible, that I had read it with the idea of finding contradictions and problems. I was trying to prove to myself that it wasn't worth reading.
>
> I observed to them that the Bible wasn't clear to me. It didn't make sense.
>
> They told me that it contained *spiritual truth*, and that I had to read it spiritually in order to understand it. It

should be read prayerfully. My friends (in the afterlife) informed me that it was not like other books. They also told me, and I later found out this was true, that when you read it prayerfully, it talks to you. It reveals itself to you.

Approaching the Bible in this way, insight came to me, helped through the teachings on a cassette tape by the prominent English Bible teacher David Pawson. His talk was titled 'Between Death and Resurrection', which is the time slot we are in after we die, and thereby within which NDEs take place.

My overall understanding regarding death and NDEs has remained essentially unchanged over many years of reading and listening.

What better place to start studying death than to contemplate the death of Jesus on the cross? This is where my personal understanding began.

Consider John 19:30, which reads: 'When he had received the drink, Jesus said, "It is finished." With that, he bowed his head and gave up his spirit.'

We see that Jesus died when his spirit left his body, when he 'gave up' his spirit! There was a moment in time when the two separated, and that was the moment of his death. What is more, his body hung there for all to see, but his spirit was elsewhere doing other things – which we will probe later.

The scripture that states, 'The body without the spirit is dead' (James 2:26) clarifies death, including that of Jesus. What could be clearer? It does not say that if the spirit returns to that body, it revives, but such is logically the case.

Jesus revived at least three people during his earthly ministry, and Father God revived others, including those who were raised from their graves at the time of Jesus' Resurrection (Matthew

27:52). It follows that to God the Father and to Jesus, death is a reversible process. As thousands have testified, it is God who revives NDErs, just as he did people in the Bible; nevertheless, when physical death is not reversed another scripture applies: 'people are destined to die once, and after that to face Judgment' (Hebrews 9:27).

We find other cases in the Bible where death is equated to the spirit leaving the body. In Acts 7:59 Stephen's dying prayer was 'Lord Jesus, receive my spirit' and not, 'receive my body', while Paul wanted to 'depart and be with Christ' (Philippians 1:23) because it was preferable 'to be away from the body and at home with the Lord' (2Corinthians 5:8).

What might Paul have meant by saying it was preferable to be away from the body? Paradise is the garden idyll to which most spirits go at death, and as millions can now testify, it is far better than life on Earth – and a fantastic place to wait for the final Judgement, not least because of the quality time that may be spent there with God the Father, Jesus, angels, relatives and friends.

What is Death?

Death, then, can be defined as the spirit leaving the body *permanently*. I soon learnt to stop thinking of death as an irreversible instant in time, but rather as a process completed only if the spirit does not return.

While this 'process' definition of death is accurate, it is not easy to apply and it opened up more difficulties than I imagined when I first perceived it as a young Christian. For example, I ran it past a couple of Christian doctors who are friends, who explained that clinical death could not use such a definition because there was no way of knowing the moment that the spirit left the body. So from the medical point of view it was a useless definition – they would continue to need to rely on physical measurements such as brain waves and heart function. Consequently, while of necessity practical, this approach means that the medical profession cannot determine the moment true (irreversible) death begins, a fact that vexes it to this day.

Dr Mary Neal[2] changed her mind regarding the moment of death subsequent to her own NDE. Note that she writes of the 'soul' departing, which is usually in combination with the 'spirit' departing, as discussed later:

> I have come to believe that the departure of the soul defines and determines the moment of death, rather than the body's physical death determining the moment of the soul's departure.
>
> With the use of modern medicine and technology, the organism that is our human body may continue to physically function and appear to be 'alive', but unless God sees a purpose to return the soul to its body, the person is essentially dead. Not only had I witnessed this during my surgical training, but also there are far too many accounts of near-death experiences in which there is a description of the soul departing the shell of its not-yet physically dead body to ignore this reality.

One doctor friend mentioned to me that a study had been done to determine whether there was a change in mass when the spirit left the body, but that the results were inconclusive. For my own interest I looked into that research, done in 1901 by Dr Duncan MacDougall[3], which decided a body lost a tiny mass of 21 grams when the spirit left. However, the sample size studied was too small and the methods of measurement too imprecise for the results to be reliable. Nevertheless, a movie titled *21 Grams* was made in 2003 based around these inaccurate results!

To summarise – it appears that death begins when the spirit separates from the body. Death is complete if the spirit no longer returns to its body. If the spirit does return, the event is termed a near-death experience.

The Soul, Spirit and Spirit Body

Once I grasped that dying and death are a process, I wanted to consider the steps involved.

Before proceeding, I need to define what is generally understood by the terms 'soul' and 'spirit' that I have begun to use freely.

> Spirit = the eternal essence of who we are that gives life to the body. It is the God-conscious part of our being.

> Soul = the self-conscious part of our being – including our intellect, self-awareness, emotions, memories, personality, likes and dislikes, reasoning ability, appreciation or criticism of things, sociability, attitudes... i.e. the aspects that make us conscious individuals.

The early church appears to have believed these divisions in essence. For example, from about AD 177 Irenaeus[4], the bishop of Lyons in Gaul, preached that the soul exists after it is separated from the body at death – and that man is comprised of body, soul and spirit.

Early on in the NDE, the consciousness that drifts away from the body finds it is within a new 'spirit body', a process that thousands have now described. This spirit body has new abilities, so it is more than simply a consciousness that experiences the afterlife.

So I will add to my usage of the terms 'spirit' and 'soul' that of 'spirit body'. In most NDE descriptions, 'spirit' is an inclusive word understood to include all three components. Taken together, these comprise the 'real' person following separation from the body.

Some new abilities discovered in the spirit body include sharper perceptions – for example blind Vicki Umipeg[5] could *see* in Paradise, but returned to being unsighted when back in her physical body. This one account reflects a common theme that runs through NDEs, that Earth lacks the perfection and beauty experienced in Paradise. Dean Braxton[6] and others describe Paradise as where 'everything is right' – a strange description, but one that denotes a region of perfection where God is in total control, which is not the case on Earth where other personalities and forces are involved, along with our own free choices. But I am getting ahead of myself. First I need to probe what actually happens to people when dying.

A word of caution before we continue: God is involved in NDEs, and God does not necessarily operate according to the rules of human logic. Logic, in fact, is given to us to enable us to get through the day and plan ahead, because it makes the world predictable, and therefore science depends on it – but in an NDE one enters new venues where new rules apply. God has the ability to do whatever he chooses however he chooses, far beyond the constraints of human logic, which makes NDEs themselves unpredictable. In the Bible we learn: 'For my thoughts are not your thoughts, neither are your ways my ways, declares the LORD' (ISAIAH 55:8-9), AND, 'With man, this is impossible, but not with God. All things are possible with God' (Mark 10:27). Overall, this makes NDEs a bit frightening and very exciting, rather like the first time we went on a roller coaster or other scary ride over which we had no control.

Pre-NDEs, OBEs and Deeper NDEs

I am excited by the progress science is making in clarifying the input of the dying brain in the NDE process. Important information is emerging from which we can all learn a great deal. It is fascinating and explains many of the weirder experiences reported as being NDEs. For the purposes of this book, though, I will label these dying-brain experiences as pre-NDEs as they generally precede the actual separation of body and spirit and are body-centred. They will be discussed further in the following chapter.

The stage following the pre-NDE is the consciousness/spirit leaving the body and observing it accurately from another vantage point. This is the OBE stage and can signal the start of a 'deeper' NDE when the spirit body leaves Earth for other venues.

A genuine OBE is not a hallucination and will enable the floating spirit to observe the surroundings and activities accurately. This case described by the cardiologist Dr Maurice Rawlings[7] is typical. Rawlings was prominent in his field, serving as physician to President Dwight Eisenhower and also to the Joint Chiefs of Staff. His example involved a patient who was interviewed after his OBE:

> I remember getting out of my body headfirst and floating over to the corner of the room. My wife was crying and I tried to tell her to look over here at me. No one paid any attention. I moved past the two doctors and looked down at my body. The clothes had been burnt from the fire and my face was a mass of peeling skin. The doctor said, 'Is the machine charged to four hundred?' and then he put two metal discs on my chest that were wired to the machine. I saw my body jump.

This experience describes the features of an OBE – where the spirit has separated from the body and accurately observes the body and activities on Earth. However, 'buyer beware', because there are reported OBEs and NDEs that are imagined and not real. This is because NDEs have become part of the expectation of many dying people, such that dreams and hallucinations mimicking these can be thrown up by a traumatised or dying brain – often mixed in with more dream-like fantastic imagery – mythical creatures like centaurs, talking animals or plants, hostile nurses, celebrities living or dead, and so on. As one researcher Dr William Serdahely[8] has observed, confusion between NDEs and brain-generated hallucinations may occur. A man who was electrocuted described an encounter with a centaur, but Serdahely suggested that the experience might have been a hallucination misidentified by others as an NDE. This strange content is in any case uncommon, and taken in the context of other experiences, it is most likely to be pre-NDE and hallucinatory. To quote J. Steve Miller[9], regarding NDErs encountering people who were not yet dead, or mythological creatures, or predictions that did not come true:

> I did my own study of 100 complete NDEs on Dr Long's NDERF site. None of these contained any of these elements, indicating to me that they must be extremely rare.

Nevertheless, it is a fact that weird content may readily be thrown up by a traumatised brain. The difficulty is that pre-NDEs are far too often identified in error as NDEs. Not making this distinction leaves reports and statistics regarding NDEs in tatters. Furthermore, the veracity of what is reported is also often doubted because the pre-NDE hallucinations smack of fantasy. Unfortunately, later stages of the NDE sequence can be tarred with the same brush and discredited unfairly.

Bruce Greyson[10] makes a challenging and perceptive observation, "Without exception, every report of a large study of NDEs published in a mainstream medical journal has concluded that these phenomena cannot be explained as hallucinations. Such unanimity among scientific researchers is unusual and should tell us something. Why is it that scientists who have done the most near-death research believe the mind is not exclusively housed in the brain, whereas those who regard NDEs as hallucinations by and large have not conducted any studies of the phenomena at all?"

The NDE Sequence

This is an introduction to my model of afterlife experiences. It looks like this:

Pre-NDE (brain function is changing) → NDE begins as the spirit leaves the body (OBE) → 'Deep' NDE as spirit travels from Earth to different afterlife venues.

When death is reversed, we find:

NDE → Spirit re-entering body (revival) → Restoration of brain function.

Does its position in this sequence make a pre-NDE invalid as a spiritual experience on the basis that the spirit has not left the body? By no means – our souls, spirits, brains and bodies are always interacting. From my Christian perspective, God designs all processes of life and death, and that includes the dying processes in the brain which feature in pre-NDEs. These are perfectly valid and are often life changing, as God apparently designed them to be. We seem to 'live' in our brains while on Earth, and the chemical, neurological and other brain changes in pre-NDEs are part of who we are and they influence who we may become. Remember that we are a spirit (our God-conscious dimension) and a soul (our self-conscious dimension) that reside *temporarily* in a body; while they are in the body, the brain and other functions of the body feed into our soul and spirit.

To clarify – I have chosen to divide the progression through the dying process as experienced by an NDEr into these three main phases – the pre-NDE, death itself as an OBE when the spirit leaves the body but is still on Earth, and then a 'deep' NDE as the spirit enters venues in the spirit world. This is not a rigid order because experiences can ebb and flow between these stages.

A pre-NDE may or may not progress into an OBE. An OBE is the first stage of a true NDE because the spirit has parted from the body. Nor can all OBEs be classified as initiating death – for example protective OBEs such as the OBEs of pilots spun in centrifuge tubes where the spirit returns quickly to the body, are hardly the initial step of dying. Nevertheless, all true NDEs pass first through an OBE stage because the spirit has to separate from the body, and in almost all cases will observe the dead body below before moving to other venues.

Furthermore, an NDE may begin and end at the OBE level alone. I have used the term 'deep NDE' to distinguish those that continue by leaving the Earth for other afterlife venues. However, to enable the script to flow better and put it in line with common parlance, I will use the generic term 'NDE' rather than 'deep NDE' and trust that the context will enable readers to distinguish for themselves which stage the account is describing.

Some examples may help to clarify this. Dr Maurice Rawlings[7], as a resuscitation expert, had the privilege of hearing some patients describe their NDEs immediately on their return to life. He describes an incident where a man began with a graphic and frightening experience of being in a pit with snakes before Dr Rawlings revived him. This shook him up, and it surprised Dr Rawlings too, because the man was a professing Christian and they both would have expected him to have only pleasant experiences after death. That same man had two further episodes of dying, from which Dr Rawlings revived him. On both subsequent occasions the patient had pleasant NDEs that followed the classic path of his spirit leaving the body; he had then enjoyed the nearby spirit world before returning to his body.

Can we explain why this patient had such different experiences? The first was a pre-NDE, occurring in his dying brain alone, with no record of his spirit leaving his body and seeing it lying below him. While graphic and very real to him, this pre-NDE was on the same level as a bad dream or hallucination. No doubt it will have served a purpose, such as encouraging him to put his affairs in order. This was followed by two 'deep' NDEs where his spirit truly left his body and entered the invisible spirit world, in which his experiences were pleasant and exciting, and included reuniting with his dead brother in the garden environment of Paradise.

> I found myself on a rolling green meadow that was slightly uphill. I saw my brother, and he was alive, and yet I remember when he had died. He was so glad to see me! We put our arms around each other right there in the middle of the meadow. I had tears in my eyes. Then we strolled arm in arm up the meadow. I remember that it was uphill a bit and then we came to a white fence that looked like a split rail, but I couldn't get over it. Some force seemed to keep me from getting over that fence. I didn't see anybody on the other side and there didn't seem to be any reason why I couldn't get over that fence!
>
> The next thing I remember I was feeling this thud on my chest... I woke up looking into your face!

Imagine the relief this account could give to surviving relatives, to know that the brother was fine and happy!

The fence the patient described was perhaps a boundary into another section of Paradise. Others describe similar boundaries.

His third NDE appears to have been a preview of Heaven itself, because of the beautiful city over which he floated – 'the prettiest city I have ever seen.' Heaven is distinguished from Paradise by having buildings. He did not get the opportunity to investigate further: 'I was about to drift down and walk around in this city when I found myself back in my body.'

Rawlings[7] describes in some detail two different but similar experiences of patients who had a number of NDEs, which progressed from an unpleasant experience to pleasant ones. His summary is significant:

> In separate clinical deaths occurring in the same individual, which itself is a rare thing, it's always a bad-to-good conversion [progression].
> I've never seen a transition from good-to-bad.

This highlights a principle in which I have come to believe, one that I have alluded to previously and which is a vital key to understanding NDEs:

An NDE appears to be designed personally by God to be of maximum benefit for one individual.

Consequently, afterlife experiences are appropriate to who that person is – including his or her background.

Furthermore, NDEs encourage returnees to progress spiritually and to conduct their lives back on Earth differently – more lovingly – more morally – more healthily – more in keeping with God's nature.

NDEs are Individualised

Evidence abounds from NDEs themselves that they have been individualised by a supreme intelligence.

Living Beyond

Returnees, please grasp this – your NDE involved seeing your own body below you, not another body, and meeting your friends and relatives, not someone else's, and seeing your own life in review, not someone else's, and so on – depending on how far your NDE progressed and who you are. It was obviously designed for you alone, without mistakes, and your experiences were therefore also chosen and planned carefully and appropriately. And the plan can only have originated in an omniscient intellect – which by definition is God.

Unfortunately, too much effort has been spent by investigators on seeking a formula approach for NDEs – kind of a general description of what to expect when one dies. This has limitations. It is similar to trying to produce a general description in advance for one individual's life on Earth. Sure, we are all born, but that's where the differences begin, and thereafter they widen, until a description in advance for the life of any particular person becomes nonsensical, excepting in the broadest of categories – we all have to breathe, to feed, to grow through childhood into maturity etc. It is the same with the next world – there is no formula – no 'one size fits all'. The experiences have been carefully engineered to the best advantage of that particular NDEr, and take into account individual differences that include background and culture. Consequently every NDE will exhibit differences. Part of the adventure lies in discovering precisely what God has planned. Nevertheless, apparently to ease the NDEr into afterlife venues, there are sufficient similarities to life on Earth such that he or she does not feel totally alien. This easing into the new venues I call the 'Transfer Principle'; it includes the people and circumstances met with there. This is a term I will use again later in this book.

And just as it is on Earth, that we all belong to different families in diverse cultures and beliefs, it is hardly surprising that the NDE reflects this difference. This is how it can provide a transfer of relevance on return to the person's original circumstances – the Transfer Principle in action. Lessons learnt in the afterlife can thereby readily be imported back to Earth and implemented there. The principle is not precise, but I have found it to be a useful tool and guide for understanding NDE features. It has many applications – each new afterlife venue acting as a kind of halfway house to the next, such that all changes are progressively phased and easier to comprehend. For example, life on Earth can be like a halfway house to Paradise, which can be like a halfway house to Heaven.

The Transfer Principle means that, to a significant extent, previous life experiences, choices and expectations drive the subsequent NDE.

If NDErs found themselves with strangers from dissimilar cultures having different expectations, they would most likely be confused or distracted by the novel situations.

Indeed, different NDErs have described features that suggest God has arranged things carefully to enable their entry into the afterlife to be less traumatic. For example, an early meeting with a favoured relative, or pet, or the particular scenery encountered, or even a display of beloved items such as jewellery or a child's toys, may be provided to help to facilitate the transition. However, please bear in mind that what an NDEr from one culture finds especially interesting or calming may not be so to someone from elsewhere!

Perhaps for the purpose of not confusing the NDEr, the Being of Light and the angels seldom identify themselves, leaving it up to the NDEr to draw his or her own conclusions.

Nor do the spirits of prominent people who have pre-deceased the NDEr identify themselves on the rare occasions they have been encountered in the afterlife. Where there have been exceptions to this, they have mostly identified themselves as persons or beings described in the Bible, and usually to those who would have no issues with this identification, people to whom this information would not be perplexing. It is as if there

Living Beyond

is sufficient novelty for the NDEr to adjust to in the afterlife without the addition of further confusing elements.

Split NDEs

Interpretations of these can be confusing. In a 'split-NDE', events occurring in an afterlife venue can be viewed separately but simultaneously with events occurring on Earth. The martyr Stephen, while being stoned to death, nevertheless could see 'Heaven open' and Jesus Christ standing watching at the right hand of Father God (Acts 7:56). His was not an NDE because he did not return to life on Earth, but his death nevertheless illustrates a split-experience involving Earth and a separate afterlife venue.

Ashlee[6] provides a good example of a split-NDE. She was in a bad car crash trying to steer with her knees while changing a CD. She knew she was dying, but felt a peace inside and experienced a bright light coming from the spiritual dimension: comforting, loving, 'like a hug'. She was aware of rescuers trying to reach her on the driver's side, the left hand side of the vehicle, while she was simultaneously talking to an angel, dressed like a cowboy, on her right hand side. Ashlee, living in Texas, was not alarmed by cowboy garb. In other situations, angels have been known to take on a presentation that will not frighten, or will even encourage, the person they have been sent to help.

Her experience arose from her spirit becoming aware of the nearby spirit world before her brain function had ceased.

This cowboy/angel was in the spirit world on what appeared to her to be the other side of the vehicle, the RHS. She could turn from the one reality to see the other and then back again.

In Ashlee's case, the spirit world (the angel) and the living world (the frantic attempts to revive her) were sufficiently separate that she was not confused. She spoke to the angel about her life and how she wanted to get through this crisis. The angel reassured her that she was just visiting the afterlife.

A Care Flight helicopter arrived, used the Jaws of Life, and extricated Ashlee from the smashed up car. She then died and experienced an OBE, watching attempts to revive her body as it lay on the stretcher.

> I am sitting on the helicopter, on the edge, looking down on them about to put my body onto the helicopter, and I am thinking to myself, 'I've never been on a helicopter. I'd better remember this.'
>
> The spirit that looked like a cowboy, I saw him as they put my body on to the helicopter. And he said, 'Don't forget, this is going to be scary, this is going to be hard, but you are going to be OK.' And, boom, I was back in my body.

As the angel had warned, Ashlee's recovery and rehabilitation were difficult, but worthwhile, and she is now happily married with three lovely children and has also achieved a Master's Degree in Counselling.

In many NDEs the separation of the spirit world from the material world is not as clearly defined as in Ashlee's experience, and 'mixed-NDEs' result. In these, events occurring in the afterlife venue may become superimposed on events on Earth. The reverse also occurs, where events on Earth somehow become incorporated in the NDE. In the NDEr's memory, they may become blended and difficult to distinguish.

This effect raises further questions. Does the spirit have to be hovering *very near* the body for the brain's activity 'brain waves' to reach it? What process transmits the brain's information to the spirit, if in fact this ever occurs? If the brain is anaesthetised, will this prevent mixed NDEs? If, during an operation, a burst of brainwave activity is observed, might this equate to the entry of a fictional person, animal or activity into an otherwise 'classic'

NDE, or perhaps the appearance of a living person during the NDE? Suppose a grieving mother was at the bedside and calling out to her dead child, might that child, perhaps already in Paradise, receive hallucinations about having a meeting with that mother? There are many questions – but as yet only tenuous indications as to their answers.

Mixed-NDEs are extremely rare events in the thousands of reported NDEs. Consequently, they are comparatively poorly described as yet, and more examples need to be recorded before any reliable conclusions can be drawn.

Traditional Science, pre-NDEs and Classic NDEs.

I trained as a scientist and I am a fan of traditional, evidence-based science, which has achieved an amazing amount by a fairly rigid application of the Scientific Method. However, if the boundaries of knowledge are to be extended, it is appropriate for science to loosen up a bit in a number of fields – NDEs being one.

Science already helps us to comprehend pre-NDEs and will open doors to deeper understanding in this area year by year as our knowledge of the dying brain moves forward. However, some scientists hope to explain away all NDEs in terms of brain activity. Some cannot even conceptualise memories forming outside the brain because their prior experience has been memories forming within the brain – any more than scientists of earlier eras could conceptualise continents drifting, a hypothesis that they ridiculed year after year; none-the-less, continents continue to drift.

Science becomes severely limited when it comes to probing post-separation NDEs in the spirit world, as its scope is sadly tied almost exclusively to the material Universe. It does not need to be so to the extent that it is, but its development has been such that to theorise and investigate outside of the material box is a difficult challenge, but one that hopefully more and more research scientists will accept. There are constraints in doing so. For example, the self-imposed requirement for reproducibility – it is obviously difficult to conduct reproducible experimentation in a parallel but linked spirit world out of human control.

Dr Michael Marsh[11] and Dr Sam Parnia[12] express an important point of view when they argue that a dead brain doesn't make memories. Nevertheless, NDEs have produced provable memories of events happening around the corpse and afterwards.

Resuscitation specialist Dr Sam Parnia[12] explores the significance of this:

> We know from clinical tests that the brain doesn't function after death, therefore you can't even hallucinate. It's ridiculous to say that NDE people are hallucinating because you have to have a functioning brain. If I take a person in cardiac arrest and inject them with LSD, I guarantee you they will not hallucinate.

Remember, NDEs beyond the OBE stage happen outside of the brain's immediate proximity.

Despite the huge difficulties, certain scientists are interested in how consciousness survives beyond death and are turning their attention to a study of NDEs. Sam Parnia is one. Regarding NDEs he said during an interview[12]: 'As a scientific community we have tried to explain these away, but we haven't been successful.' He points out that the brain might be dead for a time, or damaged, but nevertheless if the patient is revived, the consciousness may return unchanged. This indicates that consciousness probably exists beyond the brain.

> I don't believe that your consciousness is annihilated when you reach the point of death. How far does it continue? I don't know. But I do know that at least in the

period of time in which we can bring people back to life, that entity of the human mind has not been annihilated.

On the 7 October 2014 Sam Parnia[13] published the results to date of the AWARE study, involving 2060 patients from 15 hospitals, the biggest study of its kind of NDEs. It raises issues for further study, and it quotes individual cases. In particular, the case of one carefully investigated patient caught my attention. This patient reported 'memories of visual awareness compatible with so called out-of-body experiences' that corresponded with actual events. This validation by scientists of what thousands of NDErs have already reported may prove a game changer for the thinking of some scientists. The AWARE study also suggested that 'A higher proportion of people may have vivid death experiences, but do not recall them due to the effects of brain injury or sedative drugs on memory circuits.'

Society is being impacted by a growing awareness of the afterlife, and good information is needed to set appropriate social, moral and spiritual compasses here on Earth, such that people are not led down blind alleys regarding matters of life after death.

To do this, we need to lay bare the essentials of each stage of an NDE as best we can, beginning with the mysterious pre-NDE.

3
Pre-NDEs

There is much to learn from the varied, intense and sometimes fanciful occurrences of a dying brain. Whether or not an NDE follows, I term these a pre-NDE.

A Pre-NDE – What It Is:

A pre-NDE occurs on Earth before the spirit departs the body. It will become better understood as brain research progresses, because it occurs within the dying brain.

Where a person's brain is damaged or expiring, but where there is no record of spirit separation from the body resulting in seeing the body below, we may anticipate any fanciful descriptions that follow to be pre-NDE in character.

Typically, a pre-NDE brings confusion because it is a definite and often life-changing experience, but does not fit the usual sequence of an NDE. This is because consciousness still remains within the body. Nevertheless, important experiences may have been occurring in the dying brain.

Because pre-NDEs involve memories stored in a brain, they are very varied and individual, sharing few common features with other people's pre-NDEs. Consequently, detailed descriptions of pre-NDEs may hold significance for those who have experienced them, and for psychologists and counsellors, but less so for readers. Accordingly, most of this book will concentrate on post-separation NDEs – whose characteristics describe realities in the afterlife and not simply occurrences in the dying brain.

Pre-NDEs, like drug trips, occur entirely on Earth and not in the spirit realm, although those who have experienced them may believe this to be incorrect.

A Pre-NDE is not an NDE

A pre-NDE is a stand-alone experience.

A true NDE that may follow a pre-NDE is different from both drug trips and having hallucinations. A number of NDErs who have previously experienced drug trips or hallucinations assure us that these past experiences are not even similar to their out-of-body NDE. Raymond Moody[1] quotes an example:

> It was nothing like a hallucination. I have had hallucinations once when I was given codeine in the hospital, but that happened long before the accident which *really* killed me. And this experience was nothing like hallucinations, nothing like them at all.

Dr Maurice Rawlings[2] MD confirms these differences:

> It is true that certain stimulated areas of the brain can produce images, but there is no sequence, no consistency, and no predictability. Out-of-the-world experiences rarely, if ever, occur from the damaged brain.

This conclusion regarding the independence of NDEs from brain function has been reached and supported by a number of other researchers. For example, oxygen deprivation as a possible cause of NDEs has been discredited. In Dr Morse's[3] studies, there was no more oxygen deprivation measured in children having NDEs than those not having NDEs. Cardiologist Dr Fred Schoonmaker[4] discovered patients experiencing NDEs had sufficient oxygen in their blood for normal brain function, and so on...

No chemical or electrical stimulation of the brain has managed to generate a sequence of images remotely similar to those described by thousands of patients who have experienced NDEs. However, some of the fanciful images recorded are similar to those described during pre-NDEs, because chemical imbalances or electrical malfunctions in the brain might be involved in certain pre-NDEs.

There have been major studies of NDEs in the last thirty years and ongoing research renders obsolete previous hypotheses that these experiences are caused by a lack of oxygen to the brain, or that they are hallucinations caused by chaos in the brain, or psychological disorders, or temporal lobe seizures, or replays of the birthing process, or are the consequence of the drugs given to dying patients. Some of these might well contribute towards pre-NDE experiences because they may affect brain function in certain cases. However, none have satisfactorily explained the OBE and beyond.

To summarise – attempts to link brain malfunction or psychological disorders to NDEs have been discredited; nonetheless these may contribute to our understanding of pre-NDEs. As explanations for NDEs, they have fallen short when compared with data collected during subsequent investigations. J. Steve Miller[5] gives an excellent overview of the failure of these and other naturalistic theories.

Dr Jeffrey Long[6], an NDE researcher and Radiation Oncologist, made this penetrating analysis:

> What near-death experiencers see correlates to their time of cardiac arrest and it is almost uniformly accurate in every detail. That pretty much refutes the possibility that these could be illusionary fragments, or unreal memories associated with hypoxia, chemicals, REM intrusion, or anything that could cause brain dysfunction. I looked at over 280 near-death experiences that had out-of-body

observations of earthly ongoing events. If near-death experiences were just fragments of memory, unrealistic remembrances of a time approaching unconsciousness or returning from unconsciousness, there is no chance that the observations would have a high percent of completely accurate observations. They'd be dream-like or hallucinations. But 98% of them were entirely realistic.

Further recent theories have been proposed to try to debunk NDEs, and still others will be suggested in the future. Their stumbling block, however, is that they will remain with a localised material brain in a material body in a material Universe, and so will never explain the OBE and beyond, when the consciousness leaves the body behind and begins a series of afterlife experiences in novel venues. In addition, the consequences of NDEs are startling. For example, thousands of returnees no longer dread death and many are living transformed lifestyles. Something unique and powerful has happened to these people. They deserve to be listened to carefully.

From a scientific perspective, pre-NDEs will be better understood in the future as brain research powers ahead, but NDEs will not yield readily to traditional scientific investigations.

However, from a Christian perspective, as taken by this book, NDEs are explicable as spiritual experiences, and years of confusion can be rolled away.

Pre-NDE and Pre-Death Experiences

A pre-NDE occurs in total on the Earth.

In a pre-death experience, the dying person does not return to life on Earth.

In both instances, people may communicate what is happening to them and around them while in the dying process. Sometimes these accounts may provide insight about the dying process and the beckoning afterlife. Doctors, such as the Paediatrician Dr Diane Komp[7], may hear these spoken descriptions from their patients and record what they have heard. Here are comments about Diane related by Elizabeth Stalcup[8]:

> In the early years of her practice, Dr Diane Komp reported to the bedside of dying children out of duty. But one day just before seven-year-old Anna died, the child mustered the strength to sit up in bed and cry out: 'The angels – they're so beautiful! Mommy, can you see them? Do you hear them singing? I've never heard such beautiful singing!' Then she lay back on her pillow and died.
>
> Anna's vision was the first of many supernatural visitations that Dr. Komp witnessed at the bedside of dying children. Although Komp was an atheist at the time, the children's visions forced her to re-examine her atheist beliefs. She reasoned, 'Surely dying children have no agenda, no reason to deceive me. They simply report what they see. They are reliable witnesses.'

That was more than thirty years ago. Today, Diane is a convinced Christian who finds it a privilege to serve families and young children facing extreme medical challenges.

Further Features of Pre-NDEs

Pre-NDEs are readily confused with the effects that may occur during heavy drug use, appropriately called a 'drug trip' since drugs can cause a person to feel as if they have flown away from their bodies into strange and sometimes mysterious experiences. Some pre-NDErs recover and place an emphasis on the universality of spirit and knowledge, as is common after an LSD trip; some describe transcendental experiences of music, cosmic unity, rapid travel, and merging with space or the Universe; some even become delusional about knowing the future. Others feel a 'unity of vibration' (or a disunity – less common) with other people or situations.

Some Examples of Pre-NDEs

Pre-NDErs may have their lives changed as radically as any NDEr. After all, we 'live' in our brain activity while resident in our material bodies, so what happens there is 'happening to me'. As in the aftermath of NDEs, the changes brought about are generally towards a more loving life and simpler lifestyle. Pre-NDErs often report a great deal of satisfaction with the resultant changes.

However, in some cases personal disasters have followed. Darlene is a case in point.

Darlene[8] was a novice scuba diver when her mask filled with water that she failed to clear. She became frightened, hyperventilated and then she found herself paralysed.

> Terror crept through my body – 'Dear God, please help me!' 'You'll be all right, Darlene. Everything will be all right. Just surrender.'
> She let go of the fight. 'Now I was seeing beautiful bubbles around me. It was like a kaleidoscope, beautiful... I was vibrating like a tuning fork. I was vibrating my song – everything I had experienced in this body. I was a part of the ALL; I was a part of Love. I was singing along with billions and billions of other vibrations, and my vibrational life was part of Heaven's music. I understood why I lived and who I was... I was being lifted from the ocean [which showed that she was still in her body] and was aware of a voice saying they did not know who this person was.

To this point Darlene had been experiencing a pre-NDE and was still in her body. Feeling herself to be a vibration in tune with the Universe is a common feature of pre-NDEs. But then a true NDE began: she had an OBE, watching from above as those strangers who had rescued her tried to revive her. While looking down at her body from above, Darlene experienced an attraction towards it, and zipped back down into it.

Was Darlene happy to be resuscitated? Not at all! She had wanted to stay in the afterlife that she had tasted. Unfortunately Darlene turned her anger towards God. 'I don't think that I had ever been so mad at anybody or anything in my life.' This anger presaged an emotional and spiritual breakdown from which it took her years to recover.

As in Darlene's case, pre-NDEs may be identified at a first level by an awareness of remaining in the physical body, or sometimes by feeling like a ball of energy or some other non-human presentation, but no spirit body is experienced.

Pre-NDEs may display other features too. As with dreams, pre-NDEs can change venue very quickly, and the experiences can be vivid but contribute no deeper meaning. Kerry[8] smashed into a truck on his motorbike, somersaulting over it and losing a leg in the process; he also suffered horrendous injuries to his head. In addition, a torn abdomen exposed his intestines. He summarised his situation: 'My lungs had closed down and I couldn't breathe. I had no blood in me. There was no way I could have been alive.' But his brain continued generating a pre-NDE before closing down completely, after which he had an OBE. Here is his pre-NDE.

> The first memory I have, I was in this place – a small brick house. I felt the presence of protection around me and a warm feeling. I had never felt more secure in my life as I did then.

Living Beyond

> In a split second I was in a room. It was a large room, almost like an abandoned room. The roof had been blown in; the top was hanging down.
>
> There was a man and a woman, a young couple. There were fifteen to twenty of these little kids running around, playing. I had a feeling that they were there for some kind of care, almost like a day-care. The young couple were looking after the kids very well. They were having fun, laughing and shaking my hand.
>
> All of a sudden I am not there anymore. I am at another building, like a truck stop. There were several tables and chairs, like a diner would have in it. As soon as I sat down, a man asked, 'Does anyone know how to drive a truck?'
>
> Having the requisite licence, Kerry parked the 18-wheeler alongside the building. 'That was all I remember about that place.'

Note how the scene keeps changing rapidly as it does in dreams, and there is no connecting thread or obvious lessons to be learnt from the experiences. Both these features are tell-tale signs of a pre-NDE. Pre-NDE scenes like these often take place in buildings in an earthly environment. True NDEs are designed by God to be a learning experience while they move from one real scene to the next. Deep NDEs take place in afterlife venues that are strikingly different to earthly ones.

Kerry's pre-NDE then moved smoothly into the OBE phase of a true NDE as his spirit separated from his body. 'I was hovering at a low altitude, about three feet; the only time I saw myself lying there. I looked down and saw this metal contraption holding my skin away from my internal organs; I could see my intestines and stuff. I was in no pain; I was "no worries" '.

His descriptions, which continued, of what he saw during his OBE described precisely the reality of the scene. Kerry was no longer hallucinating or dreaming. 'It was as clear and vivid as we are here today.'

A medivac helicopter arrived and took Kerry to hospital, where he revived after flatlining nine or ten times. He survived against all odds. Today he has a computerised prosthetic leg, but nevertheless lives an active and cheerful life.

And so we see that a pre-NDE operates in the dimensions of symbolism and creativity in a distressed brain. Often the content of the experience may be akin to dreams or a nightmare; it ends, just as suddenly, without resolution. Nor will the pre-NDE descriptions follow a similar course to that of NDEs, which generally share certain similarities to one another.

There are other more subtle characteristics within the range of a pre-NDE that may cause it to be misidentified as a post-separation NDE – especially if there has been trauma to the brain. One such could be seeing a light, as occurs in most true NDEs, and sometimes even a tunnel; however, brain research and modelling of a distressed brain suggest both experiences might be possible during a pre-NDE while the brain dies.

However, on probing more deeply, misidentification need not occur. The models of the 'lights' and 'tunnels' that may be generated in the dying brain are very different in character from those found in post-separation NDEs. For example, the pre-NDE light is unlikely to be vivid enough or to persist for long enough as to illuminate a pastoral scene and provide its exquisite and indescribable colours, as recorded in multiple classic NDEs. Nor has it been reported to be as dazzlingly bright. In addition, the computer models that I have seen of what the tunnel *may* look like in a distressed brain bear little or no resemblance to the tunnels described by hundreds of NDErs.

Further features of pre-NDEs occur wherein the person feels they are travelling; there is a feeling of freedom and a reversal to their fundamental essence or, as some of them say, their 'vibration'. They typically do not have a body, not even a spirit body.

Many pre-NDEs have much in common with drug induced experiences. Nora[9] experienced a typical though short pre-NDE – although it might also have been a drug-induced hallucination, as it can be difficult to distinguish between the two:

> I had no body, no form, no name, and no persona. I was my raw 'self', clear, simple, and aware. As I realized all of this, questions arose in my mind. Thoughts like – who am I, where am I, bloody Nora, is this a LSD flashback, what is going on? – to the point that I worked out that I must be dead.
>
> Upon realizing I was dead even stranger things happened. Suddenly I was jet propelled into space, like star trek hyperspace travel – stars just shooting past me to the point they formed blurred streaks. A thumping/pulsing sensation began and got stronger as the stars blurred past faster. Then I felt the pulsing feeling take over like I was being electric shocked. This feeling got stronger and stronger until I heard voices yelling my name, screaming 'AMANDA'; I panicked. [Why 'Amanda' when her name is Nora? A nickname perhaps?]
>
> This brought me around and it was like I got sucked into reality again, absorbed like a sponge. I was completely shocked, crying and a mess. I had been out for a long time and my flat mate reported that I had showed no vital signs. I had urinated myself during the episode and was badly shaken.
>
> Although the experience greatly scared and shocked me it has given me an insight into my true essence, my centre and complete self – with no personas.

Mark J[9] provides another typical pre-NDE description which, because of his intelligent observations, provides graphic detail. As a self-confessed drug user, it is debatable whether Mark's experiences were caused entirely by drugs or simply influenced by them. Because the dying brain generates drugs that mimic some of the effects of recreational ones, some pre-NDEs may even derive from a combination effect. Here are some of his descriptions:

> I still had no 'body' that I remember, but had the 'feeling' that I was an amorphous, glowing pure intellect... This was very pleasant and comforting and went on for microseconds or billions of years, I have no idea since time just wasn't an operative construct and had no meaning or relevance to existence. I literally had the feeling that I was everywhere in the Universe simultaneously...
>
> I suddenly just relaxed completely and allowed 'myself' to dissolve (?) open up (?) merge (?) into the 'oneness' that surrounded me. The explosion of emotion and (again words are almost useless) overwhelming 'Love' that I now felt made any previous feelings I had experienced even during this episode, however 'long' it had/was/is going on, seem like nothing! I cannot possibly put into words that any human language has that feeling. I was everything, I was nothing. I was everywhere, I was nowhere. I was everywhen. I wasn't. My intellect had expanded to contain every thing, time, place, and even being that was, is, or ever would be! I was unique, yet I was the tiniest part of the whole.
>
> I know this is sounding like gibberish... it even does to me at times when I read it on paper; but to have *been* it!

As said earlier, pre-NDEs like this must not be confused with actual events. NDEs, on the other hand, are real events taking place in real venues in the afterlife.

New Abilities Following a Pre-NDE or NDE.

An unexpected characteristic of some pre-NDEs, and NDEs too, is the discovery of enhanced abilities and interests. As NDEs often follow after pre-NDEs, it is difficult to determine at which stage the new abilities develop, and so I will lump them together here.

Nobel[9] illustrates positive psychological changes from a pre-NDE. From childhood, he had problems communicating with others and was something of an isolate before his pre-NDE. On recovery, he found he could communicate more freely and effectively in social situations. He also began writing poetry. His new sensitivity to others and what they were thinking enabled him to sense what they were feeling at times, helping him to empathise with them. 'I seek a level of communication and understanding that the likes of God would even smile down on. [I have a new] level of emotion and feelings to be shared with as many people as possible in my lifetime. When I die, it's only feelings and memories I'll be able to bring with me. I should hope they will be good.'

These new abilities do not always have a positive outcome in terms of relationships. Tony[8] is an orthopaedic surgeon who discovered a new talent for playing the piano and composing original music. Previously he had shown no musical talent or interest in classical music in particular, but composing and playing began to dominate his life on return, to the exclusion of his family. Divorce followed. The lesson we may draw from his experience could be not to obsess over any new gifting that might result after a pre-NDE or an NDE.

Ricky Randolph[10] handled successfully a similar gifting to Tony's. Following his NDE, he found that he could play instruments he had never played previously, but he remained careful to lead a balanced life not dominated totally by his music. Songs just seemed to come to him, and he formed 'The Master's

Touch', a touring gospel group. 'I have been able to help others in ways I never dreamed,' he concludes.

Pre-NDE and Pre-death Helpers

Angels sometimes attend a dying person before death; in rarer cases deceased relatives are seen, and even more rarely Jesus is recognised. If these helpers are seen during the pre-NDE stage, the dying patient will often describe them and even call out their names. This is often just prior to death because the spirit then leaves the body and joins those who have been sent to help. In this sense, these deathbed 'premonitions' can link the pre-NDE with the death or near-death that follows.

Natalie Kalmus[11], renowned for her contribution to the development of Technicolor in movies, described the death of her sister Eleanor Smith:

> I sat on her bed and took her hand. It was on fire. Then she seemed to rise up in bed almost to a sitting position.
> 'Natalie,' she said, 'There are so many of them. There's Fred, and Ruth – what's she doing here?'
> An electric shock went through me. She had said Ruth! Ruth was her cousin who had died suddenly the week before. But Eleanor had not been told of Ruth's sudden death!
> Chill after chill shot up and down my spine. I felt on the verge of some powerful, almost frightening knowledge. She had murmured Ruth's name!
> Her voice was surprisingly clear. 'It's so confusing. So many of them!' Suddenly her arms stretched out as happily as when she had welcomed me. 'I'm going up,' she murmured.
> Never again will death frighten me in any way.

This is a surprisingly common occurrence in the literature, a dying person identifying someone sent to accompany them.

Here is another example, of one of Dr Penny Sartori's[12] terminally ill patients, whose family were called to the hospital at 3 am to say goodbye.

> At one point, he smiled and appeared to converse with someone no one else could see. He subsequently told his family that he had been visited by his deceased mother and grandmother, and also by his sister. His sister had died the previous week, but the family had made a point of not telling him for fear of setting back his recovery. He died a few days later.

It is now time to see how a pre-NDE can dovetail into a classic NDE.

4

Blast-Off! The NDE Begins

*Pre-NDE → OBE(on Earth) → 'deep'
NDE (in afterlife venues)*

Identifying NDE Venues

The venues NDErs visit seem to be determined by what they need most at a deep level, as will be discussed later. Identifying these venues becomes seminal to understanding the NDE as a whole. In turn, this facilitates maximum benefit when returnees reflect upon the experiences that occurred there.

A major stumbling block to this vital process is the misidentification of afterlife venues by NDErs and researchers alike. Paradise is often misidentified as Heaven, and Hades as Hell, the consequences being unnecessary confusion and personal difficulties for the returnee.

A brief examination of what happened to Jesus after his death throws light on these venues, together with their different features and purposes.

Paradise is not Heaven

The thief crucified beside Jesus asked whether he could become part of Jesus' future kingdom.

Jesus made a startling reply. 'Today you will be with me in Paradise' (Luke 23:43).

Note that Jesus did not say, 'Today you will be with me in Heaven,' because his spirit was not going to Heaven, and nor was

Living Beyond

the thief's spirit. Jesus, who was always careful with his words, stated that he personally was going to Paradise, and that the thief would be there with him.

This was a kind and thoughtful answer to a man about to die, who had just acknowledged that he deserved to be crucified because of the life he had led. He had been looking to Jesus for some distant redemption: 'Jesus, remember me when you come into your kingdom', but Jesus instead offered him immediate comfort: 'Truly I say to you, today you will be with me in Paradise'. Neither of them were going to be re-embodied that day to enter Heaven or anywhere else – their bodies remained hanging on the crosses till removed later for burial. By then their spirits had long since departed and gone to Paradise.

What was the Paradise Jesus was going to that day, with the thief, if it was not the same as Heaven? The word 'Paradise' derived from an ancient Persian (Iranian) word found in the Avestan language, and simply meant a garden, generally one that had been walled in. If you have a garden at home, especially if it is walled or fenced to separate it from others, then that is your Paradise. It often referred to a royal garden, such as the hanging gardens of Babylon that were king Nebuchadnezzar's Paradise. In the Genesis account of Adam and Eve, we learn that they were in God's garden – the Paradise of God on Earth, and that God was often found in that garden. Some kings had several gardens at different palaces, different paradises that they owned, and it appears from scripture that God does too. Note that in the particular garden for Adam and Eve that God designed, there is no record of buildings – God presumably controlled conditions there such that even clothing was not necessary for them until Adam and Eve were expelled from that particular Paradise and entered the world at large, where temperatures fluctuate and clothing becomes helpful. Conditions in the Paradise to which millions of spirits travel nowadays are also reported to be very pleasant, having adequate warmth and light that some NDErs report as streaming from Father God himself, and from Jesus.

Jesus was obviously not offering to take the thief back to that original earthly Paradise of God's, because it no longer existed on Earth, so where was this garden that he was offering to take him to once he had died? One thing we can be sure about is that it was not located inside Heaven itself, because they were going as spirits and not yet as resurrected beings. The heavenly city is a place for those who have incorruptible, resurrected bodies that are comfortable within buildings. Based on the accounts of NDErs who have seen it in the distance, the city is situated amongst wonderful scenery including gardens that run right up to its walls.

God was to be found and related to in his earthly garden by Adam and Eve. Similarly, God the Father has related with millions of NDErs in his gardens of Paradise in the afterlife. He is most often described by them as a Being of Light. Jesus is also reported to meet with many NDErs in Paradise.

God is not limited; therefore he can present himself in any form he chooses to any number of individual spirits in Paradise simultaneously.

According to NDErs, there are no houses in Paradise. It appears that spirits do not need houses to live in.

Paradise is huge and described slightly differently by NDErs depending on what part their spirit may have travelled to, but common characteristics include wonderful colouring and even shades of colour not seen on Earth, exotic plants and trees, grass that is extraordinarily green, perfect and 'alive', typical garden structures such as fences, benches, patios, sparkling clear streams, rolling hills and mountains, and the prevalence of a beautiful light unlike any light on Earth, but which pervades everywhere. Paradise is picturesque but more awe-inspiring than any gardens on Earth, since spirit existence is incomparable to physical existence. There is some evidence from NDEs that Jesus enjoys Paradise, as when Richard Wright[1] met him:

> I was standing on a huge grassy hill with a big green valley below, beautiful forests on both sides, and a crystal blue lake in the distance. I was amazed. Then I looked to my left and there stood Jesus! I was astounded, and He looked down at me, smiled, and said, 'Pretty impressive, isn't it?'
> All my fears were gone, and I laughed.

Rev Royston Fraser's[2] NDE is helpful for our comprehension of Paradise. Killed during mission work in Chile, he met both his deceased mother and sister in Paradise, although he had not yet known of the death of either. Then he met previously deceased missionaries and some prominent people – all in Paradise, none yet in Heaven. Finally he met Jesus. He takes up the account:

> I asked what might seem a strange question, 'Where am I, Lord?'
> His response was, 'You are in the Paradise of God'.
> I told Him I thought I was in Heaven!
> But He replied, 'No man has entered Heaven except He that has come out of Heaven' (John 3:13).
> I said I had not really thought about it, but I did recall reading it.
> 'Do you not remember what I said to the thief on the cross?' He asked me.
> Of course I did: 'This day you will be with me in Paradise'.

This distinction between Paradise being for the spirits of the dead now, with Heaven being a future venue after the Judgement, was important enough for Jesus to emphasise to Royston.

Furthermore, this distinction holds up in word studies of the scriptures. In addition, it was understood and taught by the early church.

Unless this difference is clear, NDErs may think they have been to Heaven and not to Paradise. So what? We find a potentially disastrous attitude creeping in – 'Uncle Joe was a drunk and beat his wife, but I saw him in Heaven, so obviously nearly everyone is going to Heaven'. Not so. Only at Judgement will God assign who goes where. Just as the Earth itself is wonderful but not everyone living on it will spend their eternity with God, so it is with Paradise. Nearly every book with the word 'Heaven' in its title should have it replaced by the word 'Paradise' instead.

This is a key to understanding NDEs:

Pleasant NDEs described by adults did not generally take place in Heaven, but in Paradise.

Unfortunately, the distinction made by Jesus and the Bible has become confused in the literature. It would become tedious were I to try to draw attention to this in the titles and quotes I use throughout this book.

Nevertheless, I ask the reader to keep in mind this important distinction while reading, as it at once clarifies much of the confusion surrounding NDEs. At death, the spirits of adults who enjoy a pleasant NDE have travelled to Paradise – not Heaven. Interestingly, though, the spirits of young children often have different NDE experiences in Heaven itself – as we will come to later.

Hades is not Hell

Paradise is situated in the spirit world within a venue termed Hades in scripture, which is the destination of the departed spirits of adults. Hades has 'a bad name' that is largely unwarranted and

Living Beyond

needs further explanation. The difference between the venues Hades and Hell can be a major cause of confusion for NDErs, and others too.

Why can I state that Jesus' spirit at death did not go to the heavenly city, but rather a venue within Hades?

First of all, his body remained on the cross that crucifixion day, so it was his spirit that travelled to the world of departed spirits, which is identified as Hades in scripture. They were going to Paradise, both he and the thief, despite their bodies being left behind. Paradise is therefore in Hades; it is the garden section enjoyed by spirits there.

There is at least one other location in Hades besides Paradise. It is termed the Prison, to which spirits at death may travel – though Jesus was reassuring the dying thief that he would that very day accompany him to the pleasant, Paradise section.

From scripture, we see that our spirits and souls will live in Hades between the time of our death and our resurrection, in regions designed for spirits; we would not be within the heavenly city unless perhaps God decreed an exception for us. That is why hopeful statements like, 'She is smiling down at you from Heaven,' are a human construct that does not reflect reality.

How else do we know that Jesus was not going to Heaven on the day of his death, but to Paradise? When he met Mary Magdalene once he had been resurrected, and was no longer in his spirit body but in a physical resurrected body that could be touched, eat fish and so on, he told her that he had not yet ascended to his Father, who Jesus had taught them already 'is in Heaven'. Jesus told Mary (John 20:17) 'Do not hold on to me, for I have not yet ascended to the Father. Go instead to my brothers and tell them, "I am ascending to my Father and your Father, to my God and your God."'

For some Christians the next few paragraphs may be a little shocking, because of inaccurate, unbiblical concepts that have become entrenched in some parts of the Church and society. I will need to explain how these false concepts arose; otherwise it may be difficult to believe that Jesus' spirit went to Hades and not Heaven while his body remained behind on Earth.

Unfortunately, the King James translation of the Bible, which held sway in many churches for centuries, translated both 'Gehenna' and 'Hades' as 'Hell', which is where most of this confusion was birthed. The confusion is not found in the original Greek language of the New Testament, nor is it to be found in Jesus' own teachings, because he used his words carefully and precisely. Jesus reserved the word 'Gehenna' (which is similar in the Aramaic he spoke, in Hebrew, and in New Testament Greek) for when he referred to the place of torment for re-embodied spirits after the final Judgement – i.e. Hell.

Hell is presumably unoccupied by people at present, because the Day of Judgement has not yet happened. We find that spirits of the dead go in the interim to another place, given the name 'Hades' (Greek) in the New Testament or 'Sheol' in the Hebrew of the Old Testament. We read in Ezekiel 26:20: 'I will bring you down with those who descend into Sheol (Hades), to the people of ancient times (or olden days)'.

So we see that departed spirits will occupy Hades (Sheol) together with the spirits of those who have died over the centuries. They will remain there until shortly before Judgement.

Revelation 20:13 tells us about what happens next, as revealed to the Apostle John in a vision:

> Death and Hades gave up the dead that were in them, and each person was judged according to what they had done.

Hades was a word borrowed from the Greek language, where it is used to describe either the grave or pit, or the place of departed spirits. Although the Bible indicates accurately what is found in this abode of spirits, the original word in Greek carried with it certain inaccurate concepts linked to the Greek belief of what happened to spirits at death. But the word, in itself, has no additional meaning. Sheol was also mistranslated sometimes in the Old Testament, as 'the pit' or 'the grave', but means the same as Hades. In the ancient Greek version of the Old Testament that pre-dated Jesus' birth, the Septuagint, 'Sheol' was translated as 'Hades.' The Jews of that age understood clearly that the spirits of the dead went to Hades before Judgement. (Douglas Connelly[3] in *After Life* does a penetrating analysis of Sheol as equivalent to Hades pp 64, 65.)

Hell (Gehenna) will be a very unpleasant venue *after Judgement*.

Because of his loving nature, Jesus spoke more often about Hell than he did about Heaven, hoping to warn people from going there. He offered belief in himself as a means of choosing life with God instead, through adoption into God's family.

Hades, in contrast, is not necessarily a bad venue. In fact most NDErs describe it as pleasant and peaceful, although that does depend on which part they have been to. It does have different sections, the pleasant Paradise section being one, but in addition we learn that there are unpleasant Prison sections, also described in many NDEs. These sections may be segregated further, perhaps even arranged historically and culturally – such as the Prison section for those who had occupied the Earth before the Flood (1Peter 3:19,20) and 'all those who were leaders in the world' (Isaiah 14:9).

Jesus' spirit went to Hades at death – not to 'Hell' as a (probably) 5th century addition to the Apostles' Creed rendered it.

How else do we know that Jesus went to the place of departed spirits at death while his body remained on Earth? Consider the verse from Acts 2:31 in which the Apostle Peter is interpreting the prophecy made by King David regarding the messiah to come: 'Seeing this in advance, he spoke concerning the resurrection of the Messiah: *He was not left in Hades...*'(Holman Christian Standard Bible.) This scripture teaches that Jesus was in Hades before his resurrection, but that his soul was not left in that place of departed spirits once he had risen on the third day after his death.

And what did Jesus do while in Hades? 1Peter 3:18-20 provides us with some information:

> He was put to death in the body but made alive in the Spirit.
>
> After being made alive, he went and made proclamation to the imprisoned spirits— to those who were disobedient long ago when God waited patiently in the days of Noah while the ark was being built.

This shows that one place visited by Jesus' spirit while he was dead was a Prison section in Hades occupied by 'predeluvian' people who had died before the great flood of Noah. We deduce that they were both historically similar and distinct, and apparently segregated from the peoples of other times. Please note that they had not been reincarnated as some might expect, but were still in Hades despite the passing of millennia.

It comforts us to know that Jesus had not forgotten these ancient imprisoned spirits, but we can only conjecture what it is that he told them and must be careful not to go beyond scripture in our suppositions.

There are other interesting venues in Hades beyond the Paradise and Prison sections, but they are visited less frequently by NDErs and will not be described in this book. The vast majority of NDErs visit either Paradise or a Prison section, or both. Additional venues, while very interesting, are only experienced by a few NDErs.

NDEs are Unique: a Special Word to Returnees.

Returnees please keep in mind that God, whom you may have met during your NDE, selected where you went. He had his reasons for wherever that was and for what happened to you there. Because he made you unique, your NDE will have had distinctive features. So don't be too concerned if your personal experiences were different from those of others, but be prepared to learn of their experiences, so that your knowledge of God is expanded. That is of prime importance for you, as you will be spending eternity in God's hands one way or another. We all will.

Leaving the Body.

We return now to the moment of 'blast off', when the spirit leaves the body in the early phase of an NDE. This is usually a rapid and surprising event. Dr Mary Neal[4] reports, 'I felt a "pop". It felt as if I had finally shaken off my heavy outer layer, freeing my soul.' Iris Lemov[5] recalls, 'I was brought back to my room after surgery and was speaking to my nurse, when a strange separated feeling between my body and my brain occurred. High above my body I floated, wondering why so many doctors were around the bed.'

In the small number of cases where the NDEr has noticed something more specific, it appears that the spirit generally leaves through the head area. Some others have felt their spirit exit near the head, as in the neck area. PJ[6] recalls, 'The next thing I know, I am pulled out of my body from the back, like someone has yanked my soul out painlessly but very abruptly – or my consciousness – who I am, in other words – by the back of my neck.' A further possibility is that a bodily wound or incision provides an easy avenue for the spirit to leave, as described by Darrel Young[7]: 'It seemed that I was coming out of my body from where they had made an incision in my chest.'

Ivan Rudolph

Leaving the body is both fast and unexpected. It can be so quick that the spirit is confused and uncertainty reigns. Lucas[8] was a drunken college boy in a dreadful car accident with three friends.

> It was almost instantaneous, from being here, to being somewhere else. I almost didn't realise that I had been in the accident, that I had been a part of it. I was just watching it.

Floating above the scene, Lucas saw a friend, Alan, walk over to a body lying sprawled in the middle of the road, face bleeding, that Lucas identified as his own body. Alan put a CD under the nose and could see no mist forming.

Lucas comments: 'It did not cross my mind yet that I was dead, I was just sort of living in the moment, going with it.'

However, as Lucas began to float higher upwards, he began to wonder, 'Am I dead?'

Lisa[8] also experienced confusion at the start of her NDE as she found herself floating out of her body. 'I did not feel any different, but felt very loved. I continued floating and trying to grasp that I had passed away. I found I could not grasp things [her hand passed right through them] and thought that I could not hold hands again or hug again!' [In fact, spirit bodies have found they can react with other spirit bodies and hugs can be enjoyed!]

Arlene[8] died during childbirth in Rome. Her NDE account is especially interesting because it occurred back in 1965, before she came across other accounts for comparison. She experienced fear.

> I am dying. I am leaving my body, and I didn't know where I was going. Next thing I was in the corner of the ceiling of this room... I saw my body, sweaty, writhing in pain [note that bodily functions continued despite her spirit and

soul having already exited]. Instantly the pain stopped. I equate it to getting into a warm bath after being very cold; it was so comfortable and comforting.

PMH Atwater[9] was also confused at the start of her first NDE of three:

You don't always know you are dead when you die. It can happen so suddenly and unexpectedly that the thought of death simply does not occur to you. For this reason, I did not recognize death. I only recognized myself as floating next to the bathroom light bulb with the ceiling scarcely an eyelash away. There was no darkness or distortion of any kind; if anything, my surroundings were even brighter and more distinct than normal.

As I looked around, distance relationships differed. It was now a long way down to toilet, sink, and bathtub surfaces. Although I felt no discomfort, the distance change was disorienting and confusing. I began to bump into the brightly glowing light bulb like some kind of moth, yet it did not seem hot when I touched it.

Gradually, the confusion cleared and my mind formed lucid questions. Why was I up here bobbing along the ceiling? How was this possible? Why did I keep bumping into the light bulb? The body on the floor was a mess, so I paid it no attention. Spatial differences were all that mattered.

The process of the spirit exiting the body appears to be a natural one. It may be conjectured that once the body reaches a point of distress or malfunction, then the spirit will leave, just as when you touch a hot stove with your finger, a reflex action whips it off for protection before you even think about it.

This is analogous to how, if the body is placed under certain circumstances of stress on Earth, the automatic response is for the spirit to exit the body, and a classic OBE may then follow.

Test pilots have been placed under high gravitational forces to 9G in machines that twirl them around (centrifuges) – until in some cases their spirit exits their body. Videos show their faces contorting followed by their bodies collapsing into unconsciousness. Machines monitoring bodily functions indicate significant changes during this process, but the important fact is that the pilot knows that his spirit has left his body and that he has become an observer of his own body and the centrifuging. He has had an OBE for his protection – but his brain is still operating. The resulting interface between the traumatised brain, the soul, and the spirit is both mysterious and interesting – and awaits serious research. Dr James Winnery[10], Head of the US Air Force Aeronautical Research Unit, comments that some pilots record confusion: 'Short dream interludes were reported by some centrifuge subjects, but these "dreamlets" were confused, fragmented, and often incorporated ongoing physical sensations into dream content'.

Suffice to say that an OBE does not necessarily progress into a deep NDE, which involves a more complete detachment of soul and spirit from the body, and then moving away and into the afterlife. For example, none of the pilots tested in a 1970s study reported seeing deceased relatives or meeting with a divine presence. As a natural process, their spirits simply returned to their bodies once the centrifuging stopped, the perceived threat having passed, the protective OBE having served its purpose.

Dr James Winnery has come up with some fascinating insights linking these pilot OBEs with those that occur during NDEs. Dr Winnery noted that the experiences of NDErs had a strong correlation with the experiences of his own fighter pilots who had had OBEs. As a consequence, he states that accounts of NDErs should be listened to closely, because their stories are very accurate, as demonstrated by his experiments on pilots. His conclusion: 'As a traditional scientist, these experiments add tremendous credibility to the NDE phenomenon'.

When I was pondering these results, in particular the pilots' spirits leaving their bodies while in the giant centrifuge, I wondered whether there would be other large groups of people whose bodies had been put under high stress such that their spirits left as a protective process, but later returned when that stress was removed. I supposed torture or assaults such as rape could generate those conditions, and using my model, I predicted that there would be records to that effect from those who had been tortured. So I googled 'NDEs and torture' – and found there had been many examples! It appears that it is an open 'secret' that certain torture techniques generate such stress on sufferers that they can experience OBEs or even deep NDEs. The Chilean Commission on Political Imprisonment and Torture provides us with a striking example[11]. Working with the testimonies from more than 35,000 victims of the Pinochet regime, they concluded that *'to provoke a near-death experience, by waterboarding, is torture'*. M.J. Cooper[12] in 2011 described in detail the 'out of body experience' of an African man who had suffered torture.

Regarding rape, violence and OBEs, I discovered a few examples. Laura's father, as reported by PMH Atwater[13], abused her as a 3½ year old child: 'My father, in a blind drunken rage, raped and sodomized and beat me to death in the middle of the night. At the most extreme outpost of pain, I cried out to God and in that moment I was torn from life'. During the NDE that followed Laura met with God, whose nurturing love enabled her to make a successful return to earthly life.

I am now convinced that an OBE can occur spontaneously as a protective mechanism – even as a response to a perceived threat where none exists, or under conditions of stress where bodily function can continue while observed by the spirit hovering outside the body, similar to the pilots undergoing centrifuge training. Some OBEs will progress to the spirit world and become deeper NDEs, while in many cases the spirit will instead return directly to the body once the perceived threat has been removed.

On looking through research literature, I discovered a wider variety of causes of OBEs than I expected. Some may not be accurate, and some others may remain to be identified. Here are some: impending accidents or disasters, specific exercise regimes (such as in yoga), high fevers, toxicity, certain drugs, self-hypnosis, deep meditation, reciting mantras, and other purposeful tinkering with normal mental functioning. A warning here – some OBErs report having had difficulty returning to their bodies: Carl Jung the famous psychiatrist was one, while others known to have been deliberately seeking an OBE as an exciting experience have died in apparent good health and 'without obvious cause'. Until much more is known about this phenomenon, it is unwise and dangerous to seek after it for thrills.

So we see that whether an OBE progresses to a deeper NDE depends on circumstances. Nevertheless, all classic NDEs begin with an OBE. This is a critical evaluation of your NDE. If you saw your body below you and watched the circumstances it was in, for example observing paramedics applying CPR or paddles to try to revive you, then you were experiencing an OBE – the first stage of an NDE. Your pre-NDE stage was finishing and your NDE itself had begun, and would continue until your body reconnected with your soul and spirit.

Conversely, if you did not see your body below you, then what you thought was an NDE might have been a pre-NDE. Remember, for you personally, it may have been no less significant.

Has a Pre-NDE transformed into an NDE?

This can be difficult to decide and going from written descriptions alone it is impossible to be dogmatic. Why might it be important to make the distinction? If trying to help a troubled person unsure about what has happened to him or her, an important step is to determine whether the traumatic event was a pre-NDE, an OBE, or a deep NDE. Each is very different and involves its own particular features and issues. Here is a useful sequence to employ:

1. Was the body seen separately, usually below the NDEr?

This may occur at the start of the NDE or at the end, shortly before re-entry into the body. It is the only feature that positively identifies an OBE and perhaps the launching of a deep classic NDE. However, consider Talon's[14] description:

> As I lay suspended in mid air near the ceiling (about 15 feet), my body began to roll to the left 180 degrees. As I looked down, I was directly over my bed, and I saw something that I had never seen before. There before me was me! My body was lying in the bed! My eyes were closed, and I appeared to be sleeping. Again, I wasn't afraid, and I remember thinking, 'How peaceful I look.'

Talon's spirit needed to turn over before his body could be seen lying below! In a small proportion of cases, a spirit will separate rapidly from the body and not reorientate, but will instead pass rapidly into a nearby spirit venue. This is accompanied by a dimensional change such that the body below would be no longer visible.

2. Have standard classic NDE descriptions been given?
For example, have dead ancestors been met with? Or a Being of Light? Did a Life Review take place?... and so on.

This appraisal is not as definite as seeing one's body post-separation because hallucinations and the effect of drugs may mimic a few standard NDE experiences and cause confusion. Secondly, it appears that NDEs are designed by God specific to an individual such that each will vary to a degree; it follows that seeking for common NDE features in the evaluation can be problematic.

3. Have the events described been culturally and religiously embraced by others?
Research, such as that of Cherie Sutherland[15], shows that others seldom readily accept true NDEs in that society. This is especially pertinent within non-Western countries. If a story has been acceptable, we can suspect either a fabrication or a pre-NDE.

Spirit Bodies

If you have had an NDE, what sort of body was it you found yourself in as you exited your material one? All NDErs have problems with this question as the spirit body is fundamentally different to a material body. It is more ethereal, in accord with what Jesus said to the disciples about a spirit not having flesh and bones – meaning that the spirit body is in no way material (Luke 24:39). Nevertheless, it retains sufficient individual characteristics that the NDEr feels at home in it, and others in the spirit world can easily recognise it. Some NDErs make surprising observations, such as those of RaNelle Wallace[16] whose body had been terribly burnt before death as a consequence of an airplane crash. She observed:

> My hand was clear, like transparent gel, but there was light coursing through it like clear blood. But, the light didn't run in irregular patterns as it would in veins; rather, the light shot through my hands like rays or beams. My whole hand sparkled with light. I looked down and saw that my feet also sparkled with light. And I noticed again that *they weren't burned*. My feet and hands were perfect and whole.

Crystal McVea[17] gives a thoughtful description of her spirit body:

> I was aware I no longer had a physical body. I had left it behind. I was now in spirit form. I never examined my form, I was just aware of it – just like we know we have ten toes without having to see them!
>
> My spirit form was not a form as we know it, with defined edges and shapes, but it was still very much a form, and I was very much a presence.
>
> And even without a physical body, I knew that I was still 'me'. The same me that had existed on Earth, the same me that had just told my mother I loved her before I died.

The fact that the 'me-ness' continues demonstrates the fact that the soul accompanies the spirit into the afterlife. Other reports harmonise with Crystal's in her description below, that they perceive themselves more clearly than ever before:

> Unlike on Earth, where I was plagued by doubts and fears, in Heaven [Paradise] there was nothing but

absolute certainty about who I was. This was a far more complete representation of my spirit and my heart and my being than was ever possible on Earth, a far deeper self-awareness than the collection of hopes and fears and dreams and scars that had defined me during my life. I was flooded with self-knowledge, and all the junk that cluttered my identity on Earth instantly fell away, revealing, for the first time ever, the real me.

'Before I formed you in the womb, I knew you,' God says in Jeremiah 1:5. And now I knew myself!

Imagine that – the first person we meet in Heaven is ourselves!

Dr Mary Neal[4] is an astute and thoughtful analyst of her NDE helped by her scientific and medical training on Earth. She confirms and adds to Crystal's observations that spirit bodies are not clearly defined, and that information is communicated differently, faster and more completely – but directly into the soul without the need of language – telepathically!

> They appeared as formed shapes, but not with the absolute and distinct edges of the formed physical bodies we have on Earth. Their edges were blurred, as each spiritual being was dazzling and radiant. Their presence engulfed all of my senses, as though I could see, hear, feel, smell and taste them all at once. Their brilliance was both blinding and invigorating. We did not speak, *per se*, but easily communicated in a very pure form. We simultaneously communicated our thoughts and emotions, and understood each other perfectly, even though we did not use language.

This complete telepathic communication is described in thousands of NDEs. RaNelle Wallace[16] portrays its strange nature:

> I found that Grandmother and I could think on several levels at once and communicate them all simultaneously. You can't know something without knowing everything around it, what causes it, what sustains it.
>
> Knowledge dovetails in the spirit world, each piece fitting with other pieces. Every fact connected to it is seen instantly, in totality. We have nothing like it on Earth. We can't even approach it. Our knowledge and ability to communicate is like a child's who hasn't yet learned a language.

A further unexpected feature is the spirit body being invisible to our natural eyes, such that friends, paramedics and others on Earth cannot see you even if you try to catch their attention. Light seems to pass right through the spirit without being reflected or refracted, which makes it transparent to the natural eyes of those left behind on Earth.

Numerous NDErs have said they did not notice much about their spirit bodies because they had become so caught up with the fascinating events around them. Others have said its composition appeared to be wispy and slightly bluish, like thin smoke – one NDEr described dead relatives as if they were wearing light blue gowns. It may be that a spirit is composed of substances as yet unknown on Earth, rather than simply an energy imprint as some have guessed.

Finally, Raymond Moody[18] mentions other unexpected features of the spiritual body, as described by NDErs of those they meet: an amputee has the leg or arm restored, and the spirit person appears in general in robust health aged somewhere between 25 to 35 years old, although those who have died as youths may appear still as young people.

New Senses and Abilities

Whatever its composition, the spirit body's senses are more acute than ever. Faster cognition; deeper logic, greater clarity of thought; superior overall visual perception and other highly developed capacities are commonly described. Among a large sample of near-death experiencers, 80 percent described their thinking during the NDE as clearer than usual. This all demonstrates the poverty of any model that suggests the dying brain is producing the NDE effects!

The nature of vision in the spirit body undergoes immediate change. PJ[6] died for a brief time while in class at school and found herself floating outside the building looking back at the classroom windows.

> I am passive but comfortable and very aware of the colours and details of this ordinary landscape before me – unlike a dream, this landscape reflects the type of day it was before I fainted: sunny, blue skies, afternoon, locals. The colours are extra vivid, the sensation of being aware fully of this day and landscape all encompassing. I take in the scene all at once, not just what is before me but around me and behind me.
>
> Then I am aware of the class change bell ringing and I observe students walking from one of the outlet school buildings towards the main building. The thing that I find curious about this later is that as I focus on these students, I do not see them with the same sense of recognition that I did in regular awareness – instead a part of me – my vision, I think – telescopes right up to them while the rest of me remains back at the same vantage point in the air.

> I am aware of what each particular student that I focus on is thinking and feeling – in fact I sense what it is to be that person.

Her observations that she could sense what was going on all around her, even behind her, is a common feature of the spirit body, as is the ability to sense the thoughts and the feelings of people observed. Her projection of her new sensory capabilities, her 'telescopic sensing', is also recorded elsewhere. 'I just can't understand how I could see so far,' a returnee said. 'It seemed as if this spiritual sense had no limitations, as if I could look anywhere and everywhere.' This zoom effect could be operated at will.

As mentioned previously, blind or partially blind people on Earth can see perfectly in the afterlife. Rev. Juliet Nightingale's NDE happened in the mid-1970s – and is recorded on Kevin Williams' NDE webpage (2015):

> There was never any sense of hunger, thirst, weariness or pain. Such things never entered my mind, in fact! Alas, I was pure consciousness, embodied in a light and ethereal form, travelling about ... or being still and observing intently ... and always in a state of awe. It was such a glorious sensation where I experienced such calm and a profound sense of peace and constant trust. I also experienced no blindness, (as I do with my physical eyes being legally blind), and what a sense of awe and wonder – to be able to see!

Vision and other senses occur without using the brain. Eyes and ears are no longer needed because the soul and spirit absorb information directly, which is why vision can be peripheral and not solely directional. Why then does the spirit body retain eyes, ears, nose and other organs? Since they do not appear to be used in an earthly manner, these may be for recognition of that person by other spirits in the afterlife. Also, they may be used again, when the spirit is re-embodied before the final Judgement. Our incorruptible resurrected bodies in eternity, we are told, will be like that of Jesus, who after his resurrection interacted socially. He was readily recognised on most occasions, spoke to others, commented on things, and even cooked and ate fish (John 21:9-13; Luke 24:28-30, Luke 24:40).

The spirit perceives its surroundings differently: In many ways it is as if our five senses have been magnified and speeded up – for example vast amounts of information can be transmitted telepathically very quickly. A brain with all its complex biology is no longer required to absorb information, which is instead absorbed directly into the soul and spirit. An unusual feature appears to be that emotions cannot be hidden, but are readily perceived by other spirits.

Furthermore, the mind becomes clearer and more alert, able to think faster and do accurate calculations with greater facility. The researcher Dr Richard Kent[19] has confirmed the enhanced precision with which OBErs using their new senses remember detail, often despite the flatlining of brainwaves: 'Patients accurately report details of car accidents, operating theatres, emergency rooms, and hospital staff. Patients even report conversations whilst their heart has stopped and they are being resuscitated. Some patients have accurately reported details of drugs administered, the time on clocks, details about hospital staff who appeared on the scene only after they had a cardiac arrest, and even details of the roof of hospitals.' The point is that these same patients would not in normal circumstances recall these details with such clarity as during their OBEs.

Spirit Interactions With Earth

Interactions between the spirit body and our physical world are problematic. Generally, there is no physical interaction in that spirits cannot grasp objects or speak or be heard, which is often very frustrating to them.

Dr A S Wiltse[20] described his NDE in 1889. He stated that his spirit body made contact with one of the men in the room. 'To my surprise, his arm passed through mine without apparent resistance, the severed parts closing again without pain as air reunites. I looked quickly up at his face to see if he had noticed the contact, but he gave me no sign. I directed my gaze in the direction of his and saw my own dead body.' Incidentally, Dr Wiltse had an amusing response after his spirit finally returned into his body and he revived: 'I was in the body, and in astonishment and disappointment, I exclaimed, "What in the world has happened to me? Must I die again?"'

However, repeated effort has been known to enable a spirit to have a limited interaction with the material world. Jazmyne Cidavia-DeRepentigny[21] of Hull, Georgia, describes her efforts:

> I was floating over my body. I could see and hear everything that was being said and done. I left the room for a short while and then returned to where my body lay. I knew why I died; it was because I couldn't breathe: there was a tube down my throat and the medical staff did not have an oxygen mask on my nose. I had also been given too much anaesthetic.
>
> In my out-of-body state, I'm using my mind to try and make my right arm and hand move – my arms are extended parallel to my physical body. I want my right hand to move, anything to move – I was trying to pull the tube out of my mouth. I looked down at my face and tears were streaming. One of the nurses blotted the tears from

> my face but she didn't notice my breathing had stopped, nor did she see me [Jazmyne's spirit] next to her. At this point, I'm trying really hard to make my physical arm move, but it's like my whole body is made of lead.

Cidavia-DeRepentigny's determination in her out-of-body state to make an arm move finally paid off; and, with great clamour and commotion, the tube was pulled out, an oxygen mask attached, and her breathing restored.

Her experience is especially interesting for another reason; it demonstrates that the physical body can still be functioning, such as crying, while the primary seat of consciousness has left the physical body and has joined the spirit body.

While spirit bodies do not interact readily with material objects still on Earth, it is important not to confuse this with interactions between spiritual beings. A spirit body can feel interaction with another. For example, Mary Neal[4] recalls:

> A feeling of absolute love was palpable as these spiritual beings and I hugged, danced and greeted each other. The intensity, depth, and purity of these feelings and sensations were far greater than I could ever describe with words, and far greater than anything I have experienced on Earth.

Richard Wright[1] provides us with a different example. In his case, dead relatives came to meet him:

> My mother-in-law, who had died about 11 years previously, came up to me and hugged me. She said, 'When you get back, give this (hug) to my baby.'
> It was then that I turned around and saw my body lying in the Emergency Room!

OBEs and Earth-Bound States

Some spirits remain attached to the Earth during their NDE instead of proceeding into Hades, and can be considered to be in an Earth-bound state. An addiction or a powerful emotional force such as depression, guilt, hatred, jealousy, anger or anxiety – can also attach or attract a spirit to some place or person on Earth. For example, four NDErs from Guam[22] claim to have 'projected' thousands of miles away to see relatives living far away, with whom they felt especial ties. As the number making this claim is so small, it must be held lightly until further reports accumulate.

In America, George Ritchie[23] did something similar when obsessing about reaching medical school in time. His spirit flew at great speed across significant distances. His thoughts seemed to propel him in the correct direction despite not knowing the way, similar to a modern GPS. However, realising how peculiar this was, he panicked and stopped near a cafe in a strange town to ask directions, but was unable to be seen or to communicate with anyone there. Years later he again saw that *same restaurant* in Vicksburg, Mississippi, although he had not previously been there in the flesh. He studied the map on his lap to trace the path his disembodied spirit had been travelling from the army camp at Abilene, Texas – it had been on course to reach medical school.

During his Earth-bound adventures, George Ritchie could see the activities of others who were in a similar state, of whom there were many. Their activities took place in the real world, but were invisible to people living on Earth. He saw spirits chained to occupations frantically advising those still working there, and a mother following her son and giving him a stream of advice, none of which he heard. Ritchie wondered whether what Jesus said in the Sermon on the Mount might explain these trapped spirits: 'Where your treasure is, there will your heart be also.' Ritchie saw the power of addictions binding people to Earth. Here he relates an example concerning alcohol:

> A crowd of people, many of them sailors, lined the bar three deep, while others jammed wooden booths along the wall. Though a few were drinking beer, most of them seemed to be belting whiskies as fast as the two perspiring bartenders could pour them.
>
> Then I noticed a striking thing!
>
> A number of the men standing at the bar seemed unable to lift their drinks to their lips. Over and over I watched them clutch at their shot glasses, hands passing through solid tumblers, through the heavy wooden counter top, through the very arms and bodies of the drinkers around them...
>
> And it was obvious that the living people, the ones actually drinking, talking, jostling each other, could neither see the desperately thirsty disembodied beings among them, nor feel their frantic pushing to get at those glasses. (Though it was also clear to me, watching, that the non-solid people could both see and hear each other. Furious quarrels were constantly breaking out among them over glasses that none could actually get to his lips.)
>
> I thought I had seen heavy drinking at fraternity parties in Richmond, but the way civilians and servicemen at this bar were going at it beat everything.

Dr Jeffrey Long[24] has investigated similar reports, in which OBErs have later set about investigating earthly details seen during their OBEs:

> They can see the tops of buildings. They can see far away. In my study over 60 of these near-death experiencers later went back and independently attempted to verify what they saw in the out-of-body state. *Every single one of these over 60 near-death experiencers that reported*

checking or verifying their own observations found that they were absolutely correct in every detail.

Ritchie, Emanuel Swedenborg, Josiane Antonette and other NDErs have described the Earth-bound condition. A consensus seems to be that calling out to God for help may enable spirits to move on from this unhealthy state.

Spirit Bodies and Resurrected Bodies

Spirit bodies are only a temporary habitation for consciousness, until we are resurrected and receive bodies similar to Christ's resurrected one.

Christ's new body possessed certain novel properties, such that he could simply appear in a room and not enter through a locked door, and then disappear at will. Nevertheless he could be touched, and made the point himself *that a spirit could not* (Luke 24:39.) Many people saw his physical body in daylight after the Resurrection, including 500 witnesses at one time, most of whom were still alive while that particular account was being written. Notice that his new body was recognisable as himself (1Corinthians 15:6).

At our own physical resurrection before Judgement Day sometime in the future, our spiritual bodies that we will have inhabited in Hades will be exchanged for new and imperishable physical bodies – not with the same properties as previously, but similar to the one that Jesus has occupied since his Resurrection. We are told that he became the forerunner 'firstfruits' of resurrected people (1Corinthians 15:20-23). Some of the frustration that NDErs report at not being able to touch, feel and talk to people left behind on Earth will pass away. In our new bodies, we will be again be able to express ourselves fully, using our hands, voice, and facial expressions just as people do during this, our first physical sojourn on Earth. Here is how the Apostle Paul expressed what we can expect at the general Resurrection – taken from the Living Bible, a paraphrase rather than a translation, but one which I feel puts the difficult concepts in this passage into readily understandable language (1Corinthians 15:42-52):

> In the same way, our earthly bodies which die and decay are different from the bodies we shall have when we come back to life again, for they will never die. The bodies we have now embarrass us for they become sick, and die; but they will be full of glory when we come back to life again. Yes, they are weak, dying bodies now, but when we live again they will be full of strength. They are just human bodies at death, but when they come back to life they will be superhuman bodies. For just as there are natural, human bodies, there are also supernatural, spiritual bodies...
>
> I tell you this, my brothers, an earthly body made of flesh and blood cannot get into God's kingdom. These perishable bodies of ours are not the right kind to live forever. But I am telling you this strange and wonderful secret: we shall not all die, but will be given new bodies! It will all happen in a moment, in a twinkling of an eye... [at the return of Christ].

In the meantime, after we die, we will inhabit our spirit bodies in the afterlife.

Into The Spirit World

Spirit bodies nowadays may leave earth and undergo a variety of adventures in new venues. An account of an OBE that progressed further is that of Captain Dale Black[25], a pilot, who died in a terrible air crash in July 1969. Dale's training enabled him to record observations concisely, accurately, and objectively.

> As the trauma team worked feverishly, I felt surprisingly detached. I recognised myself on the table, but felt no anxiety, no sense of urgency, no pain, no sadness, nothing.
>
> It was a schizophrenic feeling, being in two places at once, your body on the table below, another very real part of you floating near the ceiling above. That may be my body, I thought, but I'm up here. I can't be dead because I feel so alive! Amazingly, I wasn't shocked by all this, just curious, still wondering what had happened...
>
> I began moving higher, slowly but steadily. I noticed details in the light fixtures as I approached them. I saw the air-conditioning ducts in the ceiling. I was moving away from my body, slowly... out of the room... down the hallway.
>
> I began picking up speed. The movement was effortless and I had no sense of self-movement. I didn't know where I was going, but I was distinctly aware that some irresistible force was drawing me there.
>
> The speed of my movement increased. I couldn't stop it, couldn't steer it.
>
> I moved faster, faster and faster still.
>
> Then suddenly...
>
> I was gone!

Dale had moved away from our familiar world. The next phase of his exciting NDE was about to begin in the spirit world.

5

Entering the Spirit World

OBE → tunnel <u>or</u> direct → Hades (Paradise or Prison)

There are different possible routes to Hades, a venue that comprises both Paradise and Prison sections.

NDEs are Pre-Planned

NDEs involve a journey. Since we seldom if ever initiate a journey on Earth without an underlying purpose, planning is needed. For example, whom we are expecting to meet often determines where we go, when and by what mode of transport. NDEs appear to involve a similar style of pre-planning; furthermore, their sequence seems to be arranged by someone with our best interests at heart.

NDEs Are Purposeful

For a particular NDEr the order or nature of the events depicted in the model above might be different. I must stress again that because God made us different and individual, he deals with us individually, as he did with each person we read about in scripture. Nevertheless, certain general truths about how he works in human lives remain, summarised by his never acting outside of his character. This means that while an NDEr may be able to relate to many of the common features of NDEs as experienced by millions, it would be surprising if his or her particular NDE did not feature unique differences.

PMH Atwater[1], who has personally had three NDEs and has researched hundreds of others, has come to recognise that deeper *purposes* drive the NDE.

> Experiencers seem to get what they need – whatever it will take to get their attention and make an impression – as if near-death experiences were *purposeful* somehow... Sometimes what seems unloving is exactly the opposite of that in its impact on the individual.

Some NDErs realise this and it is helpful to them – Dr Mary Neal[2] states: 'Many have described my accident as terrible and tragic. I describe it as one of the greatest gifts I have ever received,' because of the NDE that followed.

God is mystifying, and his dealings with humanity can be too. Did you know that you were designed and pre-planned by God before the foundation of the world? (Psalm 139:16 and Ephesians 1:4). And did you know that God monitors your thoughts and holds you accountable for them? (Psalm 139:1-3 and Psalm 94:11). I found that God knew my 'private' thoughts as a consequence of a strange experience when I was a new Christian, years before finding it to be so in scripture. It still blows my mind, and makes me uncomfortable. God not only knows all our thoughts, he has recorded them – as NDErs find to their astonishment during their Life Review.

It is entirely to be expected, with all this planning, knowledge and prior concern, that God designs NDEs for the betterment, on return to Earth, of those to whom he grants them.

**NDEs are individualised and personalised,
for the greater good of the recipient.**

To summarise, God designs the particular features of an NDE depending on whom it is for. NDEs are thereby unpredictable to our mortal minds. Period.

Unexpected Meetings During NDEs

It might be planned for you to meet unexpected persons, living or dead. Sometimes these persons are only met in visions, which facilitate deep reflection on your life to that point. One of the unusual visions God may give you at any point during an NDE is of yourself as a young child. Crystal McVea[3] describes her experience of this.

> I became aware of yet another presence in the tunnel, just ahead. This was the person God had brought me to meet.
> This presence was smaller than my angels and also much more distinct. This figure had a body, and a face, and arms and legs.
> It was a child.
> It was a little girl.
> I had the sensation of locking in on her and soaking up everything about her. She was small and no more than three or four years old... The girl was skipping and prancing and laughing, just like little kids do on Earth. She was bending and dipping her basket into the brightness at her feet and filling it up like she was filling it with water. She would dip the basket and scoop up the brightness and pour it out and do it again. And every time she dipped the basket and came up with it dripping this magical brightness, she laughed.
> Every time she laughed, my spirit absolutely swelled with love and pride for her.

God then revealed that this vision of a charming innocent girl was Crystal herself, as he had delighted in her many years before! In real life, Crystal's innocence had been brutally taken from her while she was still three years old, through sexual abuse, a situation that had reoccurred many times over the years and had driven her to despair – thinking herself totally unlovable and shameful even to God. But by showing Crystal how he saw her at that age as a beautiful child whom he loved despite the abuse, God released her from self-loathing.

> Seeing the child was the most profound and powerful thing that ever happened to me, because it did something I didn't think was possible.
> It made me whole.
> In that moment, chains that had bound me all my life fell away. Chains of shame and secrets and lies and pain. Chains too heavy for anyone or anything to free me from on Earth. Chains that simply dropped away in the presence of the truth.
> That was the key sensation – that the truth of truths had been revealed to me. I was imbued with this penetrating understanding that God had always loved me, like he loves all his children. And so for the first time ever I was filled with love for myself.

At other times God may give the NDEr a vision of someone still alive that he knows will need to be interacted with when the NDEr returns to Earth. This vision can come with relevant deep knowledge imparted by God, and is sometimes a call to the NDEr to forgive and relate correctly with that person on return. In other visions, a relative or child may be seen who is still alive but the vision imparts some important information, guidance, or allaying of fear. RaNelle Wallace[4] experienced an unusual variation of this. To encourage her to return to Earth, she met her future son. 'His name was Nathaniel, and he hadn't been born on Earth yet. He said that if I didn't go back, his own mission would be hindered.' On returning to Earth, RaNelle went on to have a son named Nathaniel and at times when looking at her boy, she could see the adult she knew he would become.

Throughout my research on NDEs, I have been confronted by one great truth, that they have been planned in minute detail for the NDEr. Perhaps that is the take-home message of this book. Thousands more examples than I mention in these pages illustrate this foundational fact.

Moving Into The Spirit World.

At some point the OBEr begins moving away, perhaps directly through an earthly barrier such as a ceiling. The view of the room below may fade out or simply 'disappear' because a new reality is beginning. On rare occasions this can cause confusion – for example Dr Peter Fenwick[5] and his wife Elizabeth, prominent NDE researchers in London, mention a woman who had three OBEs during her second pregnancy. In her third OBE, Mrs Ivy Davey had already most likely begun to move into the spiritual dimension while on the ceiling, because she lost sight of her body below her. Other NDErs have commented on this effect, that as the nearby spirit dimension starts to appear, physical surroundings on Earth can become indistinct – even wall clocks, windows, pictures on the wall – become no longer visible and disappear as the next world 'invades'. Some NDErs report that a 'fog' appeared, rendering the earthly surroundings less clear. Gary R[6]: 'I was aware of a sort of shimmering fog that surrounded the area (a fog) that was growing more distinct and substantial by the moment'.

Sometimes the movement into spirit space is presaged by a sound: musical in some cases, or buzzing, clicking, tinkling bells, ringing, roaring or banging. However, in the majority of NDEs, no sounds intrude and subjects describe silence and peaceful feelings.

The movement itself may be at great speed, as described by Ken Mullens[7].

> I felt movement, as if I was going somewhere, but I didn't know where. I was drifting, but I wasn't sitting up or standing up. I was just drifting in the form that I was in, whatever form it might have been. At what speed I don't really know, but I know it was incredibly fast, as fast as electricity you might say. That speed factor was an important point; it was very, very quick.

Estimates of speed vary; some even believe they were zipping along 'faster than the speed of light', or at the speed of thought perhaps, while others describe far more sedate movement. Travel is exceptionally easy because physical objects represent no barriers to spirit bodies.

Moving Along a Tunnel

Many NDErs describe a tunnel similar to a space-time wormhole appearing, into which they move. They begin to travel through the surrounding darkness. The tunnel can take a variety of forms and presentations: some describe it as a funnel, cylinder, well, enclosure, or even vacuum.

The variety of tunnels experienced may depend on where they are leading, and what they cross to reach their destination – for example, they may be crossing different parts of the dark Void. The tunnel takes the NDEr *precisely* from where they are dying to where it has been planned for the NDE to continue. For example, to meet a group of ancestors in Paradise is a common experience, so the tunnel takes them there directly, or to a specific grouping or position in the Prison.

Part of the variety of tunnel types may lie in the language problem, in that to describe the passage to Hades may lie outside people's normal descriptive language. PMH Atwater[1] helps us to see this problem more clearly in her analysis, which suggests that after the term 'tunnel' became used by Raymond Moody[8] in *Life After Life,* it provided a word that people could seize on to describe their passage to Hades. Nevertheless, she believes that the word is not really appropriate.

> Suddenly, people spoke about tunnels, lots of them. I was attending a near-death experiencer group meeting after that and personally witnessed experiencers changing the term of what they went through, to 'tunnel.' No, I do not think anyone lied. What I think has happened over the years since, and because of continued media attention, is that we now have a word [tunnel] to use when we're not sure what it was we saw or travelled through during our episode. Words, after all, are a huge challenge for all of us [NDErs]. What do you call things when the language we speak doesn't cover or describe what we encountered? Tunnels? Yes, interesting word, and now affixed to the near-death phenomenon, whether it truly fits or not.

Her analysis may be a little influenced by her own NDEs, during all three of which no 'tunnel' was experienced. Nevertheless, her points about the problem of matching earthly language to afterlife experiences remains. What is difficult enough to identify and describe for those familiar with the English language becomes almost impossible for those whose first language is not English. Consequently, a number of researchers have wasted fruitless hours combing NDE reports from other cultures and various religions trying to identify 'tunnels' when instead they should be looking for two essentials that particularise the experience – darkness and fast, progressive movement.

Here are a few descriptions to illustrate how different these 'tunnels' may appear to be to the NDEr:

Dr Maurice Rawlings'[9] example of what an NDEr said: 'Next I was hurtling down this dark tunnel at a high speed, not touching the sides. It made sort of a swishing sound. At the end of the tunnel was this yellow-white light.'

Arlene[10], floating just below the ceiling, found herself 'being navigated towards what might best be described as a cylinder, and I was ascending into this cylinder. At the top of this cylinder was a light.'

Another patient reported by Dr Maurice Rawlings[9]: 'All at once I started ascending upward rapidly through this huge tunnel, round and round, not hitting the sides at all. I was saying to myself, "I wonder why I don't hit the sides of this?" Then I was stopped by this brilliantly lighted person.'

Sandy[10] who drowned during a kayaking accident: 'It felt incredibly quiet, no sound, no lights, no anything. But it was very much *me*, my personality. I got pulled into this black, circular tunnel, kind of like a big tube, and I was just pushing down this thing as fast as you could imagine, just so fast, faster than anything I had ever felt. All my worry was gone; I was no longer concerned with holding my breath. I wasn't afraid at all; I was in awe at everything that was happening. It was almost like I was this ball of energy going through this tunnel. Although I could feel myself moving, I wasn't hitting against rocks as I had been before; I was not being bounced around, there was no pain, no fear – just awe!'

Guides and Helpers

On Earth, people sometimes seek after guides from the spiritual realm for a variety of motives. However, this may lead to a plethora of problems because of the involvement of satanic forces, smarter than we are and whose goal is to harm people. Personally, I have seen problems developing in the lives of a number of people who have dabbled in spiritism, some close to me. For our own sakes, the practice is warned against and is condemned in scripture.

> When someone tells you to consult mediums and spiritists, who whisper and mutter, should not a people inquire of their God? Why consult the dead on behalf of the living? (Isaiah 8:19).
>
> I will set my face against anyone who turns to mediums and spiritists to prostitute themselves by following them, and I will cut them off from their people (Leviticus 20:6).
>
> The Spirit clearly says that in later times some will abandon the faith and follow deceiving spirits and things taught by demons. (1Timothy 4:1).

The guides arranged by God to help NDErs in the afterlife are totally different from demons and spirit guides. Turmoil and fear at times invade NDErs at their first entry into the spirit world. Guides and helpers from God may appear to allay this fear and assist with their passage. Angels or relatives most commonly fulfil this role, less often an unidentified person or even a 'Presence' does so. Many children report being put at ease on being greeted by a beloved pet that had died previously.

Fear is seldom felt on meeting angels for the first time, rather a feeling of 'I know you'. Dr Mary Neal[2] suggests they have been invisible companions during our lives on Earth, which could explain the familiarity NDErs often feel when meeting them face-to-face in the spirit world.

> Although we are rarely aware of angels or their intervention in our world, I believe there are angels all around us every day of our lives. Angels are spirit beings who are mentioned more than 250 times in both the Old Testament and the New Testament of the Bible... They care for, protect, and guide God's people.

Angels can present in different physical forms, from strong masterful men capable of dealing with scary situations, to beautiful gentle women who put the spirits of dying or dead children at ease. Often they are robed. The colour of the belts they wear or the threads woven into their garments have been perceived by NDErs as significant, perhaps for identification purposes or to denote rank. Dale Black[11] provides a typical description:

> At this time, I became aware that I was not travelling alone. Accompanying me were two angelic escorts dressed in seamless white garments woven with silver threads. They had no discernible gender but appeared masculine and larger than I was. Their skin tone was light golden brown and their hair fairly short. I could see their emotions, clearly delighted to be ushering me through this wonderland. They moved just behind me, one to the left of me, one to the right.

Angelic guides such as these two are especially helpful during the NDE in indicating what to expect ahead. They subsequently arrange the travelling. Some NDErs record angels even carrying them to Paradise. Jesus in the description of the rich man and

Lazarus in Hades, said in his parable 'The time came when the Beggar died, and the angels carried him to Abraham's side'. Abraham's side or bosom is a term used by Jewish rabbis interchangeably with Paradise, to denote the resting place for spirits after death and before Judgement Day. Hippolytus of Rome and other early Christian writers employed the term similarly.

Several examples follow of helpers sent to guide and support some NDErs in their journey towards Hades.

*Dr Mary Neal[2] was met by a group of spirits. 'They greeted me with the most overwhelming joy I have ever experienced and could ever imagine... I knew they were sent to guide me across the divide of time and dimension that separates our world from God's. I also had the unspoken understanding that they were sent not only to greet and guide me, but also to protect me during my journey.'

*Linda[10] was met by her son Scotty, who had died two years previously, but who came in his spirit body to be her escort. 'I was hovering over the top of the [MRI] tunnel. I was bathed in light, and Scott was bathed in light; it was a sensation of peace... he had his arms around me.'

*Lucas[10] was met by a helper who guided him along the tunnel. He was helped further, as others have been too, by a kind of instinctive knowledge. 'I *knew* that at the end of this tunnel there were people waiting for me... I *knew* why I was there, I *knew* what the light was, and I *knew* what was happening. I had no doubt that I was dead.'

*Julie and Robyn[10] died in an accident and entered the afterlife together. 'This spiritual presence was sharing that we were going to have the experience of rising. That we were going to go someplace that was incredibly beautiful, blissful; nothing that our life experience could possibly begin to prepare us for – but that one of us was going to have to come down again and that trip was going to be extremely painful, and only I would have the strength to do it.' Julie later revived, while Robyn remained in

Paradise. It is significant that until they parted in Paradise, the two women had shared very similar experiences. This suggests that those who do not return have similar afterlife experiences to those who do, at least initially.

A Light Appears

At some stage in the NDEr's journey, a mysterious light is encountered. It often appears at the end of the tunnel, towards which the spirit appears to be drawn like a moth to a lamp. Lillian Oaktree's[7] experience is typical. 'In a flash I was transported into a dark tunnel, travelling fast towards a bright, golden light. There was something warm and appealing about the light. I wasn't scared anymore. Within seconds I was out of the tunnel and in a lush, green countryside.'

Rose Richter[7]:

I went up. It was very, very, very dark. There were no stars. And I don't know if there was wind; that I cannot tell you. But before I became frightened, there was a tunnel there... I went through the tunnel like 'shwoosh,' and at the end of the tunnel was a light. I followed it. I had no choice. I came out by the light. There was no sun. It was all in a golden, warm, loving light.

Some mention that while travelling in the tunnel, they hear distant voices, often calling out to them, as if to encourage them, and to remove any fear.

Brian Johnson[7]:

Suddenly, I could see this tunnel or whatever it was, and the sides of this tunnel thing looked like a blinding bright corrugated metal, and a kind of very bright bluish/white pulsating light, and this light was like a strobe light on high power, but this light was about a 100 times faster than a strobe light, it was pulsating so fast that it was almost a steady light. Next, I could hear people were calling my name, when I found myself travelling to a place that was beyond my comprehension. I was no longer feeling the pain that I was feeling before this wonderful experience started.

In some cases, a tunnel is not seen at all, only the startling light in various presentations. This demonstrates that the *purpose* of that tunnel is to reach the light, but that methods other than tunnels may be used to achieve this primary objective.

None-the-less, the tunnel most commonly delivers NDErs to the light in an awe-inspiring destination that we will visit next – Paradise!

6

Paradise and God

Hades (Paradise section).

God may be found in the beautiful gardens of Paradise, just as in Eden in Genesis 2.

If your NDE included a visit to the Paradise section of Hades, then you have enjoyed a sublime experience. You have been particularly privileged.

Here is a mainstream description, this one given by Baptist Minister Don Piper[1].

> Heaven's [i.e. Paradise's] light and texture defy earthly eyes or explanation. Warm, radiant light engulfed me. As I looked around, I could hardly grasp the vivid, dazzling colours. Every hue and tone surpassed anything I had ever seen. I realised that everything around me glowed with a dazzling intensity... Never, even in my happiest moments, had I ever felt so fully alive.

RaNelle Wallace[2] was also astounded by Paradise's radiant beauty.

> A garden cannot exist on Earth like the one I saw. I had been in gardens in California that had taken my breath away, but they were struck into insignificance by the scene before me now. Here was an endless vista of grass rolling away into shining, radiant hills. We have never

seen green in our world like the deep, shimmering green of the grass that grew there. Every blade was crisp, strong, and charged with light. Every blade was unique and perfect and seemed to welcome me into this miraculous place.

And the whole garden was singing. The flowers, grass, trees, and other plants filled this place with glorious tones and rhythms and melodies; yet I didn't hear the music itself. I could feel it somehow on a level beyond my hearing. As my grandmother and I stopped a moment to marvel at the magnificent scene, I said to myself, 'Everything here seems to be singing,' which was woefully inadequate to describe what I felt. We simply don't have language that adequately communicates the beauty of that world.

There are thousands more descriptions given by NDErs of this Paradise. It is huge and may even stretch as far as the massive walls and gates of the present heavenly city.

Some accounts suggest that NDErs experience colours not perceptible on Earth; they record that the plants seemed lit up. Jim Sepulveda[3] noted: 'I was standing in a field, surrounded by acres of green grass. Every blade glowed as if backlit by a tiny spotlight. To my right stretched a dazzling expanse of vibrant flowers, with colours I had never seen before. Above me the endless sky was a deep and pure blue. The air around me was permeated with love.' Dale Black[4] emphasises the sensory impact of the kaleidoscope of colours: 'If millions of jewels had been gathered into one place and the brightest sunlight shone through them, it wouldn't begin to describe the colours I saw.'

No descriptions of Paradise mention dead leaves or dying grass – there seems to be no energy cycle of life and death as on Earth. It seems that God alone provides directly all the energy needed in Paradise.

Crystal McVea[5] even suggests that new senses are activated, opening up a deeper interaction with the environment than on Earth. 'In Heaven we don't have just five senses; we have a ton of senses. Imagine a sense that allowed us to not only see light, but also to taste it. Imagine yet another sense that isn't taste or touch, but some new way of experiencing something, creating a more amazing and rewarding connection than any of our earthly senses allow.'

Dr Mary Neal[6] felt an inadequacy when trying to describe what Paradise was like.

> It is impossible for me to adequately describe what I saw and what I felt. When I try to recount my experiences now, the description feels very pale. I feel as though I am trying to describe a three-dimensional experience while living in a two-dimensional world. The appropriate words, descriptions and concepts don't even exist in our current language.

As Mary discovered during her NDE, the afterlife *is* strange and God *is* mysterious to our thinking.

For example, different returnees observe that a curious unity and interconnectedness links all living things in Paradise. Some feel that they become a part of this strange unity.

Dean Braxton's[7] cardiac arrest lasted nearly two hours and his descriptions are especially detailed. To Dean Braxton everything *seemed* to him to exude life and even intelligence. Here are his words: 'It is a landscape of *more* because nothing is dead; everything is alive. It moves. *It thinks!* You say, "Whoa, that is way out there!" It was way out for me too!'

Weird, but those were Dean's impressions, and we know that the spirit world runs on different principles from our own. God is in total control in Paradise, so that the issues of a fallen world and fallen nature do not apply there. Instead we discover his life, love and unity pervading, around and in all living things. In addition, we should not try to equate plant life in Paradise too closely with that on earth. It is obviously different in nature, structure and function. Besides visual resemblance, there may be little other similarity.

Perhaps by synthesising different descriptions of Paradise, we can dimly conceive of what might await us there.

Dale Black[4] expands on the amazing music that appears to permeate Paradise.

> Music was everywhere. The worship of God was the heart and focus of the music, and everywhere the joy of the music could be felt. The deepest part of my heart resonated with it, made me want to be a part of it forever. I never wanted it to stop. It swelled within me and without me as if it were inviting me into some divine dance.
>
> The music was a seamless blend of vocals and instrumentals, the voices enhancing the vocals. Neither diminished the other but rather enriched the other. There was no competition, only cooperation. Perfect harmonic order... Perhaps this is what love sounds like when put to music.

This unity within diversity that was apparent in the music characterised all of Paradise. Dale noted it as a principle that appeared to drive everything.

> One of the things I somehow seemed to 'understand' was that heavenly order was everywhere and in everything... God was the heart of Heaven – His love, His will, His order.
>
> The multitudes of angels and people were responding to the will of God and acting in perfect order to accomplish His will.

> Even light – the way it travelled and reflected – was highly complex, yet mathematical and precise.
>
> The melodies and rhythms of the music were all in perfect order.
>
> Nothing was out of sync. No part of Heaven was independent of the whole. There was complete unity...
>
> The flowers in Heaven fascinated me – again, a delightful and delicate balance between diversity and unity. Each was unique [nevertheless] all were one. And they were beautiful to behold. Each petal and leaf illuminated with that glorious light – and added just the right splashes of colour to the velvety expanse of green grass.

Dr Richard Kent[8] summarises Paradise as seen through the eyes of a number of his patients in the UK.

> Each flower is absolutely perfect, and a work of art in its own right. Each flower radiates a light of its own causing a coloured hue all around the individual flower. Each flower is alive, and clearly moving, swaying gently. To observers' astonishment each individual flower is a self-contained orchestra of light and music. However, this music is music unlike any music that the observer has ever heard. This music spans many octaves simultaneously, and to the amazement of everyone, the music can be seen as well as heard... Perhaps this description gives new meaning to the Scripture in Isaiah 55:12, 'The mountains and the hills shall break forth into singing before you, and all the trees of the field shall clap their hands'.
>
> The observer is also instantly aware of the most beautiful perfumes arising from different parts of Heaven, mostly from the trees and the flowers. Patients describe a heightened awareness of smell, as well as all

other senses. Many patients have said that the different perfumes in different parts of Heaven are their most lasting and beautiful memories of Heaven.

Being in Paradise is described by almost all NDErs as the most wonderful experience they have ever had.

Confusion at times begins right here if an NDEr feels particularly unworthy to have arrived in such a pleasant environment. One violent criminal returned and asked cardiologist Dr Maurice Rawlings[9], 'Does God ever make mistakes?' What he was forgetting, or perhaps did not know, is that God is not judging the spirits that arrive in Paradise – Judgement is a major event that the Bible teaches will come later for all of us together. Paradise is a little like all of us who share the same wonderful Earth: we don't choose where and when we will be born on it, and the Bible specifically tells us that God's sun rises on both evil and good people, and that his rain falls equally on the just and the unjust while on Earth (Matthew 5:45). God loves us all, and it is his choice to provide a magnificent Earth for us, followed by an even more magnificent Paradise. We could not deserve anything like being on Earth or in Paradise – it is purely a gift from God. Why then don't all spirits of the dead go to Paradise automatically? That is a question to be explored later in this book. Right now those who have experienced Paradise during an NDE can rejoice in how wonderful it was and is.

The fact that NDErs have gone to Paradise is because of God's goodness; they cannot presume that they will automatically find themselves consigned somewhere pleasant after Judgement, any more than someone living in a beautiful environment on Earth can make that assumption. That could be a very serious misconception.

We move now from descriptions of the garden itself to common events that happen to NDErs in Paradise.

These experiences, if they do happen to an NDEr, can occur in any order. Just as each person's experiences on Earth differ, so too in Paradise.

Unfortunately, too much research has focussed on the commonalities in NDEs, and the individual differences have not received sufficient attention as yet.

I will attempt to record some differences as well as similarities in my descriptions.

The Person's Spirit Encounters Unearthly Light.

A bright light in the distance or at the end of the tunnel may attract the spirit as one enters Paradise.

Iris Lemov[10] recalls: 'The light at the end of the tunnel was bright but easy on my eyes.' Hundreds of NDErs record similar surprise that such a bright light is not one from which they had to turn away, as might be our automatic response on Earth. Perhaps this is because vision is very different in Paradise and does not depend upon physical eyes and the brain. It also makes the experience different to earthly ones and hard to describe, as noted by Dr Mary Neal[6.]

> In Ned Dougherty's account of his NDE in the book *Fast Lane to Heaven*, he writes 'Suddenly I was enveloped in this brilliant golden light. The light was more brilliant than the light emanating from the sun, many times more powerful and radiant than the sun itself. Yet I was not blinded by it. Instead, the light was a source of energy that embraced my being.' His description, like my own, probably seems nonsensical to anyone who has not shared this type of experience, but it is really pretty accurate.

Linda[7] gives us an artist's eye on the light.

> This light invaded the tunnel – pure white – it's not like a white that we experience here on Earth. The most beautiful white light! I'm an artist; I've never seen such pure whiteness! And when I saw the light, it was as if it was now being revealed to me, 'This is where you are going', and I knew we were moving.

This amazing light evokes deep responses from the NDErs. Descriptions such as 'ecstatic', 'dazzling', 'peaceful', 'loving' and 'embracing' permeate the reports. Here is a range of accounts to illustrate how different NDErs responded to this stunning light:

Crystal McVea[4] emphasises both its brilliance and also the peace and love it carried, in an interesting analysis:

> It wasn't just a light – or at least not light as we know it. It was closest to the colour we call white, but a trillion times whiter than the whitest white you've ever seen or could imagine. It was brilliant and beaming and beautifully illuminating, and that's why I call it a 'brightness'...
>
> But there was another dimension to it. There was also the sensation of cleanliness. It was a feeling of absolute purity and perfection, of something completely unblemished and unbroken, and being immersed in it filled me with the kind of peace and assurance I'd never known on Earth. It was like being bathed in love. It was a brightness I didn't just see, but felt. And it felt familiar, like something I remembered, or even recognised.
>
> The best way to put it is this: I was home!

Some researchers identify interaction with this mysterious light to be transformative at a very deep level. The timing, and venue for such an important event, appears to be quite individual:

Robert[7] found himself in a tunnel with gleaming light at its end, towards which his spirit gravitated – which is the most common experience.

Bill[7] who died in a construction accident, describes his encounter as one that began even before his spirit left his body: 'I started to be enveloped by this bright white light. There are no physical things you can see around you, you are just in this white light and it's the most awesome, incredible feeling that a person can experience. I didn't hurt anymore. I started to be overcome with joy. It was probably the first time in my life that I had felt unconditional love. When I felt the white light and the warmth and the joy, it felt so good and seemingly would go on forever, and I never wanted it to end!'

Ray[7] who died in a judo accident, saw a pinpoint of light 'ten million times brighter than the sun' into which he was sucked.

Cameron[7], who died in a drive-by shooting from massive blood loss, experienced the light coming to him 'like a movie projector' shining from a gap in the wall.

The NDEr Encounters a Being of Light.

The focus for most NDErs quickly changes from that startling light to a loving and intelligent presence that is sensed as being its source. Jim Sepulveda's[11] Paradise experience is typical.

> I walked over a hill, a short distance away, then stopped beside the base of a large tree. A light began to appear beside the tree. The blinding aura was too bright to look at directly. I squinted down toward the ground, and then saw a pair of sandals beginning to appear at the bottom edge of the light. As my eyes moved upward, I glimpsed the hem of a seamless white gown. Higher, I could make out the form of a Man's body. Around His head shone an even brighter brilliance, obscuring a direct view of his face.

Numerous NDErs intuitively identify this someone as God the Father, almost as if the character of God and his loving nature pervades it.

Many others, including Jim, have identified this presence as Jesus, and a number of them state that they were told this.

It is interesting that Christ exhibited a similar effusion of bright light on the Mount of Transfiguration (Matthew 17:2): 'There he was transfigured before them. His face shone like the sun, and his clothes became as white as the light.' There was intuitive identification of Moses and Elijah by the disciples at the time, similar to that which NDErs commonly report to take place in Paradise nowadays, including 'knowing' that the bright shining figure in front of them is Jesus – or God the Father – or some significant person or angel previously unknown to them.

George Ritchie's[12] encounter with the light quickly progressed into recognition of the person within that light. Remember, George was so obsessed with reaching Virginia and medical school that he decided he was not ready to leave the Earth just yet. The light came to him while he was still in his spirit body on Earth. Suddenly, the room he was in filled with an intense white light, and Ritchie saw that a man made of light had appeared within the light. From inside himself he heard the words, 'You are in the presence of the Son of God.'

> I have called him 'light', but I could also have said 'love', for that room was flooded, pierced, illuminated by the most total compassion I have ever felt. It was a Presence so comforting, so joyous and all-satisfying, that I wanted to lose myself forever in the wonder of it.

This was similar to how Jesus appeared to Paul with dazzling light on the road to Damascus, described in Acts 26:13-15:

> About noon, King Agrippa, as I was on the road, I saw a light from Heaven, brighter than the sun, blazing around me and my companions. We all fell to the ground, and I heard a voice saying to me in Aramaic, 'Saul, Saul, why do you persecute me? It is hard for you to kick against the goads.'
> Then I asked, 'Who are you, Lord?'
> 'I am Jesus, whom you are persecuting,' the Lord replied.

Before leaving the topic of a brilliant light announcing the arrival of Father God or of Jesus, it is interesting to note that hundreds of people on Earth have experienced similar interactions without having had an NDE. For example, the co-founder of Alcoholics Anonymous, Bill Wilson[13], reported that he was a despairing alcoholic when God's presence came into his room.

> He was aware first of a light, a great white light that filled the room. Then he suddenly seemed caught up in a kind of joy, an ecstasy such as he could never find words to describe... When it passed, when the light slowly dimmed, the sense of a Presence was still there about him and within him.

Bill Wilson never had another alcoholic drink. The wonderful work of AA, which has rescued thousands from a degrading lifestyle, began as a consequence of Bill's encounter with God. It is interesting that hundreds of alcoholics while still on Earth have reported their own encounters with this loving Being of Light, and that these experiences have been pivotal to their rescue. Those rescued in this particular way are a minority, though, of those whom AA helps. Why doesn't God appear to every hopeless alcoholic to rescue him or her in a similar fashion? Why do some have to struggle so hard, and many fail altogether? That we do not know.

We should not look to make God to comply with our expectations; his ways are not ours. God knows his business. Thankfully, he is still going about it.

Conversing with the Being of Light

The appearance of this marvellous Being of Light heralds the beginning of an interaction with him. Most NDErs identify the figure inside the light to be God. For most, this appears to be an instinctive identification, regardless of whether they had believed in him previously or not. Ian McCormack[14], until that time an atheist, used logic in his identification.

> Coming out of the end of this tunnel I found myself standing in the presence of awesome light and power – it seemed as though even the constellations in the Universe must find their energy source from this focal point.
>
> As I stood there, I wondered to myself if this was just an energy source in the Universe, or if perhaps there could be someone standing in the midst of this light!!!!!
>
> A voice immediately responded to my thought and asked me 'Ian, do you wish to return?'
>
> I responded 'I don't know where I am, but if I am out of my physical body I wish to return.'
>
> The voice responded 'If you wish to return – you must see in a new light.'
>
> 'New light', I thought, 'I'm seeing the light. Are you the true light???'
>
> Words appeared in front of me *'God is light and in Him is no darkness at all.'* I had never read a Bible before in my life so I didn't know this was straight out of the scriptures (1John 1:5).

Ian, as an atheist, had always employed logic to work things out. He turned to logic now, using the words that had appeared in front of him. *'God is light and in Him is no darkness at all.'*

> God is light, I thought – that is pure light – I see no darkness here, I have just come from darkness – I see no evil, no shadows – this is pure light – am I standing in the presence of God??? He knows my name and I didn't tell him, only God could do that. He knows what I am thinking before I even speak, only God could do that. Then he must be able to see everything I have done wrong in my life ... no ... I don't want God to see that!

Ian felt totally exposed and wanted to retreat into the darkness where he felt he belonged. He wondered whether a mistake had been made for him to have encountered God.

He drew back towards the darkness, but a wave of light shone out and swept through him.

> I felt pure unadulterated love flow over me.
> Love! I thought, how could God love me – I've taken his name in vain – I've slept around – I'm not a good man.
> But no matter what I said, waves of His unconditional love continued to flow over me.
> I found myself weeping uncontrollably in His Presence.

I should mention that just before he had died, despite his atheism but aware that he was dying, Ian had prayed for forgiveness to the God his mother had told him about.

Which representation of God did Ian encounter? Crystal McVea[5] gives an unusual analysis from her experience: 'Nor did I make any distinction between God, Jesus and the Holy Spirit, as we sometimes do on Earth. They were all One – the One before me now.' This would support the Christian perception of the Trinity, three in one, but note that God did not specifically identify himself in this way to Crystal: this was her personal deduction and interpretation.

On rare occasions, the Figure of Light does identify himself as God the Father or as Jesus, or as some angel (more rare). Because angels are heavenly beings, they can give off a glorious light, though it is not perceived as being of the same intensity as that of the Father or that of Christ. Note that I have termed angels as 'heavenly beings'. This is because they do not dwell in Paradise but in Heaven itself, but may be sent to Paradise or Earth 'on assignment', as was the case in scripture on numerous occasions.

Regardless of one's prior belief, or lack of belief, there is an instinctive recognition that this Being of Light is to be respected – as seen in Crystal McVea's response[5].

> There was a Being on my right, and instantly I knew who this was. And I felt as if my spirit form just crumpled and fell before this Being, as if – had I a physical body – I'd fallen to my knees and raised my arms and bowed deeply in praise and worship. Me! Crystal! The sinner and the sceptic, the one with all the questions! Here in the presence of God! Many others who have met with God in Paradise, describe how divine love characterised those meetings.

Crystal McVea expresses this: 'That is what I experienced in the presence of God – a beautiful new way of receiving and sending love. I was completely infused by God's brightness and His love, and I wanted to enter into his brightness and intertwine myself completely with it. I felt a miraculous closeness to God, but wanted to feel even closer. This was the Creator of the Universe, and I was in his presence! The sheer ecstasy of it! The beauty of it, the joy and the grace, the way my spirit soared and my heart burst – how I wish I had the words to convey just how miraculous this was! It was the blessing of all blessings, and I knew that I was changed forever.'

The greatest impact of God on many thousands of NDErs is his character – he effuses pure love, a love unlike anything experienced by them on Earth. Mary Neal[6] says:

> Don't get me wrong – I have been very blessed in my life and have experienced great joy and love here on Earth. I love my husband and I love each of my children with great intensity, and that love is reciprocated. It's just that God's world is exponentially more colourful and intense. It was as though I was experiencing an explosion of love and joy in their absolute, unadulterated essence.

Despite the glorious light that is effusing from this Being, normal interaction can still be maintained, often face-to-face. This reminds us of a strange experience of Moses in the Old Testament (Exodus 33:21-23). Moses had asked to see God, but had been informed that this would damage him – nevertheless Moses was allowed to see the back of God after He had passed by the cleft of a big rock in which Moses was sheltering. Here we find God appearing as a man, but one from whom powerful energy radiated, similar to the one modern NDErs meet, the Being clothed in unearthly light. The difference is that Moses' earthly eyes would have been damaged had he seen the glory of God directly.

NDErs Meet Jesus Christ

God the Father becomes central to those NDErs who meet him personally. So does Jesus Christ, whom hundreds of NDErs claim to have met, including some mentioned already in this book such as Howard Storm and George Ritchie.

Ian McCormack[14] also believes he met with Jesus and describes a typical encounter:

> Standing in front of me was the most awesome sight – I could see a man standing in front of me, but he was not like anyone I'd ever seen before in my life. His garments were shimmering white in colour – garments of light – I could see His bare feet and His hands were outstretched towards me as if to welcome me.

On a personal level, what does Jesus look like?

Dean Braxton[15] emphasises Jesus' radiance, but in addition a strange transmission of divine love, as described in scores of other accounts. 'The first thing that comes to me is that He is bright – it is like what John says, He is brighter than the noonday sun (Revelation 1:16 – 'His face was like the sun shining in all its brilliance.'). And the next thing is, we can look at him despite the brightness, without damaging our eyes or having to look away. And what you are looking at is not the physical part of it, you are really experiencing the love he has for you! It is like he only loves you and no-one else.'

Just as different witnesses to the same event on Earth may produce dissimilar descriptions, especially when the event has emotional impact, so it seems to be with descriptions of the person of Jesus in these highly-charged interactions. One associated problem is that the very bright light that accompanies the Being can mask details. Then the fact that the Being of Light seldom identifies himself adds to the uncertainty because, as Howard Storm[16] points out, sometimes angels may have been misidentified as Jesus. Angels, he assures us, can be pretty impressive. Nevertheless, even in the NDE accounts of children who have had no prior teaching about him, the Jesus they met with was similar to the long-haired, tall, slim, white-robed, loving person that most NDErs expected him to be.

It is possible, of course, that Jesus may change his presentation to best suit whoever he is meeting with, perhaps with the intention of not alarming them, for which again there is biblical precedent.

Divine Knowledge

God is unfazed by the questions thrown at him during afterlife interviews, and all interviewees report that they were satisfied by his answers, even though on return to Earth the details of these appear on the whole to have been lost.

Crystal McVea[5] provides typically insightful observations:

> And you know, back on Earth, I had so many questions for God. 'If I ever meet him,' I'd say, 'I'm going to ask him how he could let someone molest me when I was a child. How could he abide brutality against children or the suffering of starving people or cruelty against the weak? How could he allow such evil to exist in the world?'
>
> 'Why,' I would ask him, 'was he such a punishing God?'
>
> But in Heaven, all those questions immediately evaporated. In his presence I absolutely understood that in every way God's plan is perfect. Sheer, utter perfection. Does that mean I can *now* explain how a child being murdered fits into God's plan? No. I understood it in Heaven, but we weren't meant to have that kind of understanding here on Earth. All I can tell you is that I know God's plan is perfect. In his radiance, it all makes perfect sense.

Crystal expanded on these concepts later, after a time during which she had reflected on them more deeply:

> God allowed me to see the absolute truth about everything that matters in life. Before I could even ask the questions,

> God gave me all the answers. But then, when I returned to my human form, I no longer had those answers. I still understood that God's plan is perfect, but I didn't know what that plan was or why it was perfect. Try as I might, I couldn't remember what had passed between my angels and me, though I knew we exchanged mountains of insight in a constant, free-flowing, wordless, beautiful conversation...
>
> Perhaps we're not meant to have that kind of infinite understanding here on Earth. If we were, we wouldn't need to have faith, because we'd be so sure about everything. There's a reason we can't have that knowledge now, and God knows that reason. All we can do is have faith in God and in his plan for us.
>
> The incredible gift God gave me is the certainty that his plan is perfect.

Why isn't the specific knowledge people are given in Paradise retained on Earth? King Solomon in Ecclesiastes explained that 'people cannot see the whole scope of God's work from beginning to end.' Perhaps because when the brain kicks in again on the NDEr's return to Earth, it is too limited to process the vast amounts of information transmitted directly into the soul by God in the afterlife. Or perhaps the wealth of what they knew could divert returnees from the main commandments, which are centred exclusively in practising love rather than possessing special knowledge.

Dale Black[4] makes an interesting distinction between knowledge and truth. 'I somehow realised that knowledge is flawed and did not seem to be of great significance. Truth is what prevails and has supremacy in Heaven. When I had questions or needed understanding it seemed to be imparted automatically and directly into my heart.'

Dale like others cannot now remember certain specific details which had been given to him, and had to learn answers for himself through personal study and practice. Perhaps lessons hammered out on the anvil of earthly experience by this process become more deeply embedded in a person's character.

Divine Character

What can an NDEr learn about God from meeting him in the afterlife?

Dean Braxton[15] died following a kidney operation and was absent from his body for around two hours. He adds an interesting dimension when talking about his feelings in the presence of the Being, who in his case he identified to be Jesus. 'I know everything is right where Jesus is, and there is nothing wrong!! Some say it is peaceful, but it far exceeds peace because there is nothing to be peaceful from.' He reiterates this concept, that in the presence of this Being, the feeling is 'beyond peace'. He likens it to the peace of God described in Philippians 4:7, which 'transcends all understanding'.

Dale Black[4] provides further insight on the same theme:

> Part of the joy I was experiencing was not only the presence of everything wonderful, but also the absence of everything terrible. There was no strife, no competition, no sarcasm, no betrayal, no deception, no lies, no murders, no unfaithfulness, no disloyalty, nothing contrary to the light and life and love.
> In short, there was no sin.
> And the absence of sin was something you could feel.
> There was no shame because there was nothing to be ashamed of. There was no sadness because there was nothing to be sad about. There was no need to hide,

because there was nothing to hide from. It was all out in the open. Clean and pure.

Here was perfection. Complete and utter perfection.

In these accounts there is striking support for the Christian model of life after death in that this glorious Being effuses love, often to the surprise of the recipient. Christianity readily identifies the fundamental nature of God as being Love, so people of other faiths, or none, are often shocked by such an encounter, because it is far from what they might have expected. No other religion emphasises the revelation that *God is Love* as Christian scripture does. 1John 4:16-17 informs us:

> So we have come to know and to believe the love that God has for us. *God is love*, and whoever abides in love abides in God, and God abides in him. By this is love perfected with us, so that we may have confidence for the Day of Judgment (English Standard Version).

Dale Black[4] gives a typical description of experiencing God's love while in Paradise: 'God's love was transforming. To experience something so sacred, so profound as the boundless love of God was the most thrilling part of Heaven. It satisfied a longing in the deepest part of me.'

PMH Atwater[17] summarises her extensive research findings regarding NDErs: 'Most fall head over heels in love with God... they were bathed in God, immersed in God, filled to overflowing with God; and they return convinced of God... They know God is.'

However, meeting this person who is love – not who 'has love', but who *is* love – can give rise to misconceptions. The commonest is that at death we are all accepted forever by God regardless of the lives we have led. We will probe this .misunderstanding more thoroughly later; suffice to say for now that a parent may love a child, but if that child is opposed to the principles of the household or is violent towards that parent, the relationship and continued co-existence will inevitably change.

Meeting God in Paradise is more than a 'getting to know you' exercise – it has far deeper purposes, some of which are extraordinary and unexpected, as we will discover in the following chapter.

7

The Life Review

Usually in Hades

*O would some power the gift give us, to
see ourselves as others see us.
— Robert Burns 1785, in poem 'To a Louse'.*

Many NDErs who have progressed far enough are shown a Life Review, usually during the encounter with the Being of Light in Paradise, although the the venues vary. Masses of information can be presented in a flash in the spirit realm, directly into the soul, which is very different from how the human brain ponderously accesses and processes information. Consequently the Life Review can occur with events reviewed simultaneously; alternatively it may be presented chronologically. Differing styles of presentation are also used. As always, the experience is tailored to the individual for their understanding. For example, Susan Finlay[1] drowned in the River Thames near Oxford. She was just seven years old. After a brief experience of the beauty of Paradise, she found herself sitting in a large room with an enormous screen on one wall.

> As I looked I began to see my whole life go before me. At the age of seven my life story was not extensive, but everything was projected on to that screen, and I knew it was a summary of my life.
>
> I was shown key moments during my brief period on Earth – what I had done, followed by what I should

Living Beyond

have done. Sometimes it was what I had said, followed by what I should have said. I didn't feel condemned, but I knew that what I was witnessing was true – that what was being said or shown was not something that I could argue against because it was fair and right.

I could hear a voice explaining things to me, but I did not see anyone or anything, other than this huge screen.

Then, as quickly as it had started, the whole thing was over, and I was back on the riverbank in Oxford, with my friends standing around me, pumping the river water out of me!

The intent of a Life Review or 'debriefing' is sensed as being primarily for education and reflection, as we see in Grace Bubulka's[2] description that follows. Grace is a nurse and educator who died a decade ago. She describes the sweep covered in her review.

> Suddenly, I saw it all. I saw me as I was as a baby, a child, a teen, and adult, all at once. At the same time, I saw everything I ever did, everything I ever thought, everything. I saw events and people in my life that I previously considered important. Also, I saw many things that seemed-not-so important. I was aware of everything in my life all at once and I was aware of every response that others had to what occurred in my life. It was all there for me to understand ... everything 'good', 'bad', or 'indifferent.'

Grace then illustrated her review by describing one episode in detail, which is seldom done, but which gives us insight into the possible significance of what to us may appear to be a trivial incident.

> For example, I remembered knowing deeply about a situation that I dealt with in first grade as a six-year-old child. I was in class and it was a few minutes before recess. Sister Celine had positioned three holy cards on the edge of her desk in the front of the room. The holy cards were to be awarded after recess in the spelling bee that our class would have. I was at the front desk and could see the holy cards well. The one in the middle depicted a gossamer guardian angel watching over two small children crossing a bridge. I wanted that card so badly! As we filed out for recess, temptation overtook me and I stole the holy card. I slipped it quickly into my uniform pocket. No one saw me.
>
> During recess, I felt sick with guilt. I snuck back into the classroom while the other first graders were playing at recess and placed the holy card back on Sister's desk.
>
> In my near-death experience I remembered everything about that situation. What was really impressive, though, is that I was aware how very wrong that action was.

Grace did not feel condemned at learning this. It was embarrassing that others in the afterlife were witnesses of her misguided actions and weaknesses, but she felt enveloped by a comforting love that softened everything.

> I was enveloped in a loving feeling and given insight into areas of my weaknesses.
>
> I suddenly realized aspects of my life that were not compatible with eternity in the Light. I also knew now how to correct this. I was charged with the accountability of the remainder of my life.
>
> I knew that more was ahead in the Light that continued forever, but I could not go there now.

> Seeing my life left me with the impression that my life mattered and was somehow significant as to how far I could go into the Light. My work was not yet finished. My work was to begin inside me and within my family.
>
> I was able to concede to my impending return now that I fully understood the message.

The Life Review is incredibly detailed, vivid and real, and the emotions and feelings that are associated with each memory or image may be re-experienced, together with the emotions of the observers. For example, the NDEr may see himself or herself being born, and feel the emotions of the mother at the time, and of the attending medical staff. Of course, only an omniscient God has that level of knowledge about people, even to what they and others were thinking and feeling, such that any suggestion that the Being of Light is Satan or some other evil force during these reviews is clearly incorrect.

Some NDErs are able to recall Life Review events, unknown previously, in minute detail. These events had been presented graphically and carried an immense emotional impact.

The nature and purpose of the Life Review are fleshed out in these further examples, just a few of the hundreds reported.

Dr George Ritchie[3] described his Life Review as following an encounter with Jesus in which he sensed 'you are in the presence of the Son of God'. Jesus subsequently became his interviewer.

His whole life, 'every event and thought and conversation, as palpable as a series of pictures,' passed before him to review. He watched himself being born by Caesarean section and looked at the face of his dying mother for the first time 'whom I had never laid eyes on before'. There was no first and last scene, they appeared to him together in a single presentation, presenting the question: 'What did you do with your time on Earth?'

At first he tried to answer by things he had achieved, such as becoming an Eagle Scout, and taking out an insurance policy.

Jesus found this amusing and the light surrounding him shook with what Ritchie interpreted as mirth.

Then Jesus repeated, 'What have you done with your life to show me?'

Ritchie was offended by the question, thinking, 'Of course I hadn't done anything with my life! I hadn't had time!'

This thought was immediately 'picked up' by Jesus. The answering thought came as gentle teaching, 'Death can come at any age.' This was not presented in a condemnatory way, but as a simple loving truth for Ritchie to ponder.

He then realised that the question about his life was not about performance or accomplishments, but instead about relationships. 'The question, like everything else proceeding from him, had to do with love. How much have you loved with your life? Have you loved others *as I am loving you*? *Totally*?'

> Hearing the question like that, I saw how foolish it was even to try to find an answer in the scenes around us [Life Review]. Why, I hadn't known love like this was possible. Someone should have told me, I thought indignantly. A fine time to discover what life was all about – like coming to a final exam and discovering you were going to be tested on a subject you had never studied! If love was the point of everything, why hadn't someone told me?

Ritchie had attended Sunday School as a child, and Jesus reminded him that, 'I told you by the life I lived. I told you by the death I died.' Studying the life and death of Jesus teaches anyone on the deepest level about love.

George Ritchie had his Life Review while still a spirit inhabiting Earth, albeit out of his body. RaNelle Wallace[4], however, was moving quickly through the tunnel towards Paradise when she had hers. She makes some insightful observations regarding it:

> I didn't just understand the events; I relived them. I was that person again, doing those things to my mother, or saying those words to my father or brothers or sisters, and I knew why, for the first time, I had done them or said them. 'Entirety' does not describe the fullness of this review. It included knowledge about myself that all the books in the world couldn't contain. I understood every reason for everything I did in my life. And I also understood the impact I had on others.
>
> A part of me began to anticipate certain events, things in my life I would dread seeing again. But most of them didn't show up, and I understood that I had taken responsibility for these actions and had repented of them. I saw myself repenting of them, sincerely wanting God to remove the weight and guilt of those terrible actions. And He had. I marvelled at His sublime love and that my misdeeds could be forgiven and removed so easily.

Did this mean RaNelle had a clean slate, with little left to improve? Her Life Review continued.

> But then I saw other scenes that I hadn't anticipated, things that were just as awful. I saw them in horrible detail and watched the impact they had on others.
>
> I saw that I had let many people down in my life. I had made commitments to friends and family that I had just let ride until they were irreversibly unfulfilled. People had depended on me, and I had said, 'I'm too busy' or 'it's not my problem', and 'just let it go'. My cavalier attitude

had caused real pain and heartache in others, pain I had never known about...

I re-experienced myself doing good things, but they were fewer and less significant than I had thought. Most of the 'great things' I thought I had done were almost irrelevant. I had done them for myself. I had served people when it served me to do so. I had founded my charity on conditions of repayment, even if the repayment was merely a stroke to my ego.

Some people had been helped, however, by my small acts of kindness, a smile, a kind word, little things I had long since forgotten.

Consider next a different style of Life Review that took place on Earth just prior to a three-vehicle accident. Mary Beth Willi[5] reports that the light of God gently came to her as she desperately manipulated her car in an attempt to avoid the impending crash.

I was in my body but was taken out of Earth's time frame. There was no sound; all was quiet and calm. I spoke out loud throughout the entire conversation while His replies were in the form of thoughts placed in my head.

With time stopping came a huge feeling of enormous love that just kept growing stronger and stronger. The panic was replaced with love that gave me such a calm feeling that I was no longer afraid. I was being hugged, big time! I had never felt love like this before! Instinctively, I knew this was God. Think of someone who loves you dearly, now multiply that feeling by about a million and maybe you will come close to how loved I felt...

Most of us go through our lives being taught to believe in God. I was brought up in a very strict Roman Catholic household by parents who taught us what they learned from their parents. OK, I did believe, but I was very angry with Him because of things that had happened to me in my childhood and life in general...

She swore at realising that there really is a God!

I was mortified at my language and by this knowledge. I quickly said 'Oh ...sorry!'
His reply to me was even greater love, and a feeling of 'My child, *calm down*, everything is just fine.'

During this interchange, her foot was on the brakes and a head-on crash seemed inevitable with a car bearing down on her and a fast truck on her tail.

Placed in front of me to see and feel was a review of my life, in colour. I had to see and feel all the good I had done, and the good I didn't even know I did. I actually could feel the joy each person felt when I touched their life in a loving way. I was getting 'caught' doing something right for once in my life! During the good He was telling me 'I am so proud of you!' I felt such joy for making Him so proud because I never realized what that felt like, because I always felt like I couldn't do anything right.

Reviewing my random acts of kindness gave me the most joy because I was able to feel the difference I made in someone's life that I hadn't realised at the time, even if I didn't even know them. I was shown it is not the big things we do in life that make the difference. It's all the little things we do each day that make the difference. Little acts of kindness mean so much to God.

Even with the accident imminent, God was not finished with Mary Beth. There had been more to her life than achieving good things.

I had to see and feel all the hurtful things I had done, even the hurtful things I didn't know I did. I had to feel the person's hurt I caused. But, you know how we are taught that we will stand before God and be judged one day? God was not judging me. I was looking at my actions, with God at my side loving me while I was judging myself, and believe me, no one can judge me any harsher than I already judge myself. It was like getting 'caught' by my parents when doing something wrong, only worse. During the hurtful review I was so ashamed and there was no hiding. My immediate thought, and I said it out loud, was 'I'm ready. I belong in Hell. I don't deserve to go to Heaven!'...

'You don't understand and I'm going to explain this to you.' He then asked me, 'What different choices could you have made? What are you learning from this?'...

He let me ask him questions.

My only question was how could He give me the parents I had? How could he forget all about me and leave me so alone to work my way through those years? What was He thinking? I have to admit I was pretty angry.

He showed me why I had the parents, childhood and life I had experienced.

Mary then followed an urgent divine instruction to stop braking and step on the gas, and only clipped the car bearing down on her instead of having a head-on collision – sending it out of harm's way. The truck behind her then simply pushed her forward rather than sandwiching her, and she escaped physical injury, as did the other drivers and passengers.

Mary's life was changed as a consequence of her Life Review and encounter with God. She reflects on its significance.

Living Beyond

> By what I was shown, I understood that Earth is school – and when we are done we have a 'Life Review'; and then we get to graduate and go back home...
>
> The *lesson* was so simple – it's all about love. How much God loves us, and how well we learn to love others and ourselves during this life on Earth, despite what we have to go through in our lives.

Mary subsequently served others lovingly, both as a nurse and later in the field of hospice care. She has written a booklet *Learning How to Let Go* available through Amazon, which states: 'This is a fantastic tool for those with loved ones in hospice or receiving palliative care.'

The fact that Mary had her encounter while still on Earth and only circumstantially 'near death' illustrates a seminal principle:

Life Reviews are <u>purpose</u> driven, not process or venue driven.

In fact, the Life Review has been recorded as happening at any stage of an NDE, perhaps because of its importance. PMH Atwater[6] experienced hers while still in the Void (a venue discussed later).

> I expected some kind of theatrical showing of my 'Life as Phyllis', or perhaps something like a television replay, but such was not the case.
>
> Mine was not a review; it was a reliving. For me, it was a total reliving of every thought I had ever thought, every word I had ever spoken, and every deed I had ever done; plus the effect of each thought, word, and deed on everyone and anyone who had ever come within my environment or sphere of influence whether I knew them or not (including unknown passersby on the street); plus the effect of each thought, word, and deed on weather, plants, animals, soil, trees, water, and air.

It was a reliving of the total gestalt [totality] of me as Phyllis, complete with all the consequences of ever having lived at all. No detail was left out. No slip of the tongue or slur was missed. Neither mistake nor accident went unaccounted for. If there is such a thing as Hell, as far as I am concerned, this was Hell. I had no idea, no idea at all, not even the slightest hint of an idea, that every thought, word, and deed was remembered, accounted for, and went out and had a life of its own once released; nor did I know that the energy of that life directly affected all it touched or came near. It's as if we must live in some kind of vast sea or soup of each other's energy residue and thought waves, and we are each held responsible for our contributions and the quality of 'ingredients' we add. This knowledge overwhelmed me!

The old saying, 'No man is an island,' took on graphic proportions. There wasn't any heavenly St. Peter in charge – it was me judging me, and my judgment was most severe.

As when I previously realized my body was not me, I also came to realize Phyllis wasn't me either. She was a personality or a facade I had once projected. She was an extension of me, a part I had played, a role I had acted. She was a particular development I was engaged in, a particular focus I had become, and that focus had not developed quite as planned! [She has changed her name officially later to 'PMH' Atwater rather than staying 'Phyllis' Atwater.]

I was disappointed and saddened at this, but I took interest and satisfaction from one characteristic she had repeatedly displayed, and that was her desire to try and try again. She always did something, even if unwise. She was not one to sit back and wait upon others or capricious fate. She was relentless in her determination to make of herself a better person and to learn everything possible. She was a doer, willing and able, a person who would reach and stretch. This pleased me and at last I pronounced her personality good and the life she had lived worth its living.

During this judgment [reflection] process, 'The Void' in which I dwelt began to pull away and separate from my dining room in Boise. These two worlds separated as they had previously merged, but I was still next to the light bulb, having never at any time altered my location or the space I occupied. Only my environment had changed [into the Void], not I.

As I looked down at the body of Phyllis on the floor, I was so filled with love and forgiveness that I floated ever so gently back into her body.

I believe God's purpose is to tailor the Life Review for the *best benefit* of the NDEr, and that this becomes the deciding factor regarding the variations seen in the above stories – of style of presentation, venue, order, length, and detail. Life Reviews demonstrate that God is intensely and comprehensively interested in every living person.

Having looked at many Life Reviews, I find that they reveal the overriding importance of love – loving God and loving others.

What is the nature of this love that is emphasised during NDEs? In each case it has been an active, practical, compassionate love; it is neither a self-indulgent feeling, nor a search for God in practices that do not involve actively loving others. There seems to be a mysterious link between loving both God and others at the same time – they are not independent actions, it seems that the one keeps adding to the other, and that real success comes from doing both together. Ritchie[7] found this, and wrote in 1963:

> Today, over 20 years later [post- NDE], I feel that I know why I had the chance to return to this life. It was to become a physician so that I could learn about man and then serve God. And every time I have been able to serve our God by helping some broken-hearted adult, treating some injured child or counselling some teenager, then deep within I have felt that He was there beside me again.

There are many different styles of Life Reviews. Different personages may be delegated to take the NDEr through the appraisal process. Lisa[8]: 'There were three spirits or angels, all females, older – suddenly I am being shown my whole life. It was like watching your life on a fast forward video or DVD. It was something I saw in my mind.'

An important fact to keep in mind is that the information for the reviews exists right now, 'stored' somehow in the afterlife.

Here are some further NDEr accounts, each chosen to illustrate different points, the first recorded by Raymond Moody[9]:

> He made comments here and there. He was trying to show me something in each one of these flashbacks. It's not like he was trying to see what I had done – he knew already – but he was picking out these certain flashbacks of my life and putting them in front of me so that I would have to recall them. All through this, he kept stressing the importance of love.

Living Beyond

A few Life Reviews are reported to be uncomfortable throughout. Deborah Talor[10], who died in 2002, experienced one of these unpleasant reviews.

> As I lifted my head and looked over, I saw myself at five-years-old, and my sister when she was six. We were bigger than life. I held my head in shame as I saw myself being *evil* to my sister. At that point, I felt humiliated beyond belief. I couldn't handle the pain, and begged for it to stop.
>
> The pain I felt stopped, but immediately started again with more fury. You see, I was no longer feeling my pain and humiliation; it was all turned around to where I felt my sister's pain. I had a taste [foretaste] of Hell. I was begging for the pain to stop, but it wouldn't. Her pain that I felt was so profound, I would have given anything for it to stop!

Deborah's humiliation and hurting were not private; they were on display. God knew all the distressing details that she had not known herself until that moment.

> Thankfully, the pain stopped and the line started moving again, but I knew I wasn't going to Heaven. In fact, I had been given a preview of what was in store for me, and that was Hell! I was crying, and full of terror. I was going to Hell, something I had feared my whole life.
>
> Then all of a sudden my line stopped again. I understood by the Light that I would be going 'back' (at the time I didn't know where 'back' was), but I would not be going alone. I further understood that I would be carrying my sister's pain with me until my death on Earth. I understood that, not only would I feel her pain every day, but that it would serve as a constant reminder of how what I say to a person can really hurt them.

> I assure you, I do feel her pain each and every day!

The question hangs in the air – was she able to make the changes required on her return to Earth? Did the negative Life Review have a positive result in her everyday life?

> It took me months to tell my husband about my experience. In fact, to this day, it is still hard for me to talk about it. But I assure you it has changed my life for the better! For the first time in my life I have felt amazing. I was able to let go of my past, and now feel no pain. I want to tell the world about my experience, and how it has changed me! I am finally free, free to love, and free to be me!

As Deborah's experience confirms, even unpleasant Life Reviews are intended for our benefit, and will be so providing the lessons learnt are *applied*. One of those lessons is the significance of what we say to others. Jesus confirmed this (Matthew 12:36,37): 'But I tell you that everyone will have to give account on the Day of Judgment for every empty word they have spoken. For by your words you will be acquitted, and by your words you will be condemned.'

However, the Day of Judgement is not yet. Opportunities abound to love God and to love others, and for us to make things right that we have done wrong.

Because many NDErs do not have 'deep NDEs' that progress as far as a Life Review, this experience is not as common as some early researchers such as Raymond Moody[9] supposed. Peter and Elizabeth Fenwick[11] in England found Life Reviews were described in only 15% of their 350-NDE sample. A similar frequency of Life Reviews among NDErs (13%) was found by Dr Pim van Lommel[12] and his team in Holland.

Whatever the statistics, hundreds of detailed Life Reviews confirm that God takes our lives and life choices seriously, as we find confirmed in Psalm 33:13-15.

> From Heaven the LORD looks down
> and sees all mankind;
> from his dwelling place he watches
> all who live on Earth –
> he who forms the hearts of all,
> who considers everything they do.

— but, thankfully, not yet judgementally.

However, Judgement Day is still to come, sometime in the future. For the present, it is enough to know that God not only sees us as we are, but also that there is no fooling him, because he has recorded it all in astonishing detail. Often the events presented in the review have been long forgotten by the NDEr, or have even been unknown, such as the feelings of others, but God has held them as significant none-the-less. One returnee felt the blows he had inflicted on another man during a fight[13]: 'He felt his teeth cracking. He felt the blood in his teeth. He felt everything that this other person must have felt at that particular time. There was a complete role reversal.'

Howard Storm[14], who was rescued from unpleasant afterlife experiences by the Being of Light, experienced a Life Review shortly afterwards which he found to be intensely discomforting because it highlighted the selfishness of his life. 'With Jesus, and the angels he called to us, we went over my life from beginning to end, and it was very disturbing to see so many of the negative things that I had done. But the thing that made it bearable was that I knew Jesus and the angels loved me despite the wrong things I had done with my life, and that I could be forgiven for those things.'

Note that while there was the potential for forgiveness, it would not be automatic.

To his surprise, the spirit beings that took him through his life were more interested in his relationships than his personal achievements. In his book, Storm said that he was appalled to see how he had hurt others, especially his wife and children. He said that the beings acted with love and empathy, but told him he needed to see these things. Otherwise, how would he perceive what to change in his life? We must conclude that the driving purpose of Storm's NDE was for a course correction on his return to Earth. We can perceive this same principle in operation over and again in NDEs.

God appears to be very concerned about the influence and effect our actions have had on others, much of which, despite being a Christian for many years, I (the writer) had not fully realised until hearing so many of these stories. The depth of an NDE Life Review is astounding and still shakes me up when I read different accounts. I am very uncomfortable that the bad things I have done, consciously or unconsciously, have been recorded in such extraordinary detail. Personally, I am not looking forward to seeing them. Nevertheless, I need to learn from Howard Storm[14] who, as mentioned already, had a hard time watching his Life Review:

> Most of the time I found that my interactions with other people had been manipulative. During my professional career, for example, I saw myself sitting in my office, playing the college professor, while a student came to me with a personal problem. I sat there looking compassionate, and patient, and loving, while inside I was bored to death. I would check my watch under my desk as I anxiously waited for the student to finish...

Living Beyond

      I feel strongly that the whole Life Review would have been emotionally destructive, and would have left me a psychotic person, if it hadn't been for the fact that my friend [Jesus] and my friend's friends [angels], while we watched the whole thing, were loving me. I could feel that love. Every time I got a little upset, they turned it off for a while and they just loved me. Their love was tangible. You could feel it on your body, you could feel it inside of you; their love went right through you. The therapy was their love, because my Life Review just kept tearing me down. It was pitiful to watch, just pitiful... it was nauseating. But through it all was their love.

In Life Reviews, God is modelling the efficacy of love in counselling, and how to gently counsel those who are hurting or distressed. To some extent, the Life Review process is one giant modelling session, with beneficial lessons – including how to support others by loving them during life's challenges.

Maurice Rawlings[15] makes a good point – the NDEr appears never to be asked what church if any they attended or denomination they followed, or whether they believed this or that theological position, or trivialities such as how successful they were financially or what they looked like or whether they dressed fashionably or not – the challenge was how much had they loved their fellow man, and to what practical degree had they loved their God? If this Life Review is a prelude to final Judgement, one would assume these will remain very important challenges for all mankind, not only the few who have tasted death and returned.

Is this fair? Has God given each person a capacity to love others and to love him? Is the ability to love in the heart of each person on the planet? And can we do better?

While the meeting with God or his assistants, and the Life Review, are the most significant events reported by NDErs in Paradise, there are an interesting variety of other people and spiritual beings there too – it is a polyglot society full of surprises. Let's socialise!

8
Society in Paradise

Hades (Paradise section) continued.

Contact with Dead Relatives and Friends

In Paradise, NDErs rediscover feelings of childlike wonder. Everything is new but familiar, with certain similarities to things on Earth. This enables them to feel at ease readily, muting the shock of finding themselves there. These elements of similarity illustrate the Transfer Principle in action, and some NDErs even record that they immediately felt at home in Paradise. In personal correspondence (June 2015), Dale Black helped me to understand this feeling better with his observations:

> I felt that I was in a place that had been created just for me. I also sensed that I had been created for that place from the beginning. It was somewhat like being able to breath effortlessly compared to struggling to breath during an asthma attack. That's how different it seemed to me. It must have been the lack of sin that contributed greatly to the extreme sense of peace. Pure love and holiness was more than amazing and impossible to describe. It felt PERFECT to be there! At first, I never wanted to leave that place. But shortly thereafter, I sensed the mission I was given back on earth, but which would be only for a time.

Soon figures and forms may be seen clearly. Deceased loved ones commonly appear in the light as a welcoming committee.

Accompanying them may be pets recognized by the NDEr. Less commonly, the meet and greet group may also comprise spirit beings variously described by NDErs as angels, guides, guardians, beings of light, or holy ones.

Thousands of NDErs describe meeting with dead relatives and friends. This is not anti-scriptural – even King David expected to meet with his dead son in the afterlife. In 2Samuel 12:23, David states: 'Can I bring him back again? I will go to him, but he will not return to me'.

An intuitive knowledge that these people have come to greet the NDEr is very common, as with Teresa[1]:

> I was suddenly standing before my mother and my brother, who had passed on before me. There was a tremendous light around them. I stood watching them, but I was very aware of this glowing light that came out from around them, and just seemed to surround them and came out toward me. Oh, I was so joyful after I saw them just standing there, just knowing they were OK! Knowing the joy and the happiness they were experiencing was just exactly what I would want to have known. This was my baby brother with my mother! They wanted me where they were, and I wanted to be there. We were ready to embrace each other. At that moment, it didn't happen, I was taken away.

Amongst the dead relatives are often ancestors, perhaps not known previously and only recognised in some old photograph after the return to Earth. Dr Maurice Rawlings[2] gives a graphic example. During an NDE, his patient had met both his mother and stepmother.

> He 'saw' his mother for the first time. She had died at age twenty-one when he was fifteen months old, and

his father had soon remarried. This man had never even seen a picture of his real mother, and yet he was able to pick her picture out of several others a few weeks later when his mother's sister, after hearing of his experience, produced some family pictures for identification. There was no mistake – the same auburn hair, the same eyes and mouth – the face was identical to the lady he saw in his experience [NDE]. She was still twenty-one years old! There was no doubt it was his mother! He was astounded, and so was his father.

The fact that elderly people can look much younger in Paradise can be confusing. Chuck[1] described how his deceased Mum and Grandmother both looked in their prime and a similar age to one another.

> All of a sudden I look up and see my mother and my grandmother standing about forty to fifty feet in front of me. They looked absolutely gorgeous, from thirty to thirty-five years, dressed in black and with pearl necklaces on, and they looked the best that I could imagine they looked in their lives.

Chuck of course had not known his grandmother in the flesh on Earth when she was that young. Did she and his mother appear dressed similarly and together to facilitate his identification of her, or did he remember her from an earlier photo? Chuck does not elaborate. But she was a special favourite of his, whom he recognised at once despite her apparent youth, and he rushed forward to greet them both.

Fathers and mothers who have pre-deceased the NDEr are often the first to be met again in Paradise. Arlene[1] who died in Rome during childbirth in 1965, met with her beloved father who was waiting for her as she emerged from the 'cylinder' tunnel.

> I was so excited. I lost my father when I was ten. I loved him.
>
> I said, 'Daddy, Daddy, I've missed you so much! I want to be with you.'
>
> I knew I was dead. I knew that, or else I could not have seen my father. But I also knew immediately that there was life after what we call death, that there is an existence of our dearly departed on the other side.
>
> You are aware of complete tranquillity and great love and warmth. I said to my father, 'I will not forget this day as long as I live, so help me God.'
>
> I did not want to come back. I wanted to stay with him.
>
> My father took command of the situation as he would have taken command of any situation, and he said, 'You have to go back.'
>
> But I said, 'I don't want to go back, Daddy, I want to be with you. I missed you.'
>
> He said, 'You've just had a baby, and you have another baby, and you have to go back. It is not your time.'

Her father pushed Arlene back down into the cylinder/tunnel, and she re-entered her body.

Another daughter who described meeting her father during an NDE was Kat[1]. Her emphasis was on how well her father looked, which matches thousands of descriptions of people met in Paradise. I have not yet come across descriptions of relatives who looked unhappy or sickly.

> Suddenly my father appeared in front of me. My father had been gone for about ten years, but he looked wonderful. His skin was bright and vibrant; his hair was the auburn I had remembered. His eyes were bright and shiny and he looked so healthy, and he looked so happy.

Living Beyond

He was close enough for me to touch, and he had his hand out as if to welcome me. I was trying to reach out to hold him.

He told me everything was going to be all right, but there was more to do... It was not my time.

And I knew right away that's what I had to do; I had to fight.

I had to come back.

RaNelle Wallace[3] died as a consequence of a dreadful air crash and fire back in 1985. She met with her grandmother, who introduced herself.

She was my mother's mother, but she looked different than I had remembered. She was full and rounded and vibrant. She appeared to be about twenty-five years old, but her hair was glorious white, and everything about her was radiantly beautiful. Her body was glorious, and I began to understand why I hadn't recognized her. She had been frail and sick all the years I had known her.

Then the realization hit me – Grandma was dead; she had died a couple of years before. And I thought; if she's dead, then what am I doing here?

'Oh, I'm dead.'

Now everything fit. The colourful lights, the Life Review, and now this light of glorious love, all of it naturally occurred as my life continued in this next world. This definitely wasn't some dream or some drug-induced vision. I was more keenly aware and alive now than I had ever been in my body. I immediately accepted this and wanted to know where everybody was.

Grandma giggled. Her lips didn't move, but her spirit giggled.

> 'Aren't people supposed to meet me when I die?' I asked. 'Aren't there supposed to be people singing hallelujah and coming up to hug me and saying, "Welcome"?'
>
> She giggled again, and I thought it was the most delightful giggle I had ever heard.
>
> 'Well,' she said, 'everybody is quite busy. Come on, you have a lot to see.'

Others confirm RaNelle's discovery that there is a lot to do in the afterlife, and that spirits are busy.

Don Piper[4] fills in a little about the content of the communication he had with friends who had passed on previously.

> Our conversations centred on the joy of my being there and how happy they were to see me... They looked exactly as I once knew them – although they were more radiant and joyful than they'd ever been on Earth... I felt loved – more loved than ever before in my life.

Similar meetings with friends are described by other NDErs, but there are far fewer examples than meetings with family members. Nevertheless, friendship continues to be important after death, which confirms that the 'brotherly love' aspect of who we are on Earth remains significant in the afterlife.

Learning in the Afterlife

One of the unexpected individual or group activities in Paradise appears to be study and the acquisition of knowledge. This is confirmed in interviews, for example those conducted by Raymond Moody[5].

> Many others have emphasised the importance of seeking knowledge. During their experiences, it was intimated

to them that the acquisition of knowledge continues even in the afterlife. One woman, for example, has taken advantage of every educational opportunity she has had since her death experience. Another man offers the advice, 'No matter how old you are, don't stop learning. For this is a process, I gather, that goes on for eternity.'

Surely knowledge can simply be given to us in the afterlife. Why, then, should we study to acquire more? We don't know, but perhaps beyond our days on Earth there will be similar character development and satisfaction flowing from effort in this field.

Energy and Health in the Afterlife

Another surprising fact is that NDErs do not appear to need sleep or to suffer earthly restrictions from lack of energy. Consequently, one earthly activity is clearly missing – there have been no reports of anyone eating food of any sort. That makes it very different from the role of food in both survival and social interaction here. Whatever the ephemeral spirit body is composed of, it does not appear to require energy from food. Considering that communication is by thought alone, which also drives effortless propulsion of the spirit body, the need to renew a robust energy supply seems minimal or certainly different. The only energy source described to date is the brilliant light and perhaps heat and other unknown energies emanating from God the Father and from Jesus, and perhaps to a lesser extent from the associated beings who give off light.

Dale Black[6] noted:

> My energy seemed boundless, and even though I had always worked hard to be in excellent condition, I have never come close to feeling as strong and healthy as I felt now. It was as though I could accomplish anything.'

> The people Dale saw there were also healthy. 'None were skinny, none overweight. None were crippled, none were bent or broken. None were old, none were young. If I had to guess, I would say they appeared to be somewhere around thirty years old. They had no wrinkles, no signs of shifting or sagging, no signs of aging at all. I somehow understood that time was not an enemy here. Although some form of time does seem to exist in Heaven, no one aged. No one died. Nothing decayed.'

However, while most forebears appear to NDErs as they had been in their prime, others presented as they had looked when older. Was this perhaps their choice? Perhaps specifically for recognition by the NDEr, to help him or her feel more at ease? I have read several NDE reports that make the claim that spirits in Paradise may choose their age when meeting relatives, and what they wear for the occasion, but I would need further examples of this before accepting it as a generality. Regardless, they look in brimming good health, as seen in the Christian minister Don Piper's[4] description.

> The first person I recognised was Joe Kulbeth, my grandfather. He looked exactly as I remembered him, with his shock of white hair and what I called a big banana nose. He stopped momentarily and stood in front of me. A grin covered his face. I may have called his name, but I'm not sure.
> 'Donnie!' (That's what my grandfather always called me). His eyes lit up and he held out his arms as he took the last steps towards me. He embraced me, holding me tightly. He was once again the robust, strong grandfather I had remembered as a child.
> I'd been with him when he suffered a heart attack at home and had ridden with him in the ambulance. I had

been standing just outside the emergency room at the hospital when the doctor walked out and faced me. He had shaken his head and said softly, 'We did everything we could.'

My grandfather released me, and as I stared into his face, an ecstatic bliss overwhelmed me. I didn't think about his heart attack or his death, because I couldn't get past the joy of our reunion.

While his grandfather looked much as Don had remembered him, his great-grandmother looked so much better than he recalled her!

My great-grandmother, Hattie Mann, was Native American. As a child I saw her only after she had developed osteoporosis – her head and shoulders were bent forward, giving her a humped appearance. I especially remember her extremely wrinkled face. The other thing that stands out in my memory is that she had false teeth – which she didn't wear often. Yet when she smiled at me in Heaven, her teeth sparkled. I knew they were her own, and when she smiled it was the most beautiful smile I had ever seen.

Then I noticed something else – she wasn't slumped over. She stood strong and upright, and the wrinkles had been erased from her face. I have no idea what age she was, and I didn't even think about that. As I stared at her beaming face, I sensed that age has no meaning in Heaven.

Lillian Oaktree[7] describes when she first saw her dead parents, Abe and Jacqueline, standing at the front of the crowd, motioning her to come with them. 'Mum had died five years before,' says Lillian. 'She was 74 and died from kidney failure. But here she was standing before me looking like a young woman. She was radiant and healthy and her hair was a shimmering blonde. She was wearing a blue top and blue trousers. There was a glow all around her and I could feel her sending me massive waves of love. It felt amazing.'

Of interest to the fashion conscious, perhaps, are the reports that suggest people in Paradise may have the choice to be wearing whatever clothing they want. Lillian's mum was in a blue top and trousers. In another case, RaNelle Wallace's[3] grandmother wore a dress in Paradise that she had never worn while alive on earth – it was the one she had been buried in, bought especially for that purpose by her loving, grieving daughter.

Family Units in the Afterlife

Why do relatives and occasionally dead friends meet NDErs? We should contemplate this mystery, as it may have deeper significance than is at first obvious.

Scripture teaches that there are three 'eternals' dealing with character that we take into life after death. They are the most vital personal qualities that we can develop on Earth – Faith and Hope and Love, which I have capitalised to emphasise their importance. The Bible informs us about them in 1Corinthians 13:13: 'These three *remain*: Faith, Hope and Love, but the greatest of these is Love'. This means you will take whatever degree of love for others you have developed on Earth into Paradise with you, as have relatives, ancestors and personal friends who have pre-deceased you. Logically, then, because love is eternal, you can expect your ties with those you loved to feature in Paradise. It is no surprise, then, that you will meet at least some of them and the love you developed for them previously on Earth will continue.

Literally thousands of reports describe meeting family members in Paradise, which raises another interesting question. Just as there are sections in the Prison area of Hades, might

Living Beyond

loose family gatherings be a primary grouping of Paradise? Dr Des Sinclair[8], the New Zealand evangelist who died for 25 minutes, claims he noticed family clusters including ancestors being a basic grouping in Paradise. Other NDErs indicate they have seen or been told this during their NDE. So do we spend at least some of our time in Paradise in family gatherings, which would need to be flexible and mobile because we all belong to different and very long family lines? Friends have also been part of the meet-and-greet group – so additional mobility between groups seems likely.

This is such a primary question that I would like to make some additional observations that might pertain. In the Western mindset, family ties have loosened – but they remain the primary grouping in most other cultures on Earth, where knowing one's ancestry assumes a much greater importance. Many communities in the Third World can rattle off their ancestors going back over generations – somehow they perceive this to be important to their own place in the world.

Ancestral lines are seemingly more important to God than they are to the Western mind, which may explain why even ancestors unknown to the NDEr are often there in Paradise to greet him or her. Ancestral relationships were accorded prominence in scripture. Genealogies are recorded in detail in books such as 1 Chronicles. Furthermore, we find in the New Testament Jesus' own ancestral lines both through Joseph and through his mother Mary, which speaks of the importance and significance to God of these connections.

Yet observations of life suggest that in the heart of Western man, deep down, there remains a recognition of the dominant importance of family ties stretching back into the distant past. For example, my previous book to this one was an historical biography about Edward John Eyre, an explorer and dynamic young man in Australia between 1832 and 1845, who left no family there before moving on. After publication, most of the correspondence I received about the book was not about his amazing achievements for one so young, but regarding possible ancestral links between the correspondent and Eyre, or family links to the men who served with him! And another ongoing situation grabbed my attention. A generation ago, comfortable under anonymity protection laws in Australia, a lot of students became sperm donors to raise ready cash while at university. The resulting children grew up and many began to speak of their yearning and sometimes desperation to meet their fathers, in order to know their own identity. They hope to establish a good relationship with those fathers if possible. These young people from throughout Australia and even New Zealand made – and continue to make – every personal and legal effort to trace their biological fathers. Some unexplored primeval need to know about one's immediate family is involved here. I hope it is a tiny encouragement for them and others who have not succeeded in tracing their ancestry to know that in life after death, they will most likely meet and get to know their family members!

Brian Johnson[7] adds a further dimension; while he did not recognise his 'welcoming party', he instinctively knew that they comprised ancestors.

> Then in a split second there were people surrounding me and they were people whom I had never seen before, but for some reason I knew that these people were long time passed away family members whom I had never known, seen or met before in my life, and that they had died way long before I was even born, but I knew that all of these people were there just for me and I could feel all this love from these people like no other love that I had ever felt before and I did not want to leave this place. While I was in this place, I was totally pain free and surrounded by strange people who loved me so very much.

If the purpose of the NDE is to instruct, reintegrate and redirect the NDEr, because the process itself is both strange and unexpected, the introduction of relatives and other familiar loved ones may impart confidence to the NDEr. They may more readily accept that their best interests are at heart during the experience. Mike[1] expressed it well: 'I knew that my grandpa was there, and everyone who had touched my life were all there, and relatives whom I had never met. It's an overwhelming sensation of just knowing that everyone who had ever touched your life was there, just for you.'

Forgiveness in Paradise

Some NDE accounts raise the issue of forgiveness during that first meeting with others in Paradise, Lillian Oaktree's[7] example being a case in point. She explains how meeting her dead parents enabled her to deal with some unforgiveness issues. Beside her mum stood her dad who'd died after a heart attack when Lillian was just 12.

> 'I'd been devastated and never quite forgiven him for leaving me, but all I felt for him now was love,' she says. 'He was a chef and I couldn't help smiling because he was wearing his chef whites – the white starched shirt with the double buttons and checked trousers. His hair was jet black, too. I'd only ever seen him with grey hair, but he looked like he did in photos taken in his late 20's.'

What about relatives with whom you did not share bonds of love, relatives who abused you perhaps? Considering how common abuse is, it may be significant that NDE reports do not major on those who are missing from the welcoming group. Hopefully further NDEs will reveal more about this. What about people you hated on Earth; do you meet them again – is there a time of reconciliation in the afterlife? Sometimes we feel it is impossible to forgive someone because of what they have done, such as a murderer or torturer. Nevertheless, God expects us to. Consider Dr Petti Wagner[9], a millionaire heiress and respected doctor, who was kidnapped and treated horribly before being electrocuted to death by her captors. She met Jesus in Paradise.

> The Lord impressed on me that I should forgive all those who had been responsible for my kidnapping and murder. I could not understand this.
> 'Why?' I said. 'If I could pray, I would be praying for myself!'
> God said, 'If you do not pray and forgive them right now, then it will interfere with the work you and I have to do together'.
> I said, 'Lord, I do not know how to pray'.
> He responded, 'I will teach you'.
> He told me to say, 'God, forgive them, they knew not what they were doing'.

This imperative to forgive is hammered home in NDEs, our final example being the famous case, confirmed by witnesses and doctors, of the return to life in 2001 of a dead Christian pastor Daniel Ekechukwu[10] in Nigeria during a Reinhard Bonnke evangelistic campaign there. Daniel had been dead for two days and despite rigor mortis, he was taken to the campaign for prayer from the mortuary in a coffin organised by his faithful wife, who believed that God had prompted her to do such a strange thing.

Meanwhile, during his NDE, Daniel was shown that his future would have lain in Hell despite his dedication to God, because he had fought with his wife the morning of his death and had refused to forgive her! In fact, he planned to separate from her for one year. 1Peter 3:7 confirms that unforgiveness of one's wife has the consequence in that our prayers to God may be hindered, which is what happened to him despite being a Christian leader. He was reminded that you reap what you sow – he had not forgiven her, so he would not be forgiven. Daniel wept. He was then returned to Earth so that he would have opportunity both to forgive his wife and to warn others of the Day of Judgement to come.

Bonnke makes it clear he had nothing directly to do with the miracle. Others prayed over the corpse in the basement. A follow-up investigation[11] in 2014 included interviews with the mortician, who had already injected Daniel with embalming fluid, and conversations with different doctors, the wife and other witnesses. This investigation, and others earlier, confirmed this miraculous raising from the dead.

Daniel's NDE was obviously designed especially for him, to deal with unforgiveness in his life, and thereby to empower his future ministry. Jesus taught (Luke 6:37): 'Forgive, and you will be forgiven.' Forgiveness of others was essential to Daniel's continuing relationship with God.

Each example of forgiveness given above took place in the lives of NDErs returning to Earth to live it out. Daniel and others have emphasised how important that act of forgiveness has been to them during their continuing lives. It appears to have been a lesson planned for them within their NDE, to instruct them to forgive.

Relatives and Reincarnation

Christians have long rejected the doctrine of reincarnation, in part because scripture states that 'people are destined to die once, and after that to face judgment' (Hebrews 9:27).

In scripture, we find examples of prominent followers of God returning to visit Earth briefly – Samuel being called up from Hades by the witch of Endor (1Samuel 28:7-14), and Moses and Elijah on the Mount of Transfiguration meeting with Jesus (Matthew 17:1-3). In each case they were recognisable, such that we can be sure they had not returned to Earth in the interim in some other body to 'have another go' as another being. They remained themselves.

Jesus himself met with the spirits of the predeluvians in Hades (1 Peter 3:19), people who had been dead without reincarnation for thousands of years.

Consistent with scripture are the frequent reports of relatives in Hades greeting the NDEr, including ancestors of NDErs who themselves were members of religions that believe in reincarnation. These meetings with their own ancestors should surely challenge any doctrine of reincarnation.

Spirit Beings in Paradise

NDErs report meeting not only with God, Jesus, friends and relatives in Paradise, but with other beings there too. These beings are friendly spiritual entities, similar to ourselves yet different. Many NDErs identify them afterwards as angels, but few if any have proffered self-identification. They sometimes first appear even before entry into the tunnel. They are there to help and advise, especially if there is a complex part of the planned experience that is different from the norm. Lillian Oaktree[7] describes her befuddlement at their appearance, followed by their gentle reassuring response.

> I suddenly became aware of two, what can only be described as beings, standing on my right,' she says. 'They were 6ft tall, wearing bright cloaks and totally transparent. Where their faces should have been were balls of golden light. I remember asking what was happening and one of them said in a gentle voice, 'This is the closest you've ever been to God'. I'd never felt so humbled but I was suddenly bathed in a bright light and every bit of my body was pulsating with energy.

Crystal McVea[12] gives us a more personal description of two angels she met.

> I was instantly aware of two beings in front of me and to my left, and I knew right away who they were – they were angels.
> But they weren't just any angels – they were my angels.
> I recognised them immediately. There was so much brightness coming off them that I couldn't make out any features. But they weren't shapeless blobs; they definitely had a form, which was roughly that of a human body: long and slender.
> The being on the right appeared a bit bigger than the one on the left. They didn't move or hover or anything – they were just there.
> And what I instantly felt for them was love.
> A great, sweeping love for my angels overwhelmed me. It was like they were the best friends I could ever have, though the word friend doesn't come close to describing them. The angels were: my protectors, my teachers, my mentors, my heroes, my strength, my spirit, and my heart, everything all rolled into one. I felt like they had been a part of my existence and my journey forever – as if they had been by my side for every tear I ever cried, every decision I had ever made, every day I ever felt lonely, not only on Earth but through all eternity. I felt so unbelievably safe and free in their presence, so happy and fulfilled. I understood why they were there – to greet me upon my arrival and guide me back home.

Crystal believed that these two angels had been with her since childhood, suggested perhaps in Matthew 18:10 'See that you do not despise one of these little ones. For I tell you that their angels in Heaven always see the face of my Father in Heaven' and Psalm

91: 11 'For he will command his angels concerning you to guard you in all your ways'.

> What's more, I realised there was instant and complete communication between us. What do I mean by that? Imagine a button you can press; as soon as you press it, you know everything there is to know about someone, and they know everything about you. Or a password that, if you let me use it, gives me instant access to everything you've ever said or thought or felt or written or believed in your life: past, present and future. Instantly, I would have a more complete understanding of you than is possible on Earth. Well, that is what this was like – a sensation that everything we were, everything that mattered, was passing freely between my angels and me, strengthening our profound connection and an eternal bond. There was no room whatsoever for secrets or shame or misunderstanding or anything negative.

Crystal McVea tries to place the angels in a wider context.

> The light, the brightness, the angels, the communication – everything was a creation of God.
> I understood that I too was a part of him, and that's the moment I truly realised what being a creation of God truly means.

Pets in Paradise

One might speculate that because loving connections are formed with pets on Earth, and love is eternal, those pets could be found in Paradise. It certainly seems to help an NDEr to relax when reunion with a special pet is part of their experience.

Lillian Oaktree[7] to her delight was reunited with her old dogs, Fluke, Random and Joule.

Susan[13] recalls that, 'I had seen all the pets I had as a child in heaven. Dogs and even parakeets whom I really loved. They had a caretaker – a man who took care of all the animals. So if anyone ever asks me if animals survive death, I have to say, "Yes!"'

Three-years-old Colton Burpo[14] even claimed that Jesus himself has a horse of his own – although the horse may be kept within the heavenly city rather than in Paradise. Nevertheless, the principle is the same, which is that pets exist in the afterlife.

Children in particular settle into the afterlife more readily if a beloved pet greets them - Transfer Principle. When telling us about of Heaven, some children speak quite naturally of animals and past pets that they have played with there, and a picture is emerging that these animals may have a section of their own – but more detailed accounts would be needed to establish this idea.

Music in Paradise

Iris Lemov[15] enjoyed her time in Paradise, and her description adds an extra dimension noticed by others – there was soft music playing. 'Music coming from nowhere made me feel comfortable and I began to feel as if I belonged.'

Many others extol this music. Don Piper[4] states that he never saw anything that produced the sound, which was the most beautiful and pleasant one he had ever heard. 'And it didn't stop. It was like a song that goes on forever. I felt awestruck, wanting only to listen. I didn't just hear music, it seemed as if I were part of the music – and it played in and through my body. I stood still, and yet I felt embraced by the sounds.'

Ethnicity in Paradise

Some NDErs comment on seeing strangers enjoying Paradise, who are usually in the distance. Styles of clothing vary, but they appear to be enjoying themselves.

As might be expected from the God who created and loves all people, there is no racism recorded in NDEs, nor any social divide. Dale Black[6] remarks on this:

> I did not notice racial differences, but I was aware that they had come from many tribes and nations. None were recognised by the physical or social distinctions that we recognise on Earth. All were recognised by their spirit, by the essence of who they were. Everyone and everything was full of pure life and was connected to the light somehow, and everything that was connected led to God.

Boundaries in Paradise

Some NDErs report they became aware of a boundary in Paradise that separated those allowed to return to Earth from those who after crossing it could not return. Rose Richter[7] intuitively 'knew' that there was this boundary. It gave her an unusual perception of Paradise – beautiful as it was, she says she knew it was just a place of waiting.

The barrier can take different forms: a fence, a gate, a body of water, a wall, a group of rocks, a mist, or even an imaginary line. Because Hades is a real venue, it seems to have a variety of sections, each with a different purpose and separated from others by a barrier or border, just as on Earth any country may have a variety of borders to separate it from neighbours. Thus for such a big region as Hades, a variety of barriers within it could be used to separate out particular regions or no-go areas.

Dr A. S. Wiltse[16] gave an early example of this during the NDE he described in 1889.

> This being told me, 'This is the road to the eternal world. Yonder rocks are the boundary between the two worlds and the two lives. Once you pass them, you can no more return into the body. If your work is complete on Earth, you may pass beyond the rocks. If, however, upon consideration you conclude that it is not done, you can return into the body.'
> I was tempted to cross the boundary line...

The NDErs are not generally told that 'this is the threshold between life and death', but that is what most intuitively perceive. In a few cases, such as Dr Wiltse quoted above, they have been told specifically that to cross the barrier means they cannot return to Earth. Crystal McVea[12] records: 'The instant I became aware of the gates of Heaven [as opposed to the gardens of Paradise], God said, "Once we get there, you cannot come back."'

An unwillingness to return to Earth is commonly recorded and it is easy to visualise multitudes of spirits choosing to stream past barriers of no return. Some NDErs describe seeing them doing so. Crystal McVea did not hesitate: she wanted to cross the barrier and live with God. 'I understood we were near the point of no return in my journey, and that filled me with such excitement and such expectation, I couldn't wait to get there! But in that instant, I had a vision of my four children... I was nearing the point where I would not be able to go back and see them again on Earth.' Despite this, she wanted to proceed, to remain with God rather than to return! She turned back only when feeling a pressing need to tell her mother where she was.

There are interesting variations in other accounts – some wanted to stay yet not cross the barrier, others felt obliged to go back to Earth to complete unfinished tasks or because of loved ones. Many others were sent back without being given a choice and without seeing any visible barrier to cross.

Before investigating the return of NDErs to Earth, we must examine experiences in Hades other than those that have taken place in Paradise. These may be harrowing to consider, but their message for the NDEr is similar to that discovered in Paradise.

That overall message is positive!

9

The Void

Hades – Prison section (the Void)

The Void is most likely within the Prison complex of Hades. It is a temporary venue.

Entering the Nearby Void.

The Void is our nearest afterlife neighbour. No tunnel is generally experienced between Earth and the Void; OBErs often pass into it directly through a kind of dimension wall. The Void appears to be close and adjacent to Earth.

Guides, generally masquerading as friendly but who turn out to be malevolent, can call to a spirit as it leaves the body to join them there. It is a short step for the spirit to do so, not involving a tunnel unless a short one is used to direct the NDEr to a specific position within the Void.

The Void can invade and change the nature of Earth's surroundings to the NDEr. PMH Atwater[1] describes the start of her second NDE in these words:

> I glimpsed a peculiar shift in my environment. My dining room below was slowly but surely merging into another kind of space coming down from a source past my ceiling.
>
> These two spaces or dimensions of space were merging into each other, but I was not moving. I did not change position in any way. I was where I was, but the world around me was changing and shifting and becoming

something else. My dining room faded from sight as this new space became more visible and more real. It was like nothing I had ever seen before. It encompassed me.

Atwater used the term 'Void' to describe the strange new reality in which she found herself. This same word began to appear in a number of portrayals given by NDErs who had been there, and who struggled to describe somewhere they had not known about previously. 'Void' seemed the most appropriate depiction for where they found themselves. It is now an accepted term within NDE literature.

What Is the Void?

The Void is a dark, unpleasant venue on the whole, to which only a few NDErs are taken, and we will not spend a long time describing it.
It appears to facilitate several processes:

1. Self-discovery through contemplation.
2. Direct experience of the reality of evil.
3. Development towards God.

This is not a rigid order of events. Furthermore, one or more of these steps may be missing in the experience of a particular individual.

Self Discovery in the Void

The initial purpose of the Void appears to be a season for the spirit to reflect. Pure thought exists there, enabling contemplation of one's life. Emmanuel Swedenborg[2] described this process in the 1700s following his NDE.

Immediately following death, there is a period of self-discovery in which the social masks worn on Earth dissolve away and the true self is revealed.

Each soul then shapes their own situation to correspond with their real inner nature.

The second stage after death is where people learn the inward things that belong to their mind and their true selves.

Both of these stages facilitate a deeper understanding of oneself than is normally possible during the hurly burly of life on Earth.

To facilitate this reflection and re-integration of the soul, experience in the Void often begins in total darkness and might be described as 'sensory deprivation' if it occurred on Earth.

The Russian neuropathologist George Rodonaia[3], an avowed atheist, had his NDE in communist Russia in 1976, while lying dead in a morgue for three days. He had a prolonged experience in the Void, to his shock. We sense what the Void can feel like from his description.

> I discovered myself in a realm of total darkness. I had no physical pain, I was still somehow aware of my existence as George, and all about me there was darkness, utter and complete darkness – the greatest darkness ever, darker than any dark, blacker than any black. This was what surrounded me and pressed upon me.
>
> I was horrified. I wasn't prepared for this at all! I was shocked to find that I still existed, but I didn't know where I was.
>
> The one thought that kept rolling through my mind was, 'How can I be when I'm not?' That is what troubled me.

An environment that lacks sensory cues has disturbed others too. The blank, impersonal darkness gets to them. Torment may be felt there as well. David A Smith[4] gives a typical description:

> I went to where there was only darkness, and wailing and gnashing of teeth, void of all light and of any thing good. This tells us what it's like to be totally severed from God, for God is light, He is all that is good. Where I was, there was no comfort, not of thought or feeling, there was only torment. I would have loved to have been somewhere with a little red devil with a pitchfork poking me. It would have been a relief to have had physical pain, and if there was fire there would have been light. Anything to break the darkness, but this place was totally void of God.

BJ McKelvie[5], a talented and proud non-Christian musician, found himself there after an attempted suicide because of depression. In the deep darkness, an angry voice spoke to him: 'Those who commit suicide go nowhere. You're not getting a second chance'. He concluded it was God who had spoken, and also that he would be in that place of dark nothingness for eternity. He despaired – 'I was so alone, it was horrific.'

After a prolonged period of reflection in the Void, the next step is often to learn that evil exists and that one must choose against it.

Direct Experience of the Reality of Evil

Howard Storm[6], an Art Professor, had a distressing experience of the Void. A freethinker at the time, he considered faith in God absurd.

In June 1985, Storm lay in hospital, believing he was going to die. He mentally prepared himself for death. After saying goodbye to his wife, he eventually lost consciousness.

When Storm opened his eyes again, he found he was standing outside of his body, looking down at the hospital bed, with his wife crying at his bedside. He said that he felt no pain and that his senses were suddenly very acute. He tried to talk to his wife, 'It's OK. I'm here', but she ignored him as she could not see or hear him. Frustrated and befuddled, he tried yelling at her, with no response. Very confused now, he was drawn by seemingly friendly voices from outside the hospital room calling his name and saying, 'Hurry up. Come with us. We have been waiting for you for a long time.' He followed the voices, supposing at first in his confused state that he was being called at last for his operation. The creatures, which looked like pale people, urged him to walk down the hallway, pushing him and surrounding him.

The hallway became very dark and almost foggy. With horror, he realised the malicious nature of his guides who became increasingly hostile towards him. Then they turned on him and attacked him savagely in the darkness, physically and psychologically.

These perpetrators of malevolence are called evil spirits or demons in almost all religions. These are deceiving spirits and often appear friendly at the start of the interaction to tempt the NDEr to follow after them, as they did with Howard, but they reveal their baleful nature progressively. They can vary from simple elemental spirits to powerful fallen angels. Generally invisible on Earth, they become visible in the afterlife. They serve Satan. Their activities are many and varied, but descriptions of these are only an incidental part of this book.

Storm's spirit body was severely beaten, bitten and torn to pieces by many of those shadowy creatures, and though he managed to survive, he experienced severe pain. He says that his overall impression was of a process of 'initiation'. Storm later said there were things these creatures did to him that he couldn't even talk about. We note that the demons could not destroy his spirit body, but bashed and ripped it. It seemed to re-constitute itself continuously – although wounds were still visible for a while and a degree of pain was experienced by him.

We know that earthly physical pain is seated in the brain. This pain disappears at death as a person enters the spirit world. However, NDErs report that new and different pains inflicted on the spirit body in the afterlife can be felt, although the intensity of these appears to be significantly less.

Escaping the Void

The NDErs we have mentioned reached a point where they wanted desperately to escape. Each release from the Void was different, but the common denominator was that God became directly involved.

After a time for reflection, reports BJ McKelvie[5], God's voice scolded him again for his suicide, and he responded, 'OK. I've done it. I accept it.' He felt he had no hope; he would have to endure his punishment for eternity.

The voice spoke a third time, far more gently and kindly now: 'You're not getting a second chance – *but a new beginning*!'

He awoke in his hospital bed – and today is an effective Christian musician and prominent minister. He equates his experience of the Void with Jesus' warnings about being 'cast into outer darkness' (Matthew 8:12, 22:13, and 25:30).

The Russian atheist George Rodonaia[4] adopted a novel approach during his NDE to solving whether he was still alive or not. He pondered an expression used by a philosopher – René Descartes.

> Why am I in this darkness? What am I to do? Then I remembered Descartes' famous line: 'I think, therefore I am.' And that took a huge burden off me, for it was then I knew for certain *I was still alive*, although obviously in a very different dimension.

Living Beyond

Then I thought: if I am, why shouldn't I be positive? That is what came to me. I am George and I'm in darkness, but I know I am. I am what I am. I must not be negative.

Then I thought, how can I define what is positive in darkness?

Well, positive is light.

Then, suddenly, I was in light; bright white, shiny and strong; a very bright light! It was like the flash of a camera, but not flickering – that bright. Constant brightness.

At first I found the brilliance of the light painful, I couldn't look directly at it. But little by little I began to relax.

I began to feel warm, comforted, and everything suddenly seemed fine.

George subsequently experienced common features of a classic NDE, such as a comprehensive Life Review and the peace and joy that accompanied interaction with the Light. On his return, he gave up his medical career and trained to become a Christian minister. He served as a pastor in the Methodist Church in Texas up until his death in 2004.

Howard Storm[6], trapped in the Void, tried to fend off the blows from the demons, without success. 'As I lay there in a foetal position on the ground trying to protect myself from their kicks and their taunting, I heard a voice say 'pray to God'. I thought to myself, 'I don't believe in God.' Then I heard that voice again, and another time. I tried to remember what I had prayed as a child, and it came out all mixed up with the 23rd Psalm, the Pledge of Allegiance and the Lord's Prayer, just little bits of these that I could remember. But the people [demons] around me hated any mention of God and retreated far into the darkness and left me alone for an eternity to consider my life.'

This extended opportunity for reflection that feels like an eternity is a common feature of the Void.

After a time of deep despair, Howard resorted to calling out 'Jesus, please save me!' not knowing whether Jesus was real or not, but remembering having believed in him in childhood.

A faint light appeared in the darkness and approached, becoming a Being of Light that Howard believes was Jesus Christ. 'I was lifted up to this Being of white light, and I could see the wounds in my body were healing in seconds. Never in my life had I experienced such unconditional total love, and I knew absolutely that this was the Jesus I had believed in as a child.'

Howard was given a Life Review. He was ashamed of the life he had led up until then, but was comforted by the love of Jesus and of the angels who accompanied him. Desperate not to return to Earth, Howard was nevertheless told he had to do so. His return was given the unusual additional blessing of a miraculous healing from his previous condition – diagnosed as a punctured duodenum that had required immediate surgery. The unbearable pain he had previously experienced in hospital, such that he said he would have killed himself if he had had the means, had also gone! He converted to Christianity and became an enthusiastic evangelist and pastor in Ohio before retiring.

Calling out to God from the Void provided Howard with a means of escape. Others have given similar accounts of their release from that venue.

The Void as a Section of the Prison Complex

NDErs often report simply 'stepping into' the Void, which suggests it is near to Earth but in a different dimension.

The Void has distinctive features when compared with other Prison sections. It is often pitch black to start with. Other Prison sections are characterised by dim lighting, but vision is clear – occasionally with light from flickering flames lighting up the cell walls.

The Void experience often begins without seeing other humans. In other Prison sections, prisoners are observed from the start.

The Void may not in its early stages generate the same intense fear that other Prison sections do. Bafflement is more common at the start of the Void experience.

A mysterious feeling of 'non-being' may be recorded early on in the Void, while prisoners in other Prison sections are very much aware of who and what they are.

What is the dynamic between the Void and the rest of the Prison complex? Perhaps the intransigent in the Void are transferred directly to other Prison sections of Hades. However, with the exception of a few suicides, I do not know of NDE descriptions of the Void experience that specify such a transfer. Instead, the Void for most NDE spirits appears to precede experiences in Paradise, or alternatively their return to Earth.

Tours of the Void

Often those NDErs trapped in the Void are lost in contemplation or struggling to overcome evil, such that their view is very limited and self-absorbed. They learn only what they have experienced within a restricted locale.

Certain other NDErs have been shown around the Void during a guided tour. They have been able to view the overall situation as an outsider, having aspects of it explained to them by a guide. It is interesting that the guides and 'tourists' seem seldom noticed by the spirits in the Void absorbed in their own situations. Several tourists have described the presence of angels or other beings of light hovering over the inhabitants of the Void, as if ready to help if appealed to. Spirits trapped in the Void, if typified by NDErs who have been there, seem to have a more limited view, being generally unaware that beings of light are all around them, until they decide they need help and call out for it.

Different guides have been found to conduct the tours. Dr George Ritchie[9] recorded a tour there guided by Jesus, while angels escorted the Baptist minister, Howard Pittman.

Howard Pittman[7] was taken to the Void as part of a 'learning tour' in 1979, having first died on the operating table. He had little knowledge of the nature of evil before being taken there, which he named the 'Second Heaven'. The term 'Void' seems to equate with the venue of his experience. Other writers use the term 'Second Heaven' to denote outer space, but in 1979 the term Void was not yet being generally used and accepted in NDE circles.

> When the angels lifted my spirit from my body, they carried me immediately to the Second Heaven (Void). We did not have to leave that hospital room in order to enter the Second Heaven. We entered the Second Heaven in that same room where my body was, by passing through a dimension wall. This is a wall which flesh cannot pass through, only spirit.
>
> As we moved through that dimension wall into the Second Heaven, I found myself in an entirely different world, far different from anything I had ever imagined. This world was a place occupied by spirit beings as vast in number as the sand on the seashore. These beings were demons, or fallen angels, and were in thousands of different shapes and forms. Some of the forms were so morbid and revolting that I was nauseated.

Pittman could sense the presence of evil as he watched what was happening. He was revolted by the unpleasant behaviour of the demon spirits towards the spirits trapped there.

> I experienced a dreadful feeling. It was an overwhelming, oppressive, and morbid feeling. This feeling came to me

shortly after I had entered the Second Heaven, and I wondered what was causing it.

It was at this time that I learned that my guardian angel could read my mind because he said to me, 'That feeling you are wondering about is caused by the fact that there is no love in this world.'

The angel was telling me that in this Second Heaven there is not one bit of love! Wow! Can you imagine all of those demons serving a master [Satan} they don't love and the master ruling over beings that he doesn't love? Worse than that, their companions are working together for an eternity and they do not even love each other!

He reflected on how unpleasant life on Earth would be if God had not introduced His love into in our world. 'Because of God giving us His love, we are able to return that love and then love one another. Can you imagine what it would be like in your own home or your community if it were totally void of love?'

One outcome for Christians and others in touring the Void is that they perceive first hand the primary importance of love to a meaningful life.

Consequences of the Void

Kevin Williams[8], who has studied accounts about the Void given by NDErs, believes that no one who has died remains there permanently. His comments follow:

> The Void is not punishment. It is the perfect place for all souls to see themselves and to purge themselves from all illusions. For those souls who are too self-absorbed in their own misery to see the light, there is a multitude of beings of light nearby to help them when they freely choose to seek them. The nature of love and light is such

that it cannot be forced upon people who don't want it. Choosing love/light over darkness is the key to being freed from the Void. The moment that choice is made, the light and tunnel appears and the soul is drawn into the light.

If you are an NDEr and have spent a distressing time there, be encouraged. Nancy Bush, PMH Atwater, Maurice Rawlings and Barbara Rommer's investigations all suggest that, in the long run, virtually all NDErs have ultimately found distressing experiences extremely beneficial. This is despite having to struggle first through an emotional aftermath on returning to Earth.

The Void and Scripture

The Void is not mentioned as such in the Bible, the term being a modern one.

Deep darkness, a distinctive characteristic of the Void, is however associated with death in numerous Bible verses, for example Lamentations 3:6:

> He has made me dwell in darkness, *like those long dead.*

Hell is never pictured as 'deep darkness' where those long dead dwell this side of Judgement, but rather as a place of fire after Judgement, its most enduring image being the Lake of Fire. The biblical descriptions of darkness gloom and disorder after death but before Judgement fit the Void instead, as described by NDErs.

Job is one of the heroes of the Old Testament. Nevertheless, in his time of misery, we find Job speaking about his anticipated death in negative terms (Job 10:20-22):

> Are not my few days almost over?
> Turn away from me so I can have a moment's joy,

> before I go to the place of no return,
> to the land of gloom and utter darkness,
> to the land of deepest night,
> of utter darkness and disorder,
> where even the light is like darkness.

Where was Job expecting to go at death, this land of 'gloom and utter darkness'? It was a land of deepest night, of total darkness and disorder, 'where even the light is like darkness'? It was either the Void or perhaps some similar afterlife Prison section that he was anticipating, though this degree of darkness certainly matches NDErs' descriptions of the Void.

We trust that God was merciful to such a faithful servant as Job, and that he was pleasantly surprised to find himself in Paradise rather than in the Prison. Regardless of where he went, Job was certain that he would be resurrected, as we see in Job 19:25-27 when he stated:

> I know that my Redeemer lives, and that *in the end* he will stand upon the earth. And after my skin has been destroyed [Job's death], yet in my flesh [in his own resurrected body] I will see God. I myself will see him with my own eyes – I, and not another. How my heart yearns within me!

10
Other Prison Sections of Hades

The flames from the Lake of Fire in Hell can be viewed from certain sections of the Prison.

There are no scriptural records of people being in Hell – perhaps because Hell has been reserved for the devil and his angels after Judgement and was not designed for humans (Matthew 25:41 – the eternal fire which has been *prepared* for the devil and his angels). Despite this, it seems appropriate that those who have served Satan, and are comfortable with him and his demons, should inhabit Hell with them in the future.

Here are Bryan Melvin's[1] thoughts regarding spirits trapped in Prison. His speculation is based on his experiences. Bryan was your average atheist living a life mocking the concept of God before having his NDE.

> Each person knew fully that they deserved his or her fate because each chose to walk away from God and now resided in a place without God, as they desired during their lives on Earth.
>
> God, in his great justice, fairness, and unfathomable love gave them what they desired.

Rita Chuter[2] saw her father as a prisoner during her NDE in the UK in 1969.

> Then I saw my own father in that place [Prison section of Hades]. I wanted so much to help, but knew I could not

do anything for him. My father had been a good man, and became very sick with cancer. The vicar came to see him and asked if he could pray, but my father refused any prayer, or any mention of Jesus. He wanted nothing to do with Him. Now, as I looked at him, I knew he regretted that decision to turn his back on Jesus. It was his free will choice, but what devastating consequences!

As I continued to look with horror at the situation he was in, it was as if his thoughts spoke to me again. He told me to warn my mother, so that she would not have to come to this terrible place where there was no respite, and no end to the torment. The heat was unbearable. I also knew there was nothing I could do to release my father from his 'chosen' destination. I was also terrified lest I should be dragged down and forced to stay there. In my desperation I cried out to God, 'Oh, God, please help me!'

At the moment of crying out to God, I heard another voice crying, 'We have a heartbeat!'

Please remember that each of us will only receive our final eternal destiny on Judgement Day.

Where are Hell and the Prisons of Hades?

Hell is unpeopled or at most sparsely peopled before Judgement, but the Prison sections of Hades are *not* Hell, and multitudes similar to Rita's father have been observed residing there by NDErs.

Some NDErs report visions of Hell in which people are seen in the Lake of Fire. God does occasionally provide visions to NDErs during their experiences as a part of their instruction. Visions can serve as warnings. Hell and the Lake of Fire exist already somewhere, because Jesus said in Matthew 25:41 that it was prepared (past tense) for the devil and his angels, and so was in existence. Revelation 20:10 confirms this.

A strange fact is that in a large number of unpleasant NDEs, people describe the feeling of their spirits 'going down' to the Prison, rather than floating upwards, as is more usual. The pastor Kenneth Hagin[3] provides a typical description taken from his own NDE: 'Down, until the darkness encompassed me. The lights above faded away. The further down I went, the hotter and darker it became, until I came again to the bottom of the pit and saw the entrance to Hell.'

Rita Chuter[2] provides us with further detail: 'Although my body was on the table, and the doctors were fighting to get me back to life again, part of me was above them, and began to float away from that operating theatre. I then started to go down and down. It was horrific. I could see faces in pits, contorted with agony and pain. As I continued to go down, I began to be tormented by demons of all shapes and sizes. Not only were they ugly, but also the smell was dreadful. What made this downward journey even more terrifying were the lost souls I could see. There were many other awful things of which I cannot bear to speak. I came into a room where I could smell sulphur, and I saw a Lake of Fire. I could feel the flames and heat from that fire. My thoughts were that if I hit the bottom I would stay forever.'

If Paradise is an unseen spirit world parallel to us, might the Prison regions be 'parallel' also but lower, hence the sensation of 'travelling down' there?

The Prison does not seem to have a Lake of Fire. Nevertheless, excessive heat can be experienced there, and some localised 'fire pits' and flames have been described – but nothing of the magnitude of the giant flames NDErs have seen in the Lake of Fire of the nearby Hell.

It seems that God allows some folk a glance from Prison into Hell, perhaps as a graphic warning. For example, Dr Penny Sartori[4] in England spoke to a terrified woman who had had an unpleasant NDE and who felt the flames of Hell. She was looking into Hell; it was very hot and there was a lot of smoke. At that point, she started crying hysterically because it upset her so much. They had to stop the interview and when Sartori followed up on her, she did not want to discuss the experience further. This unwillingness to talk about Prison experiences is common and makes statistics of how many NDErs go there very unreliable – and without doubt too low.

Others who have described their experiences believe that they have looked briefly into the fires of Hell, but do not describe seeing people in the Lake of Fire. Matthew Botsford's[5] account is a case in point. Matthew was shot in the head by an Uzi submachine pistol during a random shooting in Atlanta. Matthew and his brother John had just finished an evening meal out in Atlanta, and were standing on the sidewalk when the shooting occurred. One of the shots entered the back of Matthew's head, lodging itself in the frontal lobe of his brain.

> There is a real Hell. It was a cell in Hell [author: more likely in Hades] that I was thrust into, and I could also tell there was no way out. I'm shackled at the wrists with ancient black chains – left wrist – right wrist. I'm shackled at the ankles. I couldn't move to the left, I couldn't move to the right, I couldn't move up, I couldn't move down. I am confined to Hell forever, and I am outstretched over this deep abyss. I can't see the bottom; it's an endless pit. There were just red glowing embers, and this grey smoke would billow up from this lava and rose up to the ceiling [of the cell].
>
> I had no clothes on. I was naked, and my skin was exposed, and there was heat that did rise from this pit, so I felt that.
>
> Then I could hear these horrendous screams – some guttural sounding, low pitched – I couldn't understand

them but I could hear the torment and I was just terrified, and I could tell it was just pure evil where I was: no dreams, no hopes, no memories, no breathing, no heartbeat. Time was non-existent now, it was an eternal experience that was happening to me, and it was only evil that was pressing in on all sides. It was horrifying, and I could also tell that there was no way out.

Although we are not told in scripture of any humans yet in Hell, demons specialise in making frightening noises. They also torment and terrify Prison inmates. Matthew experienced unpleasant demon attack before being rescued by the literal hand of God.

As a consequence of his horrible experience, Matthew was encouraged to make changes in his lifestyle on return to Earth.

Significantly, in the parable about the rich man and Lazarus (Luke 16:19-31), Jesus did not identify where the action took place as being in Hell, but instead specified the venue as Hades. Words used to describe the rich man's condition there were 'torment' and that it was very hot where he was. There are reports by others, who at death have gone to a similar place of intense heat – one of whom was the famous French dancer, Janine Charrat[6]: 'But what was now revealed to me made me cry in terror. I was alone in a strange and unfamiliar world, surrounded by huge licking flames. The flames got bigger, and their incandescent redness so glaring that I thought I would perish in fear... The ground under me was incandescent, a lava-like boiling mud.'

Relationship of Prisoners to the Damned.

There may be some relationship between Hades' Prison *now* and Hell in the future for some inmates – as there is on Earth between Court and Gaol. Just as not everyone who stands trial will go to Prison, so perhaps not everyone in the Prison section will end up in Hell after Judgement. We simply do not know. Judgement is God's business, not ours.

Reports are that certain spirits in Hades already experience the trauma of fire and brimstone (sulphur) as a precursor to Hell itself, consistent with the account of the Rich Man in Hades in Jesus' parable (Luke 16:23) who called out in torment: 'Father Abraham, have pity on me and send Lazarus to dip the tip of his finger in water and cool my tongue, because I am in agony in this fire.'

An ongoing relationship between Hades' Prison and Hell is suggested in a number of accounts, for example Bill Wiese[7] in *23 Minutes in Hell* begins with a Prison experience: 'I landed in what appeared to be a Prison cell. The walls of the cell were made out of rough-hewn stone and had a door made of what appeared to be thick metal bars. I was completely naked, which added to the vulnerability of a captive. This was not a dream – I was actually in this strange place.' However, he was not as certain about his experience as a whole, supposing some of it may have been a vision: 'There are many examples where God gave a dream or a vision to someone for direction or warning. I believe my experience fits into the classification of a vision.' Personally, I think the next part, what he saw in Hell where he suddenly found himself and became an observer, may have been *a vision segment* of Hell in the future, post-Judgement:

> It was raining fire and burning rock, similar to the way lava falls from the sky when a volcano explodes. The smoke from the flames was very thick, allowing visibility for only a short distance, but what I could see was horrifying. I saw many people reaching out of the pit of fire, desperately trying to claw their way out. But there was no escape.

Amongst all this uncertainty, one solid fact emerges – that many returnees who have encountered the Prison or have viewed Hell radically change their lives for the better on their return to Earth. As a course-correction for their lives, the NDE has served them well.

Other Venues?

Some other venues are presumably also in the Prison section, but cannot readily be correlated with it. These include some described by NDErs from other cultures, or in unusual accounts deriving from a Western culture. There could be further divisions in Hades than those discussed so far, as was believed to be the case by the ancient Greeks – and nowadays by Tibetan Buddhists and others. Where, for example, did the following NDE take place? It is Keith's account reported by Robert Thompson Perry[8]. In 1969 Keith was a Green Beret fighting in Vietnam who cared little for the people he encountered – 'high kill numbers' of the enemy were what mattered to him. He describes himself: 'I was mean, tough, and macho. I could use every part of my body to kill. I was a trainer of such men as well.' Then one day he was slain by an exploding mortar shell: 'I floated above my body and didn't feel any pain... I felt a sucking sensation downward and was suddenly in a trench [during his NDE].'

Keith then described struggling along this trench, which was lined with those he had killed. They yelled abuse at him as he passed. There was a bright light at the end of the long ditch.

> Even though they were speaking Vietnamese, I could tell that they were screaming that I was in some way responsible for their condition and their deaths. They were so horribly frightening that I tried to stay focused only on the light. I felt that if I could just reach the light I would be safe. None of these dismembered people on

the banks ever touched me, but I felt that I was running a gauntlet anyway.

To this point, Keith had not identified any of the Vietnamese who lined the trench. That was about to change. His experience was about to become intensely personal.

> One of the most haunting memories of this torturous journey was of a six year old thin little girl I had referred to as Miss Piglet (due to the fact that she always hung around begging for food and candy and was filthy).
>
> She showed up at our camp one day and had something concealed in a bag slung over her shoulder. She looked as if she was about to do something that she knew she should not be doing. I carefully drew a bead on her from about 50 feet away and thought, 'If she pulls out anything suspicious she is history'. I saw her reach into her bag and pull out something that looked like a grenade. I thought 'She has a grenade in that bag and has been sent to blow up my guys!'

Keith at once shot Miss Piglet. Later he found out that she had been lifting a puppy from the bag to show to the soldiers. She had been trying to find an American who would hide it to save it from becoming part of the family dinner that evening. Now, during his ordeal, Keith recognised her as one of those lining the trench and screaming at him. He was horrified and filled with guilt.

> After I've gone through what seemed like miles of this trench, I heard my deceased best friend's voice from high school telling me that I can do it. I can make it. I knew he was giving me encouragement. The encouragement I needed to make it to the light.

My friend, Ed, had died one and a half years ago in a hunting accident. Yet here he was suddenly helping me out of the trench and hugging me warmly!

I felt tremendous relief, love and acceptance. Tears of joy ran down both of our faces. 'Hey man,' he said, 'I know that was rough. But you needed it, you were getting just a little bit too callous and that isn't like you. It just wasn't the Keith I knew when we played football together and hung around in high school.'

I took a good look around and was in awe by the incredible beauty of the place of where we both stood. It was like a meadow with a sparkling stream running through it. The colours were much more vivid than on Earth. I noticed for the first time that Ed was glowing, and I looked at my own arms and they glowed slightly too.

The brilliant light he had emerged into mysteriously opened up Paradise to Keith!

Following his warm welcome, Ed chided Keith, 'You're not doing the right thing; you should not be doing this killing. Your mission is to help others and to protect them.' Next, he explained that Keith would return to Earth, where he would discover his mission in full.

Keith concludes his account: 'Since my Vietnam experience, I have felt a compelling protective need toward women and children. I even help out by volunteering to build shelters for abused and displaced women and their children.'

These positive outcomes suggest Keith's NDE was successful in turning his life around, but where did it take place? It seems to have ended in the Paradise section, but where had the trench experience taken place? Puzzling. There is definitely much more to be learnt about further levels in Hades.

Selection of the Prisoners

Since we are living before the great final Judgement, no one enters the Prison section on the basis of God having 'judged' them already! We must therefore wonder why some people are sent to the Prison section? Only God knows for sure, but reading unpleasant NDEs suggests some mechanisms are in operation. For example, a person's attitudes and emotional state *at death* are likely to be contributing factors for going to the Prison section – a kind of self-selection process. Some are already prisoners of a distressed mind, as are most suicides, or perhaps of negative emotions such as hatred, greed, jealousy or unforgiveness, or of extreme fear for some reason. It appears that these or other individual circumstances can predispose them to going to a Prison section. The rich man in Prison that Jesus spoke about in his parable was there because of self-love, greed and a lack of compassion towards a beggar at his gate.

Inappropriate lifestyles also appear to be contributory factors. For example, nearly all murderers, satanists, occultists, sexual perverts and atheists report having *begun* their NDE unpleasantly.

Nevertheless, another factor that trumps these must be in operation, because not all people who have lived a debauched/violent/sadistic/criminal or otherwise antisocial life go directly to Prison during their NDEs.

I feel that the 'trumping factor' that determines the initial destination for an NDEr is most likely to be God himself! The God whose intellect designed this Universe and perhaps others is more up to deciding which venue is best for an individual's NDE than we are, which is one reason why he warns us 'For in the same way you judge others, you will be judged, and with the measure you use, it will be measured to you' (Matthew 7:1,2).

Let's theorise for a moment.

Suppose there were three people who had committed similar murders and had an NDE. One might be consigned to the Void, another to elsewhere in the Prison complex, while the third finds himself in Paradise. This would produce a confusing picture if we do not suppose that *God is not dealing with the crime but with the criminal.* He would have chosen the venue most effective to bring about change in that person. For the first murderer, reflection in the Void must have been best; while the second will have needed a different Prison experience, even contemplating a pit of fire; while the third perhaps needed to interact with relatives in Paradise and contemplate a Life Review in order to bring about a change of heart. Remember, all three would soon return to Earth to apply what they had learnt to their future life choices.

Is there a way to ensure being taken to Paradise rather than one of the less pleasant Prison venues? To date, I have found that NDErs who claimed to have a personal relationship with Jesus visited Paradise during their NDE, but many others do also, therefore this cannot in itself be an exclusive prerequisite. One other grouping seem also to go invariably to Paradise – those whose lives have consciously aimed at developing the three 'eternals' of Love, Faith and Hope.

Seeing the Prisoners

A number of accounts, across a variety of cultures stretching back centuries, describe seeing prisoners in the Prison section of Hades.

Raymond Moody[9] did not initially record significant descriptions of the Prison experience in Hades, but did so afterwards when his sample base had increased:

> Several people have reported to me that at some point they glimpsed other beings who seemed to be 'trapped'

in an apparently most unfortunate state of existence. Those who described seeing these confused beings are in agreement on several points...

He subsequently reports a woman who saw people who shuffled, as someone would on a chain gang, and who had a crushed, hopeless demeanour. The 'chain gang' description indicates that they were in the Prison section of Hades.

A number of more recent NDErs have recorded similar sightings of the prisoners in Hades, perhaps for them on return to warn family and friends of the wisdom of avoiding such a place. Teresa[5] believes this to be so. She was taken to see the prisoners after first enjoying a thrilling reunion with her dead mother and brother in Paradise. Here are her words:

> I was suddenly standing on this somewhat elevated point of view, watching a procession of people walking. The people were very fearful; I was fearful just seeing that fear – and there was no happy face there. You know, faces of torment, faces of fear, shock – it was very evident that this was a whole different place than what I had just experienced... What I saw was a form of the road that leads to Hell. [She was referring to Matthew 7:13]
>
> I know that I was not in my body as I am standing watching the procession. On the other side were these grey spiritual beings. It was almost as though they were there, these spiritual beings were there, to keep the procession of people moving. They had the shape of a hooded faceless mass. They were somewhat transparent as a mist, and there were different ones scattered in the group of people and on the other side – and it was very evident that was what the people were fearful of. That's what I was fearful of! What were these things?

> I began to question in my mind, 'Why am I here, God? I thought I was a Christian. I thought I was saved.' There was still this tremendous sense of fear. I was trying to understand why I was in this place. It represented some form of separation from God, and I knew it was a place I did not want to be.

To this point, Teresa had been a frightened observer, but had no personal contact with the unhappy prisoners. That was about to change.

> Two people in particular turned and looked at me. And the sadness in their faces!
> I couldn't do anything about it. I couldn't help.
> The one man, he had a soft look on his face, but a look of fear.
> The woman who turned to look at me, she's a very beautiful woman, she's a brunette with big brown eyes, but she looked at me with such a sad look in her eyes – 'Can you help me?'
> And suddenly I get the impression of 'what if any of my family were to come here – loved ones, people I care very deeply about? I never want them in this place!'

What happened next allowed Teresa to escape from that gloomy and upsetting region.

> As I am standing there, I get this tremendous sense of peace that just came over me, and I felt this Presence by my side. Somehow there was this assurance that I was going to be OK and I didn't have to worry, I didn't have to be fearful. The only audible voice I heard was at this moment, and I heard 'your work is not finished'; I believe it was the voice of God.

And at the time I heard those words, this energy, this marvellous energy, started over all of my body, and transported me from this place to where I am suddenly on my table at the hospital looking up at doctors.

One said, 'If you can hear me, squeeze my finger', and I squeezed the doctor so hard, because I did not want to go back to what I had just seen!

Another NDEr[10] describes:

I was going through this long tunnel and I was wondering why my feet weren't touching the sides. I seemed to be floating and going very fast. I seemed to be underground. It may have been a cave, but the awfullest eerie sounds were going on. There was an odour of decay like a cancer patient would have.

Everything now seemed to be in slow motion. I can't recall all of the things I saw, but some of the workers were only half-human, mocking and talking to each other in a language I didn't understand.

When you ask me if I saw anybody I knew or if I met a stream of light, I did not. But there was a large person in radiant white clothes that appeared when I called out, 'Jesus, save me!'

He looked at me and I felt the message 'Live differently!'

I don't remember leaving there or how I got back. There are a lot of other things that may have happened that I don't remember. Maybe I'm afraid to remember! [This supports the suppressed memories theory pertaining to NDErs who have had unpleasant experiences.]

George Ritchie[11] saw spirits of people locked into a location most likely to have been the Prison section. Its inhabitants appeared to be those obsessed with violence.

> At first I thought we were looking at some great battlefield: everywhere people were locked in what looked like fights to the death: writhing, punching, gouging. It couldn't be a modern war because there were no tanks or guns. No weapons of any sort, I saw, as I looked closer, only bare hands and feet and teeth. And then I noticed that no one was apparently being injured. There was no blood, no bodies strewn on the ground; a blow that ought to have eliminated an opponent would leave him exactly as before. Although they appeared to be literally on top of each other, it was as though each man was boxing the air.
>
> At last, I realised that of course, having no substance, they could not actually touch one another. They could not kill, though they clearly wanted to, because their intended victims were already dead! And so they hurled themselves at each other in a frenzy of impotent rage...

Besides violence and the desire to murder, other obsessions motivated these spirits trapped by their own desires – and egos.

> Even more hideous than the bites and kicks they exchanged, were the sexual abuses many were performing in feverish pantomime. Perversions I had never dreamed of were being vainly attempted all around us. It was impossible to tell if the howls of frustration, which reached us, were actual sounds or only the transference of despairing thoughts. Indeed, in this disembodied world, it didn't seem to matter. Whatever anyone thought, however fleetingly or unwillingly, was instantly apparent to all around him, more completely than words could have expressed it, faster than sound waves could have carried it.
>
> And the thoughts most frequently communicated had to do with the superior knowledge, or abilities, or

background of the thinker. 'I told you so!' 'I always knew!' 'Didn't I warn you!' were shrieked into the echoing air over and over. With a feeling of sick familiarity, I recognised here my own thinking.

Prison or Paradise?

How many NDErs have visited the Prison sections? Statistics, discussed at the end of this book, give an approximate figure of between 20% to 30% (my best guess), but the figures are rubbery and could well be higher.

One statistic we do know for certain is that 100% of those NDErs who have proceeded to the Prison complex have not gone there as a consequence of God having judged them already. This fact is demonstrated by their having returned to Earth, where they have continued to live a life of free-will choices.

I am not a theologian, but it seems to me that God is too vast for the sweep of mankind to experience all of him all the time. It would seem that from earliest times, mankind experienced his creativity, perfection and sovereignty but since Christ's first coming, we have better understood and experienced his love, forgiveness and grace. From scripture, it seems that an emphasis on God's kingship, justice and judgement will characterise Christ's second coming. We can and already do know God at a deeper level in all these areas if we have chosen to relate to him personally, but it appears that each era is *characterised* by these broad sweeps of who he is – a kind of 'general revelation' of God for mankind to ponder on and reach out for in all eras.

It would be easy to think that because we are enjoying an emphasis on his love nowadays, which is strongly portrayed in NDEs, that some of these other aspects of his nature have diminished in his dealings with mankind. That miscalculation would be unwise.

Satan and Demons

Demon spirits are often assumed to be led by Satan (the Devil, Lucifer or Beelzebub), who is revealed in scripture as a rebellious angel supported by a horde of spiritual fellow travellers. As spirits, they possess some otherworldly abilities. Demons and Satan are not a focus of this book, and their activities in the afterlife are limited and best avoided where possible. We met them earlier in Howard Storm's[12] experiences in the Void. As they are active in sections of the prison complex other than the Void, their nature and actions need to be expanded upon a little.

Dr Richard Kent[13], a prominent NDE researcher in the UK, writes:

> Although demons are very rarely discussed in churches, NDE patients very commonly observe them. Of course, demons are frequently referred to in the Bible, and Jesus Christ spent much of His ministry casting them out. They are referred to in the Bible as fallen angels [and elemental spirits].
>
> Demons are described as grotesque in appearance, often quite small, but occasionally large. They do not radiate light as angels do, and appear very dark. There are different types of demons, each type evidently having an interest in its particular rebellious nature. Unlike angels they are not at all human in shape, having hideous features. Demons are not only offensive to look at, but utter very offensive language, using all of the swear words commonly used. Unlike angels, they do not have any sort of intuition, and communication with demons is not straightforward, as with angels. Demons are most unpleasant, and have been described as abusing the spirit bodies of NDE patients both verbally and physically...

Although demons are answerable to Satan, they are much more frightened of angels, and Jesus Christ in particular...

Demons summon the spirits of the departed to Hell, initially by deception, but eventually by force. They seem to enjoy their taunting activity, and prefer to act in groups rather than individually. They have far less spiritual ability than angels, which is perhaps why they prefer to act in groups rather than individually.

Here is a typical NDE description of unpleasant demon activity. Timothy LaFond[14] – a fire engine technician who went on to become a Christian minister – provides it.

> I heard the most horrifying, tormenting screams imaginable. I heard these time and time again, and although I never saw who was screaming, I, myself, would scream because of the fear of those frightening screams.
> Besides the screaming there were also demons. Yes, there really are demons. Indescribable and the most ugly things you have ever seen. They came up to me and taunted me. Yelling in my face, 'We got you now!' Laughing at me saying, 'We fooled you!'

Dr George Ritchie and Howard Pittman both describe being taken to watch demon activity on Earth as part of their learning process during their NDEs. Here is part of Pittman's[15] description, to give you a flavour of what is involved:

> My escort then told me that they wanted me to see demon activity in the outside world. I was then escorted outside the hospital directly through the brick wall into the streets of that city. I was amazed as I watched all the activity of the humans in the physical world. Going about

their daily pursuit, they were completely unaware that they were being stalked by beings from the spirit world. I was totally flabbergasted as I watched, and horrified as I saw the demons in all shapes and forms as they moved at will among the humans.

Dr Elizabeth Hillstrom[16], a professor of psychology who has studied a number of NDE cases since 1977, states that during her research some people reported seeing a being of light who emanated evil! She linked this with the scripture in the Bible that states Satan can masquerade as an angel of light, and his servants disguise themselves as servants of righteousness (2Cor 11:14,15). As a consequence, Satan's masquerade on rare occasions, according to Hillstrom, *may* take a sinister turn for NDErs – sending them back to Earth with 'beautiful messages from God' but filled with error, such as there is no such thing as sin, or that everyone will automatically go to Heaven at death, or that we are all heading to become part of one massive cosmic vibration – or some such 'secret' knowledge. I have to say, though, that Satan masquerading in this manner appears to be rare, as I have not come across examples myself among the thousands of NDE reports I have studied. Instead, in the afterlife, most NDErs are intensely aware of their own inadequacies, the awesome nature of God, and their need to do better.

I remain unconvinced that deception plays any role in pleasant NDEs, because these generally take place on God's turf in Paradise or in tours of the heavenly city and environs. Satan and demons appear to have no influence in these venues, nor have I come across descriptions of evil spirits anywhere near God's presence. Note that, other than on Earth, demonic and satanic activities seem confined to the Void and other Prison sections, with both Paradise and Heaven filled only with positive experiences and God's presence.

Does this mean that demons are indirectly serving God's purposes by showing the NDEr in a Prison section what to avoid on return to Earth? Absolutely.

Might Satan give deceiving messages to NDErs in the Prison environment, his area of activity? Perhaps, though that would seem counter-productive.

Some Christians would like to suggest that all NDEs are the works of Satan and deceiving spirits, for the purpose of deluding the NDErs. Jesus spoke about a kingdom divided against itself falling, and he applied this principle to unveiling the work of Satan (Matthew 12:22-30). We find that even atheists return from their NDE believing in God, and that some become converts to Christianity – such as Howard Storm, Bryan Melvin, George Rodonaia and Ian McCormack becoming effective Christian ministers. They have helped many hundreds of other people accept Christ and become Christians. Thereby, using the above teaching of Jesus as our measure, we must conclude that their NDEs cannot have been experiences of satanic intervention.

Regarding returnees from unpleasant NDEs, Dr Maurice Rawlings[19] states: 'These strange, negative encounters profoundly affect their future life and their view of death. *I have not seen one such person remain agnostic or atheistic!* [His emphasis. I believe his observations confirm that God has designed even unpleasant NDEs for our greatest benefit].

Nevertheless, spiritual muscle is like other muscle; exercise leads to health and strength. To avoid being mislead by Satan (evil) posing as God (good), I suggest that the better we come to know God while still on Earth, the less chance there will be of our being deceived anywhere along the line. And because Jesus makes God the Father personal to us, it is prudent to seek to relate personally to him.

Features of Unpleasant NDEs

This has become a focus for some researchers in recent years. Dr PMH Atwater's[17] research has added significantly to our knowledge. Having had three NDEs herself, her search for truth has been personal.

Atwater's introduction to NDEs consisted of distressing ones. 'My first introduction to the NDE was in a hospital room listening to three sombre people describe what they had seen while technically "dead." Each spoke of greyness and cold, and about naked, zombie-like beings just standing around staring at them. All three were profoundly disturbed by what they had witnessed. One man went so far as to accuse every religion on Earth of lying about the existence of any supposed "Heaven." The fear these people exhibited affected me deeply.'

She subsequently researched the differences between the pleasant and unpleasant NDEs, finding:

Heaven-Like Cases	*Hell-Like Cases*
Friendly beings	Lifeless or threatening apparitions or demons
Beautiful, lovely environments	Barren or ugly expanses
Conversations and dialogue	Threats, screams, silence
Total acceptance and an overwhelming love	Danger and the possibility of violence,
Pleasant interactions	Torture
A feeling of warmth and a sense of Heaven	A feeling of cold (or temperature extremes) and a sense of Hell

She adds: 'Invariably an attack of some kind would take place in hellish scenarios or a shunning and pain would be felt. Any indifference to the individual's presence would be severe, as would the necessity of the experiencer to defend himself or herself, and to fight for the right to exist. Themes of good and evil, beings like angels and devils, I found commonplace.'

A number of other researchers, such as Dr Margot Grey[18], have uncovered very similar results to that of Atwater. Grey's emphasis is more on what the NDEr felt: the sense of being lost and helpless, fearful and panicky, emotionally and mentally anguished, utterly desperate and extremely lonely, with an enormous sense of desolation.

These awful feelings derived from a variety of unpleasant experiences. Some subjects sensed an evil force, occasionally identified as the power of darkness, dragging them down. Wrathful or demonic creatures taunted, threatened or attacked the individual. Other attacks were by different unpleasant beings, often hooded or faceless. Wailing of souls in torment were sometimes heard, or noises of maddened wild beasts, snarling and crashing about.

Here are one NDEr's[19] feelings from what he saw of the Prison.

> I not only saw Hell, but felt the torment that all who go there will experience.
>
> The darkness of Hell is so intense that it seems to have a pressure per square inch. It is an extremely black, dismal, desolate, pressurized, heavy, type of darkness. It gives the individual a despondent feeling of loneliness. The heat is a dry, dehydrating type: your eyeballs are so dry they feel like red hot coals in their sockets. Your tongue and lips are parched and cracked with intense heat. ...
>
> The loneliness of Hell cannot be expressed.

Great Escapes

A parable of Jesus suggests that escape from the Prison is not possible by one's own efforts. In Jesus' parable about the rich man in the Prison section of Hades, we discover that he was isolated from the Paradise section by an unbridgeable barrier (Luke 16:26).

Examination of accounts of those NDErs who have escaped from the Prison section confirms Jesus' parable – it has required a divine decision to extract them from the Prison. I have not heard of anyone being able to move on by his or her own efforts.

The accounts of a number of escapees follow. Imagine the terror felt by a Mrs S whose testimony is quoted by Dr Maurice Rawlings[19]. God had revealed himself to her during her NDE, but then:

> In the next moment, to my horror, I found that I wasn't going toward God! I was going away from Him! It was like seeing what might have been, but going away from it!

She begged for her life and offered it to God. He must have heard her because she returned to her body.

Matthew[5] who it was mentioned previously had been suspended over a deep pit in Hades so that he could see the glowing coals and feel the heat, had a most unusual escape – a giant hand accompanied by a brilliant white light appeared and touched him. The shackles fell off him immediately, and he could hear the sounds of music and celebration outside.

> It starts to pull me out of this horror, up and out of this cell, and I heard this voice – male – definitely a masculine voice – never heard it before, and this voice sounded like thunder, like mighty rushing waters all combined into

one. I actually heard this voice speaking – *'It is not yet your time.'* At that moment, all the fear vanished.

In scripture, we find the visible hand of God in action in equally unexpected ways, for example writing on a wall during a feast in Babylon (Daniel 5:5), and presenting a prophet with a scroll (Ezekiel 2:9).

Back on Earth, the medics in hospital managed to restart Matthew's heart. His wife Nancy was told he was not expected to live through the night. His head and face were such a mess that Nancy recognised him only by his wedding ring. She prayed, 'Lord, bring back my husband – who he is – who his personality is – who his heart is, and I promise to stay with him.'

She sat with him for 27 days and refused requests from the hospital to switch off his life support. And then, one day, he squeezed her thumb and she knew he was back.

Matthew spent two years in rehab and his left side is still partially paralysed, but he has recovered all mental function.

Matthew admits that his goal before being shot had been to make as much money as possible, but that his goals on return have shifted to warning people to choose correctly in life while there is still time, and that his relationship with his wife is now 'so much richer'.

Dr Maurice Rawlings[10], working in the field of resuscitation, saw some terrified patients undergoing unpleasant experiences from which they were desperate to escape.

> He [Charles McKaig] had a terrified look worse than the expression seen in death! This patient had a grotesque grimace expressing sheer horror! His pupils were dilated, and he was perspiring and trembling – he looked as if his hair was 'on end'.

Then still another strange thing happened. He said, 'Don't you understand? I am in Hell. Each time you quit [CPR] I go back to Hell. Don't let me go back to Hell!'

Being accustomed to patients under this kind of emotional stress, I dismissed his complaint and told him to keep his 'Hell' to himself. I remember telling him, 'I'm busy. Don't bother me about your Hell until I finish getting this pacemaker into place.'

But the man was serious, and it finally occurred to me that he was indeed in trouble. He was in a panic like I had never seen before. By this time the patient had experienced three or four episodes of complete unconsciousness and clinical death from cessation of both heartbeat and breathing.

After several death episodes he finally asked me, 'How do I stay out of Hell?'

Here is Charlie McKaig's[19] own description of what happened next.

Whenever I would come back to my body, I kept asking, 'Please help me, please help me, I don't want to go back to Hell.' Soon a nurse named Pam [Charlesworth] said, 'He needs help, do something!' At that time, Dr. Rawlings told me to repeat this short prayer. *'I believe Jesus Christ is the Son of God. Jesus, save my soul. Keep me alive. If I die, please keep me out of Hell!'*

Although Rawlings admitted later to having said the prayer simply to shut Charlie up, the immediate positive change it produced in the patient startled him. This was something far beyond any response he had anticipated. Rawlings[19] reports.

Living Beyond

And then a very strange thing happened that changed our lives. A religious conversion experience took place. I had never witnessed one before. He was no longer the wild-eyed, screaming, combative lunatic who had been fighting me for his life. He was relaxed and calm and cooperative! It frightened me. I was a shaken by the events. Not only had that make-believe prayer blown out the soul of Charlie McKaig, but it backfired and got me too. It was a conviction I cannot express even to this day. Since then, Charlie has outlived three permanent pacemakers, and it has been difficult to believe that a miserable prayer of mine had opened the road to my own salvation.

Rawlings[19] observed: 'Not only had this make-believe prayer converted this atheist [Charlie], it had also converted this atheist doctor who was working on him.'

After experiencing the Void or another Prison section, an NDEr may then be taken to Paradise and safety. Ian McCormack[20] had this experience.

Ian was an atheist who died from box jellyfish stings. 'I found myself in a very dark place, not realizing where I was. So I tried to find a light switch, thinking I was still in the hospital – but as I reached out into the dark I couldn't touch anything. Reaching to touch my face I found my hand go straight through it. It seemed so bizarre, as I knew I was standing there but couldn't touch any part of my physical body.'

Ian sensed that this wasn't just a physical darkness, but that there was something else there. 'I could feel a cold eerie feeling as though something or someone was looking at me – a spiritual darkness. From the darkness I began to hear men's voices screaming at me telling me to "shut up" and "that I deserved to be there".'

Ian believes that perhaps it was his praying mother that allowed a lifeline to be thrown to him, or perhaps it was because of his desperate dying prayer in the ambulance. 'I couldn't believe it, but as I stood there a radiant beam of light shone through the darkness and immediately began to lift me upward. I found myself being translated up into an incredibly brilliant beam of pure white light – it seemed to be emanating from a circular opening far above me. I felt like a speck of dust being drawn up into a beam of sunlight.'

From this point Ian's experience became pleasant and similar to many others in Paradise, including a long interview with God before his return to Earth.

Personally, if I found myself in any of the Prison sections of Hades, I would be calling out to Jesus Christ for mercy and pleading with him to release me. I think from NDE accounts that would be a wise approach. No guarantees from this author, though! It is more prudent to establish a relationship with Christ before death.

Good From Evil

The attitude of returnees is fundamental to the future impact of their afterlife experiences. Atwater[21] gives an example of the key role it plays.

> After a talk I had given in Williamsburg, Virginia, a man in the audience related his near-death story; one so positive and so inspiring it brought tears to the eyes of most of those attending. Yet, to everyone's surprise, he went on to reveal how cursed he felt to have had such an experience and how difficult his life had been ever since it had happened.

Then a woman jumped up and excitedly recounted her story. Even though her scenario centred on a life-or-death struggle in semidarkness at the edge of a whirlpool, while high winds and the presence of evil threatened, she was overjoyed to have experienced anything so inspiring and so revealing about how life really worked and how salvation is guaranteed by our own willingness to correct our own mistakes.

Here were two people: one traumatized by a heaven-like experience, the other uplifted and transformed by a hellish one!

Atwater went deeper. She saw a positive and definite relationship between who the person on Earth had become to that point in life, and the nature of their subsequent NDE. I believe this illustrates the planning of God, though Atwater does not reflect on this.

When you keep a person's life in context with his or her brush with death, even a clinical death, you cannot help but recognize connections between the two, threads that seem to link what is met in dying with what that individual came to accept or reject about the depths of living. It is almost as if the phenomenon is a particular kind of growth event that allows for a 'course correction,' enabling the individual involved to focus on whatever is weak or missing in character development.

Surprisingly, unpleasant or Hell-like experiences really can be quite positive if individual experiencers are inspired to make significant changes in their lives because of them.

But, pleasant or Heaven-like experiences can be incredibly negative if individuals use them as an excuse

> to dominate or threaten others while engaged in self-righteous campaigns.
>
> Even Heaven-like or transcendent experiences may be painful or hellish to an individual unfamiliar with the possibility of alternate realities, or unwilling to have his or her worldview interrupted or challenged.

Atwater goes still further, noting that those experiencing unpleasant NDEs can tread a lonelier path than those who experience pleasant ones.

> Once, when I was autographing copies of my book in a shopping mall, a man in his middle thirties stopped at my table, looked me straight in the eye, and with tight lips declared, 'You've got to tell people about Hell. There is one. I know. I've been there. All them experiencers on television telling their pretty stories about Heaven – that's not the way it is. There's a Hell, and people go there.'
>
> I could not calm this man or the piercing power of his words, nor could I inspire him to consider other ways of interpreting his experience. He was adamant and firm. To him Hell was real and to be avoided, no matter what.
>
> That's what I've noticed with individuals like this man: either there is a special kind of fierceness about them, or an empty fear, or a puzzled indifference, or an unstated panic. If they show emotion at all, it is usually tears. Many feel betrayed by religion. Many resent the endless banter on television talk shows about 'the Light': all that warmth and love and joy exuded from those who seemed to have experienced Heaven. When I would ask why they weren't on television themselves telling their own stories, most would suddenly become quiet. Eventually I came to realize that they had spoken to no one else about what had happened to them! Most often

they indicated feeling too ashamed or fearful or angry to talk about it; furthermore, the possibility of another's judgment or criticism bothered them.

Dr Barbara Rommer[22] is another fine researcher. She has found that virtually all NDErs who had distressing NDEs *'ultimately* found the experience extremely beneficial'. She offers a couple of insightful observations after careful questioning of more than 300 NDErs who had had horrible experiences.

1. Someone who had a lifelong pattern of using emotional isolation to avoid being rejected by others may have a distressing NDE of the eternal Void, in which he realized that profound, endless isolation is not what he really wants. Afterwards, he may develop his ability to be emotionally vulnerable to others, to deal with the occasional disappointments that such vulnerability brings, and to enjoy the frequent rewards of connecting intimately with others.

2. Another distressing NDEr may report that during her NDE... for the first time in her life, she genuinely called out to God for help; and for the first time she experienced the genuine presence of, and communion with, God.

Rommer then makes the point that both of these NDErs would say that without their unpleasant NDE, they would not have furthered their personal and spiritual development. In this sense, Rommer concluded that although NDErs frequently struggle through an emotional aftermath following a distressing NDE, they almost always come to see their experiences as blessings in disguise.

Nancy Bush[23], whose prominence in IANDS (International Association for NearDeath Studies) gave her access to thousands of NDE reports, probed the relative success or failure of returnees who had unpleasant NDEs. Her research confirmed Rommer's conclusions, but drew attention to the exceptions. A few NDErs tried to ignore the lessons of the unpleasant NDEs, sometimes as a consequence of bad advice given during counselling sessions once back on Earth. They achieved a measure of relief but this proved only temporary. A small number of returnees tried to search for alternative models of reality in which to accommodate their NDE, with very limited success. She categorised all returnees from distressing NDEs into three broad groups, the first being the most successful:

- Those who interpret their NDE as a warning, who are able to connect it with previous behaviours they identify as unwise or downright wrong, and who then find avenues by which to modify their lives in satisfying ways. She noted that these NDErs heal most quickly and thoroughly in the aftermath of the experience.
- The reductionist NDEr who argues away his or her unpleasant NDE as somehow less valid or real than pleasurable NDEs. Bush noted that people in this category might find psychological peace, but only temporarily. Their NDEs were too significant for their psyche to be bluffed.
- The long haul NDErs who undertake a long-term process, lasting sometimes many years, of searching for a way to accommodate the distressing NDE into a much deeper view of reality.

Her conclusion? Only those who accepted the obvious warning given during their NDE really benefitted! Her summary is worthy of reflection:

Those who insist on finding the gift, the *blessing* of their experiences, have the potential ultimately to realise a greater maturity and wholeness.

Issues about the future Day of Judgement can become a concern to those who have experienced the Prisons of Hades. According to Dr Maurice Rawlings[10], a common response is, 'It's not dying I'm afraid of. It's returning to that awful place again.' They return to Earth with a strong motivation to change their future lives for the better, and most do so.

Overall, then, research has shown that the after effects of unpleasant NDEs are enduring, powerful, and generally life-changing. We will let Dr Sabom[24] have the last word on this: 'Those who have had NDEs [pleasant or unpleasant] have had a powerful spiritual experience. The emphasis on God that they bring out of this experience is real, but they need to go to the Bible to understand what it means, and what road to walk down now. The NDE is non-directional; it can send you down many different roads, and many of these are wrong roads. And so I think it brings us back to scripture...'

Before we embark on exciting tours of Heaven, the cosmos, or Hell, we need to consider the NDEs of those who have committed suicide. There would be few readers who did not know of someone who in despair has taken their own life. In terms of those who have NDEs, what are the possible consequences?

11

Suicides: A Special Case?

Our time on Earth is but a heartbeat in the eternal scheme of creation, and yet it is the crucial moment of truth, the turning point. It determines how our spirits will exist forever.
—Angie Fenimore[1], NDEr and suicide survivor.

Suicide is not a trivial problem. For example, America[2] is losing around 38000 people to suicide each year.

The World Health Organisation[3] reported in 2013 that:

- In the last 45 years suicide rates have increased by 60% worldwide, and for every successful suicide there have been around 20 attempted suicides.
- Suicide is now among the three leading causes of death worldwide among those aged 15-44 (male and female).
- Although suicide rates have traditionally been highest amongst elderly males, rates among young people have been increasing to such an extent that they are now the group at highest risk in a third of all countries.

The NDEs of Suicides

People who have attempted suicide and who have had NDEs report them to have been unpleasant in the main. Here are a couple of typical examples.

Cardiologist Maurice Rawlings[4] quoted a despondent fourteen-year-old girl who had swallowed a bottle of aspirin:

At the time she kept saying, 'Mama, help me! Make them let go of me! They're trying to hurt me!'

The doctors tried to apologise for hurting her, but she said it wasn't the doctors, but 'Them! Those demons in Hell, they wouldn't let go of me, they wanted me. I couldn't get back. It was just awful...'

After the various tubes were removed, I asked her to recall what had happened. She remembered taking the aspirin, but absolutely nothing else! Somewhere in her mind the events may still be suppressed...

She subsequently became a missionary several years later. No despondency. I am told that everywhere she goes she brings exuberance – a contagious feeling.

A medical associate of Dr Maurice Rawlings[4] provides another 'standard' account.

At the height of his success no one could have known he was so despondent.

He told me he was searching for more than life had to offer. I didn't understand him myself. I should have listened because that night I was called to his home in Beverly Hills and found him on the floor with a bullet wound through his mouth.

He revived to consciousness and responded to resuscitation for a while before he died. I asked him if he hurt. He shook his head – No. I told him we were going to try to save him. He nodded in agreement. His last words were, 'I'm scared! Don't let me go back to Hell! I can see it now.'

I don't know what he saw.

Why are the NDEs of suicides generally unpleasant? Only God knows – but we can conjecture.

A possible reason is that the majority of suicides will have been in a traumatised emotional and psychological state when trying to kill themselves, and this state alone may have led them into the Void or some other appropriate section of the Prison for a season of reflection.

There may also be a spiritual explanation for unpleasant NDEs. Thomas Aquinas[5] argued that life is a gift from God, and that it is not man's prerogative to take it back, but God's alone. Scripture supports his thoughts by indicating that there is an allotted time to die:

> There is an appointed time for everything. And there is a time for every event under Heaven – a time to give birth and a time to die (Ecclesiastes 3:1,2).
>
> All the days ordained for me were written in your book before one of them came to be (Psalm 139:16).

While mankind does not have the capacity to increase a lifespan at will, by a free will choice to commit suicide he can shorten it. Consequently, suicide goes against God's allotted purposes. Moving outside the natural order like this may consign a spirit into a 'holding' situation in the Prison.

Suffering and Suicide

This leads us into an ethical minefield. Shouldn't a disturbed or suffering person have the societal right to take his or her own life? Regardless of our opinions, it appears unwise to do so, especially looking at the unpleasant experiences of NDErs. It seems that there is a difference between what is allowed or possible because of free will, and what is a preferred or appropriate choice to make in God's eyes.

Contrary to some popular opinion, suffering is not a sufficient reason in scripture for suicide. Paul suffered greatly for the cause of Christ to the point of despair, as in 2Corinthians 1:8, 'We were under great pressure, far beyond our ability to endure, so that we despaired of life itself'. Yet he did not commit suicide, later dying a martyr's death in Rome.

Alice Morrison-Mays[6] provides us with a modern example. Her NDE happened in 1952 and she was never free of pain thereafter. She also became wheelchair bound in later life. Nonetheless, she advised time and again that, 'There's still a quality of life available. You just have to be open enough to explore it. You can empower yourself.'

Try questioning from scriptural precedents whether suffering may have importance and even value – did Jesus suffer? Did Father God use this? Did the disciples suffer? Did God use this? Did the early church suffer? Did God use this? No wonder that in the 2nd-century Tertullian[7] wrote that 'the blood of martyrs is the seed of the Church,' implying that the martyrs' pain and death by murder, not suicide, led to the conversion to Christ of multitudes of others. That process has continued throughout history and continues in the present day, primarily in certain religious-extremist countries.

On a personal level, although none of us likes or welcomes it, suffering has a role to play in life. In Romans 5:3-5 we see a sequence of learning and growth in suffering endured with prayer and determination:

> We also glory in our sufferings, because we know that suffering produces perseverance; perseverance produces character; and character; hope. And hope does not put us to shame, because God's love has been poured out into our hearts through the Holy Spirit, who has been given to us.

NDEs reinforce that every individual has a destiny to fulfil and a 'mission' to complete on Earth. Suicide can be a selfish act that prevents personal growth and causes mission failure, to the detriment of others.

Suicide Outcomes

If God has consigned a suicide to an unpleasant NDE, and they have received insights from this before returning, it can be a positive turning point in their life. Here are some observations made by PMH Atwater[6]:

> Near-death survivors from suicide attempts can and often do return with the same sense of mission that any other experiencer of the phenomenon reports. And that mission is usually to tell other potential victims that suicide is not the answer.
>
> For example, this young man (he asked not to be identified) told me: 'Since then, suicide has never crossed my mind as a way out. It's a cop-out to me and not the way to Heaven. I wish you luck in your research and hope my experience will help stop someone from taking his own life. It is a terrible waste.'
>
> Suicide near-death episodes can lay to rest problems and conflicts, explain away confusions, and emphasize the need to remain embodied.
>
> Experiencers usually return with a feeling that suicide solves nothing, and they are notably renewed and refreshed by that feeling, using their near-death event as a source of courage, strength, and inspiration.
>
> But not all suicide scenarios are positive.
>
> Some are negative, and these can be so negative that they upset the individual more than the original problem that precipitated the suicide. This kind of devastation can

be transforming if used as a catalyst to help that person make the kind of changes that comprise constructive, long-term solutions. Such changes can come from an inner awakening, or from the fear that what was experienced may indeed herald the individual's final fate if something is not done to turn things around.

'Penalties' for Suicide

Raymond Moody's[8] early writings led many to suppose that all NDERs who attempted suicide had unpleasant afterlife experiences. Dr Moody had only a few cases of suicide-induced NDEs to study, and in each case the NDE was characterized as being nasty. Subsequent examples however show this is not always the case, even though the majority of suicides appear to experience unpleasant NDEs. Moody's analysis nevertheless remains important. He went on to note that returnees reported suicide to be a very undesirable act that might incur a 'penalty'. This penalty for an act of suicide might include witnessing the suffering this act had caused. In addition, he found that suicide-NDErs agreed their deaths would have solved nothing, and strongly disavowed suicide as a means of returning to the afterlife existence. Overall, the feelings of personal torment became magnified in the afterlife. The majority stated very strongly that they would not consider suicide again.

The implication was: 'If you leave here a tormented soul, you will be a tormented soul over there too.' Not only did the problems persist that had precipitated the suicide attempt, but also once in the disembodied state, the subjects were unable personally to do anything about it. Our sample base, however, has expanded in recent years.

Ivan Rudolph

Pleasant experiences after Suicide

Deborah Weiler's[9] description of her encounter with God is ecstatic. Her suicide attempt did not originate in feeling unloved or undervalued, factors in most other suicide attempts. 'I was loved, treasured, sought after as a friend and cherished – but I had just killed myself. To walk a path so dark that you seek death I wish on no one. I will not judge another's path home. I can only continue to try to walk mine.' She took her life in 1984, age 29 years. Here is a shortened version of her memories of God:

> All I could see was this huge, brilliant light. All I could feel was love, rolling over me as sunlight warms my skin through on a windy day. I felt examined by it. I focused all my attention on it. What I learned next amazed me. I discovered that the glowing, golden globe of light was *alive*. It was a 'self'. It was a living being. We were the same! We were both living beings! This felt like a huge revelation; 'Hey, it's another soul!' It was huge, loving and powerful, strong and gentle all at the same time.
>
> I felt the power the Being appeared to generate and that was sent out from it. It was like standing in the sunlight but, instead of sunshine, LOVE warmed you through to your centre...
>
> Then came to me the first hint of truly understanding the meaning of the word 'grace'. That Being knew all of everything I ever was and [nevertheless] loved me... Small, confused, dead by my own hand, I was cherished and loved! I was precious to it. I responded to that with my own thoughts to it of my joy in the peace, love and total acceptance it was giving me. I tried to love it back with my little self.

> The Being knew I loved it and that I was thankful for its love of me. Then it loved me more. I loved it more. A cycle of pure love between us grew.

Deborah's experiences in Paradise were effective in turning her life around.

Dr Richard Kent reports the account of Henrietta[10] who committed suicide in the UK, after being jilted by her boyfriend. She met with God in a pleasant venue during her NDE.

> I did not see Jesus, only God Almighty. I do not know what He looked like because there was just this warmth and light. Then He spoke and greeted me, and I just said, 'Hi.' His next words may sound funny, but I did not think so then. 'You are early', He said, to which I responded that I knew, and I was sorry. God then asked me what I was doing there, as it was not my time. Such was His Love that I poured out my heart and told Him I could not go on any longer because I could not stand the pain. 'I know you cannot,' He responded, 'but you cannot come home yet... there are people you need to speak to.'
>
> Although it was brightness in front of me, behind was just darkness. I turned and saw a group of people. Actually it was more like two small circles standing in the form of a figure of eight. God showed me that these people were going to Hell if I did not speak to them. There was no argument on my part; I knew He was telling the truth. I turned round to them again and pleaded with God not to send them to Hell, but to send someone else to speak to them instead of me.
>
> His reply was, 'I cannot. You are going to have to do it.'

Such an unexpected response from God intimated to Henrietta that her life had an unfulfilled purpose. This suggests that suicide can interfere with the purposes of God and even prevent his perfect will being accomplished. He had chosen Henrietta to speak to those she saw in the vision, who otherwise might be amongst the eternally lost (Matthew 7:14).

> I knew there was no arguing over this. I knew that there would be a time when I would speak to these people. Whatever it was I had to say, or whenever it was, or whether I would actually lead them to God, I really did not know. All I knew was that it was my job, and no one else could do this.
>
> As I turned, saying I agreed to go back, it hit me just what I was going back to, and again I told God that I could not go back because I could not stand the pain...

After her return, Henrietta discovered that she had been pregnant at the time of her attempted suicide, and it dawned on her that had she died then of course the baby would have died too. She believes the second group of people she saw during her interview with God, the second circle forming the 'figure of 8', are those to whom her child rather than herself will speak. It comforts her to believe that while her child was conceived in distressing circumstances, God's love and plans pertain to that child none-the-less:

> My daughter is now just turned 11, and she has brought so many people to know Jesus, it is amazing. Every time she tells me about someone else she has spoken to, I jump for joy – because I remember that group.

Afterlife Destinations

Some pleasant NDEs have been in people where mental illness led to the suicide. Where mental illness derives from a physical disorder of the brain, it ceases at death, in the same way that blind or deaf people have their brain-centred senses restored in the spirit world. Similarly with those who were suffering from Alzheimer's disease and other conditions caused by a malfunctioning of the brain: their imperfect brains have been left on Earth, and they taste a new beginning.

We might speculate about those whose life ends through euthanasia or assisted suicide. As yet I have seen no accounts by any returnees to help me explore afterlife experiences of those who make this choice or have it made for them. Of interest, Holland was the first country in the world in the year 2000 to legalise euthanasia and cardiologist Pim van Lommel[10] is their most prominent NDE researcher. Convinced now regarding the afterlife and the survival of the consciousness, he has cautioned [11]:

> The conclusion that consciousness can be experienced independently of brain function might well induce a huge change in the scientific paradigm in western medicine, and could have practical implications in actual medical and ethical problems such as the care for comatose or dying patients, euthanasia, abortion, and the removal of organs for transplantation from somebody in the dying process with a beating heart in a warm body but a diagnosis of brain death.
>
> There are still more questions than answers, but, based on the aforementioned theoretical aspects of the obviously experienced continuity of our consciousness, we finally should consider the possibility that death, like birth, may well be a mere passing from one state of consciousness to another.

It appears that, one way or another, many NDErs do not escape the consequences of their suicide. Dr George Ritchie[12] describes seeing, during his NDE, the anguished Earth-bound spirits of suicide victims.

> In one house a younger man followed an older one from room to room.
> 'I'm sorry, Pa!' he kept saying. 'I didn't know what it would do to Mama! I didn't understand.'
> But though I could hear him clearly, it was obvious that the man he was speaking to could not. The old man was carrying a tray into a room where an elderly woman sat in bed.
> 'I'm sorry, Pa,' the young man said again. 'I'm sorry, Mama.'
> Endlessly, over and over, to ears that could not hear.
> Several times we paused before similar scenes –
> A boy trailing a teenaged girl through the corridors of a school:
> 'I'm sorry, Nancy!'
> A middle-aged woman begging a gray-haired man to forgive her.
> 'What are they so sorry for, Jesus?' I pleaded. 'Why do they keep talking to people who can't hear them?'
> Then from the light beside me came the thought:
> 'They are suicides, chained to every consequence of their act.'

These scenes shook up Ritchie and remained etched in his memory. When later contemplating suicide himself, he knew that no situation on Earth was worth the misery of those spirits that he had witnessed during his NDE. Nor had they escaped from their situations as they had hoped; instead, they had become chained to them.

It is noteworthy that this unpleasant experience seen by Ritchie did not take part in the Void or another Prison section of Hades. It involved an Earth-bound experience, although the sense of captivity was almost as great.

Changing Venues

Some suicides begin with an unpleasant NDE that changes venues as lessons are learnt within it. Tamara Laroux's[13] NDE illustrates this process.

Tamara, as a troubled 15-year-old, shot herself. She called out 'God forgive me!' just before pulling the trigger.

She went first to the Prison section of Hades and experienced the torment there, becoming a 'being of fear and pain'. She felt total isolation despite being amongst a sea of thousands of others, because she perceived that they were all experiencing feelings similar to her own. Just by looking at someone, she could sense his or her thoughts, feelings of hopelessness, and details of earlier sins and behaviours. Then a giant hand scooped her out of that place and carried her over a yawning gulf separating Prison from Paradise.

Why had she been rescued from the Prison? She supposes because of her desperate cry to God as she pulled the trigger.

Other suicides may be moved from one section of the Prison to another. A number describe beginning in the Void before moving on to a section apparently designed specifically for suicides. We find both venues described by Annabel Chaplin[14]. She states that suicides are in the Void for a very long time, before moving on to a 'Land of Despair'. She describes this as an alien and strange place enveloped by a dull, heavy foreboding.

> Victims resided in the still air, completely bent over with their heads buried in mud and covered with dark shrouds. There was no communication with the victims immersed in their own bleak world of gloom and who were unaware of anything but their self-imposed misery – perhaps this

was 'his own place' to which Judas was consigned (Acts 1:25). New arrivals were powerless to reverse their descent to this awful place, even as they recognized their fate and struggled against it.

Annabel hoped that the souls who had repented 'long enough' would fulfil their need for repentance and could eventually find their way back to the light. We would all join her in that hope.

Angie Fenimore's[1] NDE

Angie's NDE is a longer, more comprehensive report than most who have committed suicide. It fleshes out important issues on the subject, and allows us to enter profoundly into her experiences. She kindly gave me an interview that helped me to prepare this account. If you want a much deeper sense of her experiences, read her excellent book or see her on YouTube.

Angie's Background

Her mother left home when Angie was just 9 years old. She had to care for the family – cook, clean and provide mothering for her little sister as best she could. Her father was an alcoholic who was lost in his own despair and ill-equipped to care for two little girls. Worse still, as time went by, she experienced sexual abuse. She put up with this to protect her sister. After these episodes she would cuddle her dolls in bed and feel utterly worthless and unlovable.

She married early at 19, but within a week her husband had yanked her off the ground by her hair. Years of abuse continued. Angie suffered a broken tooth and a broken nose, but the emotional abuse she endured was far more damaging. She eventually succumbed to addictions and behaviours that were contrary to her beliefs in abstaining from alcohol and drugs and relations outside of marriage. Angie had two boys of her own, but could not escape the inner feelings of self-loathing that trapped her. She believed that she had no control over her behaviour, her thoughts and her emotions and fell into a dark depression. She felt she would be doing her husband and children a favour by taking her own life.

When Angie was a teenager, her stepmother told Angie how, after a serious car accident, she had floated above her body in the emergency room. She heard the doctors saying that the family should be gathered because she likely would not survive. She was then enveloped in a warm and loving light filled with peace. Loved ones who had passed on met her in the light as she hovered above her body. They told her that it was not her time but that she could choose. She was told that if she returned, her life would be difficult. She chose to come back.

To Angie, this peaceful bliss sounded superb and thoughts of suicide became more urgent. She twice put a loaded shotgun in her mouth but did not pull the trigger. 'If I had, I would not have been able to return to my body after my NDE,' she remarks today.

At the age of 26, in January 1991, she slit her wrists and then swallowed nearly every drug in the medicine cabinet.

Angie's Life Review

Her NDE began in the classic fashion with an awareness of her spirit separating from her body. She was not taken to the brilliant glories of Paradise, however, but remained in darkness. She noticed a large screen in front of her on which a 3D slide show of her life began playing out chronologically in vivid detail, beginning in her mother's birth canal followed by her birth. She experienced her delighted mother cupping Angie's head in her hand.

What seemed strange as the images flew past was her adult understanding of each person who appeared on the screen – what they were thinking and feeling at the time, even those in the room when she had been a baby. 'I knew how each person felt who had ever interacted with me.'

Despite being totally captivated by the events shown on the screen and the emotions that they evoked, she became aware of a supportive 'presence' with her, without actually seeing who or what this presence was. She knew that he was male and that he knew her and loved her.

The pictures rushed along until she saw herself dead, lying on the couch. Then, just as suddenly as they had started, the pictures stopped.

The Sorting Ground.

Angie searched the darkness. Where was she? Darkness enveloped her, not the wonderful, warm light she had anticipated. The darkness continued in all directions and seemed to have no end. 'It was an endless Void,' she concluded. In spite of being surrounded by absolute darkness, she could see on a heightened level. To her right, standing shoulder to shoulder, was a line of teenagers. Otherworldly intuition kicked in and Angie deduced that they were suicides like herself.

'With a laugh, I opened my mouth, but before I could form the words, they came tumbling out, "We must be the suicides." I wasn't sure whether I had thought the words or had attempted to say them, but they were audible without my having to move my lips.'

But had the others waiting in line heard her telepathic message? They showed no emotion if so. Then the lad next to her slowly turned and looked blankly at her before turning to look forward again. He had heard her, but there had been no expression on his face, no warmth or friendliness. He returned to looking ahead in a transfixed stupor.

Angie saw a girl towards the end of the line, who looked to be about 16 years old. Might she respond? Angie drew a blank. 'She was just like the rest of them, her empty gaze fixed on nothing, staring blankly forward. They were all dead, and so was I!'

Without warning, Angie felt herself being pulled away by an unknown force, leaving the line of teenagers behind.

The Prison

Angie found herself deposited in a shadowy realm stretching as far as she could see. There were people there, apparently mumbling to themselves because she could observe no communication taking place between them. They appeared to be caught up in their own misery to the exclusion of making connection with anyone else. They stood, squatted or wandered aimlessly about.

Men and women of all ages were trapped there, but one observation struck her – there were no children.

With growing alarm as she looked around. She became convinced that this was a place where suicides were imprisoned.

The old man closest to her was in a pathetic, filthy condition, squatting on the ground and apparently resigned to his fate. He appeared to have ceased thinking altogether and took no notice of anything around him. 'He was completely drained, just waiting.' She felt his trapped soul had been there a very long time. 'In this dark Prison, a day might as well be a thousand days or a thousand years.' She even wondered whether he could be one of the most famous suicides in history – Judas Iscariot. Then she felt embarrassed for the thought, in case he had picked it up. If he did, he showed no sign of it but continued his hopeless, impassive waiting.

It struck Angie's restless, probing thought processes that this was a land of nothing – no love, no privacy, no sleep, no friends, no light, no growth, no happiness, no relief, no television, no books – no access to knowledge and no way to use it. It was an empty world, where no connections could be made. It was not how she had imagined suicide would be.

Angie found the solitude oppressive and terrifying. Her sense of being alone and helpless seemed to burgeon. How many eons would she remain in this awful condition?

Enter the Father

A commanding voice rang out and crashed over Angie like a gigantic wave. The voice expressed a strange mixture – ferocious anger, but also love at the same time, like an angry parent.

Angie cowered. 'The darkness vibrated. Every particle of darkness reverberated with the words, "This is God." I knew there was infinite power in that voice.'

'Is this what you really want?'

This great voice emanated from a pinpoint of light that swelled with each thunderous word until it hung like a radiant sun just beyond the black wall of mist that formed my Prison.

Though far more brilliant than the sun, the light soothed my eyes with its deep and pure white luminescence... I knew with complete certainty that I was in the presence of God. I didn't need to be told.

He was a Being of Light, not just radiating light or illuminated from within, but he almost seemed to be made of the light. It was a light that had substance and dimension, the most beautiful, glorious substance that I have ever beheld. All beauty, all love, all goodness were contained in the light that poured forth from this Being.

There is nothing that we are even capable of imagining that comes close to the magnitude of perfect love that this Being poured into me.

Angie became aware that none of the other suicides had heard the voice. The man closest to her could see that she was focused on something, but it was apparent that he couldn't hear anything. Others continued to babble unaware.

Then God spoke again. His words were excruciating.

> *'Is this what you really want? Don't you know that this is the worst thing you could have done? You can't take your own life; it's not yours to take.'*

I could feel his anger and frustration, both because I'd thrown in the towel, and because I had cut myself off from him and from his guidance.

Angie felt she needed to express to God how trapped she'd felt, and that she had seen no other choice but to die. So she responded, 'But my life is so hard!'

Her thoughts were not even completed before his response came.

> *'You think that was hard? It is nothing compared to what awaits you if you take your life.'*

When the Father spoke, each of his words exploded into a complex of meanings, like fireworks, tiny balls of light that erupted into a billion bits of information, filling me with streams of vivid truth. I was filled with pure understanding about the purpose of life. He continued:

> *'Life's supposed to be hard. You can't skip over parts.'*

Enter Jesus

Suddenly Angie felt another presence alongside the Father, the same presence that had stood by her during her Life Review. Similar to the Father, this presence was now radiating light such that she could see him. She discovered that he too streamed love towards her. She thought she could perceive a difference, though.

> This love was as pure and potent as the Father's, but it had an entirely new dimension of pure compassion, of complete and perfect *empathy*.
> I felt that he not only understood my life and my pains exactly, as if he had actually lived my life, but that he knew everything about how to guide me through it; how my different choices could produce either more bitterness or new growth.
> Having thought all my life that no one could possibly understand what I had been through, I was now aware that there was one other person who truly did.
> Through this empathy ran a deep vein of sorrow. He ached, he truly grieved for the pain I had endured, but even more for my failure to seek his comfort. His greatest desire was to help me. He mourned my blindness as a mother would mourn a dead child.

Suddenly she knew that she was in the presence of Jesus Christ. He spoke to Angie through the veil of darkness.

'Don't you understand? I have done this for you.'

As she expresses it, her spiritual eyes were opened. In that moment she was suddenly inside Christ's body, taken back in time and experiencing, from Christ's point of view what transpired in the Garden of Gethsemane. As if it was happening in that moment, Angie experienced Christ experiencing her life, living her entire life, as if it was His own life. She began to see what it was that the Saviour had actually achieved, how he had sacrificed himself for her. 'He showed me: he had taken me into himself, subsumed my life in his, embracing my experiences, my sufferings, as his own.'

Angie perceived where she had gone wrong. She had heard many times about Jesus before her NDE, and had hoped that there was truth to the idea of a Saviour who had given his life for her, but had been afraid to really believe it. To believe without seeing requires a great deal of trust. Her trust had been violated so many times in her life that she had very little to spare. She had clung to her pain so tightly that she had been willing to suicide rather than to believe he cared for her. 'He had wanted to comfort me and to hold me, but we were separated by my responses to the lessons of life. He had been there for me all through my life, but I had not trusted Him, until now.'

Teachings

Angie was then provided with new understanding and knowledge.

Amongst many other things, she learned that suicide produces a ripple effect, with harmful long-term ramifications remaining for those left on Earth. Her children, for example, would be greatly harmed by her suicide. She was given a glimpse of their potential futures. By abandoning her earthly responsibilities, her oldest son in particular would make harmful choices in his turn. 'I caught a glimpse of how deeply God loves my boys, and how, with my callous disregard for their welfare, I was tampering with the sacred will of God.' She still tears up when she talks about the damage she would have caused her boys.

The same applied to many others, such as her husband and her sister.

Angie still could not see how she could live her own life, but having seen what would become of her children, she uttered a hint of a response, 'Okay." Suddenly she found herself hovering above the dark plane. One gift to her of her NDE was to rekindle the desire to live and love again.

She was told that the realm of darkness where she had been sent was quite literally a spiritual time-out, a place where she was supposed to grasp the gravity of her offences.

'But I had to ask, why me? Why was it that I could see God while the vacant husk of a man next to me could not? Why was I absorbing light and being taught, while he was hunkering down in misery and darkness?'

The answer was unexpected. It revolved around willingness. When she had wondered whether the shell of the man beside her might be Judas Iscariot, she had shown she was willing to believe that Christ had once walked the Earth, lived and died. And once willing to believe, she was able to begin accepting what she was being shown. 'My spiritual time-out could have lasted a moment, or it could have taken me thousands of years to progress out of that dark Prison, depending on when I reached the point of willingness to see the light.'

The Escape

With this teaching, her spiritual eyes were opened and she suddenly saw beings of light all around her that had been invisible to her previously.

Angie found herself floating above the field of darkness and entered into a realm of scurrying spirits of light. She learnt that they were preparing for the return of Jesus Christ to Earth in the not too distant future, but she was not told when precisely.

She was filled with understanding and knowledge, everything she would need to complete her mortal existence.

Then the powerful energy source that had transported Angie to the dark Prison returned to liberate her. A rushing sensation engulfed her, and suddenly she was back in her body on Earth, lying on the couch.

Reflections

With the opportunity to reflect since her NDE more than twenty years ago, Angie has decided her state of mind had imprisoned her on Earth long before she had entered that dark Prison in the afterlife. The more she had entertained gloomy thoughts to the point of acting on them, the more her darkness had influenced and harmed those around her. Furthermore, the Prince of Darkness, Satan, had manipulated and encouraged her suicidal thoughts. The Prison section for her and those who were like her was a natural consequence, a gathering of 'like with like'. Her sufferings and torment had been magnified in that Prison environment where there was no escape from her situation except by divine intervention.

Knowing that forgiveness is important, Angie has forgiven and sought reconciliation with each person who damaged her before her suicide, including her father who had abused her, her mother who had abandoned her and her husband who had treated her so badly.

Today Angie is a spokesperson against suicide, and travels widely to teach and to warn others against taking their own lives. 'Don't do it. Talk to someone, talk to me, or get into counselling. Medicine has come a long way since my suicide. Seek medical help. If someone in your life is depressed, you must reach out. A person who is suicidal cannot always seek help. We must take responsibility for each other.'

Angie also feels that it is important to share that her near-death experience was exclusive to her. People who have lost loved ones to suicide should not assume that they went to a place of darkness during their NDE. Just as Angie's experiences were influenced by her own thoughts and beliefs, she believes that we continue to affect our circumstances during the NDE. She often prays for those who have died by suicide; she prays for their families to forgive them.

During her NDE, Angie saw that prayer and forgiveness are the most powerful tools for good that can be accessed by human beings.

Many people commit suicide during deep depression. One of life's challenges may be to learn how to cope with depression, or to overcome it. An overwhelming desire to commit suicide is one of the biggest indicators of clinical depression. As Angie points out, seeking medical help is a smart decision, as is attending support groups – if one group or counsellor has not been helpful, try others.

It is heartening to know, as Angie Fenimore attests both from her own experience and from counselling others who have attempted suicide, that an afterlife experience definitely discourages further attempts at suicide.

David Rosen[15] in 1975 interviewed 7 of the 10 known survivors who had jumped off the Golden Gate Bridge. Most striking perhaps is that each claimed to have had a spiritual experience that had subsequently transformed their lives. Consequently, none had again wished to commit suicide.

Fasten your seatbelts again; it is now time to tour some further afterlife venues.

12

Tours: Heaven, Hell and the Cosmos

In the Book of Revelation, the Apostle John relates being taken to different afterlife locations.

In the chapter that follows, I have been careful to differentiate between Heaven and Paradise. Paradise is often misidentified as Heaven by NDErs. Heaven as used in the Bible refers to where God dwells, which includes the heavenly city, while Paradise is the pleasant garden section of Hades outside the heavenly city where spirits remain before the final Judgement.

Who Is In True Heaven?

How can we be certain – it's God's turf! It's interesting to conjecture though.

Scripture teaches that 'The LORD brings death and gives life; He sends some to Sheol, and He raises others up.' (1Samuel 2:6, Holman Christian Standard Bible). We see from this and in other scriptures that God is in control of life and death despite some free choices made by man in both respects. God decides who goes where at the end of human life. And Sheol (Hades) is the likely destination of people when they die.

God the Father is certainly in Heaven – while he was on Earth, Jesus taught his disciples to pray to 'Our Father in Heaven'. God may also be found walking in his garden (Paradise) outside the walls of his city.

After his death and resurrection, Jesus ascended to Heaven and many NDErs affirm that they have seen him in the heavenly city in recent times.

Children who have died too young to understand the implications of some life choices are certainly seen by NDErs in the heavenly city in droves. Some NDErs, on return to Earth, tell of adult carers there. Some carers are angels but other descriptions suggest deceased humans act in this capacity too. We await more reports before accepting this.

As might be expected of a loving God, he sometimes allows significant adults to visit children in Heaven, presumably to put them at ease, and children describe these encounters. For example, Colton Burpo[1] describes meeting his 'Pop' (deceased grandfather) in Heaven whom he knew nothing about previously and whom he identified on return to Earth from a photograph. However, these adults do not appear to remain in Heaven. Might they return to Hades – mission accomplished?

Colton also says Jesus' cousin John the Baptist is there, and so is Jesus' mother, Mary. This would be in keeping with God's character and the fact that he has made family relationships pre-eminently important; family groupings would appear from NDEs to continue in the afterlife. Perhaps Jesus' own family group remains together as a special arrangement for him in Heaven? Descriptions given by children, however, are best held lightly, because with the most sincere will in the world, they lack adult discernment. It is only when many independent child reports say the same thing that we should accord it a high level of likelihood –which applies to adult reports too, of course.

Speaking of adults, we must keep in mind that returnees have consistently described being met in Paradise, not Heaven, by a welcoming committee of deceased ancestors and occasional friends, all in spirit bodies. When the Apostle John wrote his gospel, he noted that: 'No one has ever gone into Heaven except the one who came from Heaven – the Son of Man' (John 3:13).

He may have been referring to the living not entering Heaven in their physical bodies rather than the dead doing so in spiritual bodies. Nonetheless, it seems consistent and likely that all our deceased relatives are in spiritual bodies in Hades awaiting Judgement, and are not domiciled in the heavenly city.

And what of Enoch and Elijah? They appear to have been translated from Earth to Heaven as special cases. In the case of Elijah, the Bible specifies that he was taken up to Heaven (2Kings 2:11). It would not be surprising to find either or both of them there, or certainly in Paradise. Joseph C, NDE number 4023 on the NDERF website, says as an 8-year-old that he saw Enoch – 'I mistook him for Moses as I had not learned about him then.' And there may even be other adults who God has decided to admit to Heaven for whatever reasons. A small number of descriptions of returnees suggest this could be the case. As noted previously, it may be fun to think about who might be in Heaven today, but only God knows for sure.

Adult Heavenly Encounters

Just as spirits in spirit bodies can remain Earth-bound for a while at least and observe activities on Earth, even though the Earth is a physical environment, spirits in spirit bodies can observe the heavenly city for a time – but are unlikely to remain in those physical buildings for long.

We have examples in scripture of visitors to Heaven in spirit bodies. For example, the Apostle John was chained up on the island of Patmos and his body remained there, but in Revelation 4:2 (King James Bible) he says: 'And immediately I was *in the spirit*, and behold, a throne was set in Heaven, and One [God] sat on the throne.' When Paul visited Heaven (2Corinthians 12:2-4) he was not even sure what kind of body he was in – his physical or his spirit body! Some NDErs in modern times have experienced similar confusion. A handful of NDE adults say they have visited inside the heavenly city walls while in their spirit bodies, while others have met with Jesus at the gates of the heavenly city.

NDErs describe more than one gate into the city, and all descriptions depict the gates as strikingly ornate. Dale Black[2] gives a description of one such gate:

> The ornamentation around the entrance included phenomenal detail. It was the most astounding sight I had ever seen. As I basked in the beauty that adorned the gateway, I noticed large gold letters emblazoned above the opening. They seemed to quiver with life. The single line of letters formed an arch over the entrance. I didn't recognise the letters but knew the words were as important as any words could be. Other letters were written in honey-coloured gemstones on the ground in front of the entrance and included several lines. The entrance through the thick wall was breathtaking. The opening seemed filled with light that was the purest of white, yet it seemed to have countless hues that changed with even my slightest movement.

Several other NDErs also describe this extraordinary light radiating outwards through the translucent gates. Simon Mackrell[3] visited Heaven after dying in a road accident in 1990 in New Zealand. He noted: 'The same light that I was moving in was also radiating out from within the city, and also contained the same love, peace, joy and warmth. As I stood at the gates, I heard amazing singing coming from within the city, voices that sang in beautiful harmony.'

As with most similar accounts by adults, Simon returned to Earth without actually going through the gate and into the heavenly city.

Here are two accounts given by Dr Maurice Rawlings[4] describing the visits into Heaven by adult patients. How can we surmise that these people went to Heaven? Because of the buildings described as being there – they were not in the garden idyll of Paradise.

In this first account by Rawlings[5], the man involved had turned away from God years earlier when he had prayed for his mother to be healed; instead, her leg had been amputated and she had died. He concluded that 'God is as deaf as a stone idol. He has no use for me, nor I for Him.' Then the man died and experienced an NDE.

> I was amazed to find a brilliantly lit city, reflecting what looked like the rays of the sun, only diffused and suspended with particles of radiance. The roads were all made of gold. Some sort of shining metal covered the domes and steeples in beautiful array and the walls were strangely smooth, not quite like marble, but made of something I had not seen before. Even the air smelled good, and faint music was there.
>
> Then I saw two figures walking toward me and I knew immediately who they were – my mother and father who had died years ago. My mother was an amputee at the time of her death, but now she had two legs and was walking!
>
> 'You and father are beautiful,' I said.

Isn't it like God to assure the NDEr that his mother was in good health and her leg restored, although in the afterlife and not on Earth as the man had been expecting! That she was walking the streets of Heaven itself suggests she had been granted a new leg in a physically recognisable body, which impacted her son. We do not know why this meeting took place in Heaven and not in Paradise, as is much more common.

Rawlings'[4] second patient was a woman.

> I was floating into an area that looked like Heaven. It was wonderfully bright with buildings and streets of gold, and I saw a figure with long hair in a brilliant white robe. A light radiated all about him. I didn't talk to him. I am sure that it was Jesus. As he took hold of my hand, the next thing I remember was a jerking on my body – you were shaking me and then the pain came back!

We find from NDErs and scripture that Christ is in his resurrected bodily form nowadays and resides amongst the buildings of Heaven, which returnees describe as prolific. He is also often found in his Paradise (garden) where he generally meets newcomers. It is interesting that he stated he would be going to prepare a 'place' for his disciples (John 14:2), assumed by many to be a room or building in the present heavenly city, or perhaps in a future heavenly abode to be occupied after Judgement – possibly in the New Jerusalem (Revelation 21: 2 and 10). Meanwhile his followers would be on Earth building the Kingdom of God.

An adult who viewed Heaven briefly from a distance, but did not enter and walk its streets, was Dr George Ritchie[6]. He says Jesus was acting as his tour guide and whisked him from venue to venue.

> And then I saw, infinitely far off, far too distant to be visible with any kind of sight I knew of – a city! A glowing, seemingly endless city, bright enough to be seen over all the unimaginable distance between us. The brightness seemed to shine from the very walls and streets of this place, and from beings that I could now discern moving about within it. In fact, the city and everything in it

seemed to be made of light, even as the figure at my side was made of light.

At this time I had not yet read the Book of Revelation.

The significance of the biblical Book of Revelation that Ritchie refers to is that what he saw accords with descriptions of Heaven by the Apostle John in that book.

Baptist minister Don Piper[7] approached a gate in the walls of the heavenly city. He caught a glimpse of what was inside, but did not enter before returning to Earth. Here is some of what he saw:

> Looming just over the heads of my reception committee stood an awesome gate interrupting a wall that faded out of sight in both directions. It struck me that the actual entrance was small in comparison to the massive gate itself. I stared, but I couldn't see the end of the walls in either direction. As I gazed upward, I couldn't see the top either. One thing did surprise me: On Earth, whenever I thought of Heaven, I anticipated that one day I'd see a gate made of pearls, because the Bible refers to the gates of pearl. The gate wasn't made of pearls, but was pearlescent [as others have also described it] – perhaps iridescent may be more descriptive. To me, it looked as if someone had spread pearl icing on a cake. The gate glowed and shimmered...
>
> I paused just outside the gate, and I could see inside. It was like a city with paved streets. To my amazement, they had been constructed of literal gold. If you imagine a street paved with gold bricks, that's as close as I can come to describing what lay inside the gate.

Dale Black[2] describes how he was flown towards the celestial city by two angels:

> I was fast approaching a magnificent city, golden and gleaming among a myriad of resplendent colours. The light I saw was the purest I had ever seen. And the music was the most majestic, enchanting and glorious I had ever heard.
>
> I was still approaching the city, but now I was slowing down, like a plane making its final approach for landing. I knew instantly that this place was entirely and utterly holy. Don't ask me how I knew, I just knew.
>
> I was overwhelmed by its beauty. It was breathtaking. And a strong sense of belonging filled my heart; I never wanted to leave. Somehow I knew I was made for this place and this place was made for me. Never had I felt so 'right' anywhere. For the first time in my life, I was completely 'whole'.
>
> The entire city was bathed in light, an opaque whiteness in which the light was intense but diffused...
>
> The closer I got to the city, the more distinct the illumination became. The magnificent light I was experiencing emanated from about forty to fifty miles within the city wall. [Pilots frequently estimate distances like this.] I saw a great phosphorescent display of light that narrowed to a focal point that was brighter than the sun. Oddly, it didn't make me squint to look at it, and all I wanted to do was to look at it...

In his book, Dale provides further details of the city such as the nature of its walls and a river that flows inside. He also describes the outstanding architecture seen in Heaven, which is different from what we have on Earth.

Between the central part of the city and the city walls were groupings of brightly coloured picture-perfect homes in small, quaint towns. I'll call them townships, because I can't think of a better word for them. I focused on only three townships, but certainly there were more. A lot more, no doubt.

The dwellings in these townships were not arranged in a uniform or symmetrical manner but appeared perfectly balanced somehow. Each home was customised and unique from the others, yet blended harmoniously. Some were three or four stories, some were even higher. There were no two the same. If music could become homes, it would look like these, beautifully built and perfectly balanced.

Heaven through a Child's Eyes

It will not be surprising that many of our modern descriptions of Heaven itself come from children. Before the age of their accountability, which I believe likely to vary between children, God does not credit sin to them, which may be why they can enter Heaven itself at death, while adults typically pass into the more general venue – Hades. From their NDE descriptions, they encounter many other children already there, but no ancestors or adults from their lives greet them there on arrival as a welcoming committee. These ancestors reside outside, in the gardens of Paradise.

As mentioned previously, NDEs are not terrifying for children, who are led through the experience gently and sensitively. More often than not, God sends a guide such as an angel or relative to allay their fears and accompany the children to Heaven. A nine-year-old girl described an NDE she had on dying during surgery, recorded by Raymond Moody[8].

> I heard them say my heart had stopped but I was up on the ceiling watching. I could see everything from up there. I went out in the hall and I saw my mother crying. I asked her why she was crying but she couldn't hear me. The doctors thought I was dead. Then a pretty lady came up and helped me because she knew I was scared. We went through this tunnel and went into Heaven.

Some children report they were provided with new bodies for the duration of their stay in the buildings of Heaven. It is their spirits that returned to Earth at the completion of their NDE. Others who spent a short time there apparently remained in their spirit bodies for the duration.

So what is it like inside Heaven itself? Children describe a material world with buildings, pretty flooring, staircases, chairs, tables, writing and drawing materials, walls and gates – quite unlike the garden idyll of Paradise.

First-hand accounts are important to get a feel for the overall ambience. Here is one of many available. It is Atwater's[9] report of Clara's NDE, which she had age 10, although these memories were written down much later:

> Suddenly I heard what sounded like a city-sized playground full of kids, laughing and playing. Hearing them calmed me...
>
> I was led up a sidewalk to a large building with large doors. I walked inside and saw people all around working and doing things.
>
> I was taken to a huge iridescent white room and told to sit down on some steps that led up to a large white chair, and wait there for someone who was to talk to me.
>
> He came out a door at the other end of the steps, walked to the chair above me, and sat down. He was dressed

Living Beyond

in a white, long-sleeved, floor-length robe with a wide gold band around the mid-section. He wore sandals. His dark brown hair was shoulder length; he had a long face, broad chin, dark eyes with black around both eyelids, like eyeliner pencil, but it wasn't. His skin was olive coloured and his eyes were as liquid love.

He communicated by looking at me. No words had to be spoken, as we could hear each other's thoughts. He told me what I had to do in life and had me go to the other side of the room and look down into something like a TV set so I could see my future. What I saw made me very happy. This man, who I believe is Jesus Christ, said that once I woke up in the hospital I would forget what I was supposed to do in life.

'Nothing can happen before its time,' he cautioned.

As I was leaving the room he said I must obey his commandments if I wanted to come back.

When I revived, a nurse was sitting beside my bed and she said, 'Thank God you finally woke up.'

I told the doctor that I had watched him work on me and the colour of the machine brought into the surgery room. He didn't know what to say.

Did Jesus wipe her specific memory regarding future events because he did not want her to try to do those things she had seen on the screen before their time? Might this provide a clue as to why most adult NDErs are not shown precisely what their 'mission' will be on their return, which causes concern for them? Or might returnees become so fascinated as to encourage those around them to dabble in clairvoyance, which could be harmful?

Besides children, whom else might we find in Heaven? Colton Burpo[1] experienced both angels and Jesus. Here is the conversation, at just four-years-old, that he had with his parents – he had been three when the NDE showing him Heaven occurred:

> 'Dad, Jesus had the angels sing to me because I was so scared. They made me feel better.'
> *Jesus?*
> I glanced at Sonja again and saw that her mouth had dropped open. I turned back to Colton. 'You mean Jesus was there?'
> My boy nodded as though reporting nothing more remarkable than seeing a ladybug in the front yard. 'Yeah, Jesus was there.'
> 'Well, where was Jesus?'
> Colton looked me right in the eye. 'I was sitting in Jesus' lap.'

While it is not ideal for parents to report afterlife experiences because with the best will in the world, in clarifying their child's account, their own personal interpretation must creep in, it became unavoidable because Colton was far too young to describe all he had experienced. His parents say they tried to extricate information from him without giving him prior information and cues, a slow process taking many months, mainly while Colton was aged four, but continuing as he got older. Colton mentioned fascinating details regarding Heaven, including the clothes worn: Jesus is the only one he saw ever wearing purple. There was no darkness there but instead bright light and colours. He described the impressive throne room of God in Heaven. Besides playing together, Colton says children continue learning in Heaven, and that Jesus personally taught him things.

Colton reported that he met many children in Heaven, including his stillborn sister about whom he had not been told.

She rushed up and hugged him and they spent a happy time together. Even when he was six-years-old, his babysitter found Colton crying one night because he missed his sister so much – they had apparently bonded to that extent during his short time in Heaven. This account, and further similar NDE reports I have read, must give all parents who have lost unborn or young children great comfort.

Another child with a similar story of meeting siblings previously unknown to him was Landon Whitley[10], who died in a terrible car accident in 1997. Landon was 8-years-old at the time. He says he vividly remembers going to heaven and seeing "streets of gold" as well as Jesus and angels. 'My mom had two miscarriages before me that I had never known about, never heard about,' Landon said. 'I was able to see them.'

Landon and Colton experienced a deep truth – each stillborn child is an individual in God's eyes, a 'he' or a 'she' and not an 'it', and has a family heritage. Abortionists take note.

It became a daily theme of Colton's until his parents were tired of hearing it, that 'Jesus *loves* the children'. Many other children tell a similar story of Jesus' individual concern for them while in Heaven. For example, when Jamie Untinen[11] was only five years old, she died from meningitis. Later she drew what she saw during her NDE – three angels and Jesus himself sitting on a log. 'He was very nice. He told me it was not my turn to die.'

Many accounts of NDEs given by children speak of the loving angels, friendly beings of light, pretty women, ancestors or even deceased pets who meet, comfort and accompany them to Heaven. Atwater[12] states that 70% of child NDEs feature angelic visitations at some point.

Children also describe the variety of angels in Heaven itself. Scripture supports this, and describes a diversity of angels in Heaven including archangels, cherubim and seraphim.

Why may we suppose that angels dwell in Heaven unless they are away on assignment? A 'heavenly host' of angels announced the birth of Jesus, and when they left they went back 'into Heaven' (Luke 2:13-15). Jesus spoke of the angels 'in Heaven' (Matthew 18:10, Mark 13:32). It appears from these and other verses that they are likely to be inhabitants there, and we know from encounters on Earth that they can take different physical forms such that Heaven may have a varied populace already. Looked at from a distance, as different adult observers hovering overhead have done, this busy society might even be mistaken for people.

Interactions with children may extend our expectations of Heaven, but we must remember that the reports are given by children whose language skills and conceptual development may not extend to accurate descriptions nor to being able to answer precisely many of the adult questions asked. What comes across very strongly from numerous accounts, though, is that we are being told about a real place comprising real buildings and populated by a real God the Father, a real Jesus, and real associates. It is also a place that accords well with scriptural descriptions.

In case I have caused confusion, I must affirm that while children seem to qualify to go directly to Heaven at death, a number of those who have had NDEs report meeting ancestors or angels in Paradise instead. Perhaps for these individual children, meeting with ancestors in Paradise is more important for whatever reason than going to Heaven first? Or perhaps it is because they are only visitors in the afterlife and will be returning to Earth? Since NDEs are intended to facilitate helpful changes once a child returns, I would not be surprised to read reliable reports in the future that some children have had an experience that is unpleasant. I have only come across one report to date making such a claim, that of Richard Bonenfant[13] which describes six-year-old Scott's NDE, which began badly but ended happily with an interaction with God as a Being of Light. We await further reports.

Transcendent Tours

Tours other than of Heaven itself seem to be arranged for the privileged few. The NDEr may be shown the Universe, or parts of it. Other destinations in the spiritual realm may also be visited.

Atwater[12] describes these as Transcendent Experiences. In her opinion: 'This type of NDE involves exposure to otherworldly dimensions and scenes beyond the individual's frame of reference, and sometimes includes revelations of greater truths... It is usually experienced by those who are ready for a "mind-stretching" challenge.'

Isaiah 55:8-9 reminds us:

> 'For my thoughts are not your thoughts,
> nor are your ways my ways,'
> declares the Lord.
> 'For as the heavens are higher than the Earth,
> so are my ways higher than your ways,
> and my thoughts than your thoughts.'

Tours may even be to other creations of God unknown to us. God's creative brilliance is unlikely to have been curtailed by designing only those things we have seen or been told about; like any artist he probably continues to produce other majestic works. This is conjectural, but certain tours within some NDEs indicate that other magnificent places and dimensions exist. They would warrant more research and a deeper treatment than I could give them here.

During these tours, the NDEr may become privy to some new celestial knowledge, the details of which are largely forgotten or removed on return, or that he or she may or may not be allowed to share with others. Paul in 2Corinthians 12:4 gives an example of a man caught up to Paradise, perhaps himself, hearing 'inexpressible things, things that no one is permitted to tell,' which sounds like a transcendent experience, to use Atwater's term.

Tours of Hell

Now we turn our attention to less pleasant tours, those of Hell as distinct from the Prison section of Hades, although Hell may perhaps be viewed from the Prison under certain circumstances – most likely to act as a warning.

I know that the concept of God punishing people is an awful one. Hell is abhorrent to many, even if they believe that a person 'deserved it'. There is a temptation to tone down or dispense with the unpopular Hell altogether, as many Christian churches appear to have done. The rationale is that a loving God would never punish people in this way regardless of what they have done. All NDErs who met with either God the Father or with Jesus felt the love and compassion that streamed out of them as fundamental to their divine nature.

Nevertheless, it appears that Hell as described in Scripture has been observed as a real place by reliable NDErs. It would be unwise to ignore this. In my opinion, it is more loving to warn people about it than to pretend it doesn't exist simply because we don't like the concept. After all, John, labelled the Apostle of Love, and Jesus Christ himself, both warned more forcefully and frequently in scripture about future punishment than did any others. It is hard not to assume that it is *because* of their great love that they try to warn people not to put themselves there – similar to yelling 'watch out' to a person staggering towards danger.

Are Children In Hell?

We would not expect to find young children either in the Prison section of Hades, nor ultimately in Hell. Those who have had visions of Hell or have visited there, such as the Apostle John, and modern observers such as Bill Wiese[14], have not reported seeing any children. This perplexed the researcher PMH Atwater[15], who observed: '*Not one* of the childhood experiencers I interviewed (of 277) ever mentioned anything fearful or Hell-like or threatening. Only the adults in my inquiry reported such stories. This puzzled me. Why would some adults describe the existence of a Hell when children never did?'

The answer seems to me that it is because they have died too young to be accountable and most have gone straight to the heavenly city.

Adult Descriptions of Hell

Thomas Welch[16] was 18 or 19 years old in 1924 when he tumbled down into the murky waters of a dam. It took 75 men an hour to find and retrieve his dead body and lay it out on the mill floor. Here is part of his description of his NDE.

> I was standing near a shoreline of a great ocean of fire. It happened to be what the Bible says it is in Revelation 21:8 – 'The lake that burned with fire and brimstone [sulphur – used to intensify and prolong heat]'. This is the most awesome sight one could ever see this side of the final Judgement...
> I was standing some distance from this burning, turbulent, rolling mass of blue fire. As far as I could see,

it was just the same – a Lake of Fire and brimstone. *There was nobody in it.* I was not in it.

I saw other people whom I had known that had died when I was thirteen. One was an uncle of mine who died of consumption when I was thirteen. Another was a boy I had gone to school with who had died from cancer of the jaw that had started with an infected tooth while he was just a young lad. He was two years older than I. We recognised each other, even though we did not speak. They, too, were looking and seemed to be perplexed and in deep thought, as though they could not believe what they saw. Their expressions were those of bewilderment and confusion...

I said to myself in an audible voice, 'If I had known about this, I would have done anything that was required of me to escape coming to a place like this.' But I had not known.

In his distress, Thomas records a feeling of hopelessness, of inescapable entrapment. How long would he remain there? Until Judgement? And would he then become one of those who would be cast into that grotesque Lake of Fire?

As these thoughts were racing through my mind, I saw another man coming by in front of us. I knew immediately who he was. He had a strong, kind, compassionate face, composed and unafraid, Master of all he saw. It was Jesus himself!

A great hope took hold of me and I knew the answer to my problem was this great and wonderful person who was moving by me in this Prison of lost, confused, Judgement-bound souls. I did not do anything to attract his attention. I said again to myself, 'If he would only look my way and see me, he could rescue me from this place because he would know I never understood it was like this. He would know what to do.'

He passed on by, and it seemed as though he would not look my way, but just before he passed out of sight, he turned his head and looked directly at me. That was all it took. His look was enough. In seconds I was back entering my body again.

Tom was not a Christian at the time of this tour of Hell; he was in his own words 'an infidel' and a personal fan of the atheists Thomas Paine and Voltaire, but never afterwards doubted the reality of Hell. He emphasised the value of individual experience. 'I know there is a Lake of Fire, because I have seen it. I know Jesus Christ is alive in eternity. I have seen him.'

His subsequent reading of the Bible helped Tom identify the Lake of Fire that he had witnessed. 'This is the lake I saw, and I am certain of this one thing, that in the end of this age at the final Judgement every corrupt thing in this Universe will ultimately be cast into this lake and be forever destroyed.'

Tom was one of those few lucky NDErs who had a miracle of healing on return. His body had been terribly battered by his high fall at the sawmill, bouncing off wooden beams before dropping into the dam 55 feet below. Yet a few days following the accident, on the Friday, each broken rib bone immediately healed and he dismissed himself from hospital. He returned to work the next day to the complete astonishment of the men who had rescued him!

Another who apparently toured Hell during his NDE was Geo Godkin[17] of Canada in 1948. He described the heat and fire he experienced there.

> My guiding angel said, 'Come.' I was then guided to the place in the spiritual world called Hell. This is a place of punishment for all those who reject Jesus Christ or who

just forget God. I now had the horrible privilege of not only seeing Hell but also feeling the torment that all will experience that go there...

The breath from your nostrils as well as the air you breathe feels like a blast from a blast furnace. The exterior of your body feels as if it were encased within a white-hot stove. The interior of your body has a sensation of scorching hot air being forced through it.

The agony and loneliness of Hell cannot be expressed clearly enough for proper understanding to the human soul, it has to be experienced, but unfortunately the soul in Hell has reached the point of no return. The sad horrible fact is that the worst is yet to come, for there is a one-way road from Hell to the Lake of Fire.

Did he experience a foretaste of Hell itself? Most likely he did.

Once the tours are over, it is time for the NDEr to return to Earth. Unfortunately, for too many NDErs, 'their troubles have only just begun'.

13

The Return and Its Challenges

Marilyn: 'He (Dean) had a hard time being back here in the beginning. He had changed. Eternity coloured everything.'

—Marilyn Braxton[1]

This chapter deals with the challenges most returnees face as they attempt to settle back successfully into life on Earth. The chapter that follows majors on learning from the many NDErs who have overcome these challenges.

A Time to Live Again

An internal conflict that afflicts many returnees has its origins in Paradise.

Most NDErs in Paradise are loath to return to Earth with its pain and stress. Some psychological issues begin right there. Dr George Ritchie[2] expressed his trauma in these words: 'I regarded my return to this life as a calamity; I would have been angry, if I'd had the strength, with those who laboured to revive me.'

Despite loving her children and her husband Virgil, Crystal McVea[3] had a similar response.

> What I do remember clearly – and what lingered for a long time – was how I felt about being back in my human form. To put it mildly, I was pretty ticked off. I simply loved

> being with God so much and wanted to go back so badly that I came to resent all the people who saved my life. The doctors, the nurses, my mother, even Virgil – anyone who wanted me to come back had, in my mind, prevented me from returning to Heaven. 'Why did you make me come back?' I asked them over and over in those first few hours. 'This was not my choice!'

Sometimes teenagers and younger children wonder why God sent them back. They can feel rejected and obsess over what could be wrong with them. 'And if their attempts to talk about their experiences are dismissed,' states Cherie Sutherland[4], 'the repercussions can be long-lasting.'

A returnee's 'extra time' sometimes means many more years of earthly life, but sometimes it is only a short return. A friend of mine over many years, Vic Moore, died in June 2010 in South Africa. His wife Raewyn[5] wrote to us about something that had occurred several weeks earlier, when the family had been summoned to the hospital.

> We arrived expecting the worst, no response from Vic, then about 2pm he woke up. Said he had had a spiritual experience – saw a bright light and flowers and angels and Jesus standing there welcoming him. Jesus said, you have a choice: you can either come with me or go back. Vic chose to come back to us, for which we are truly grateful and absolutely gob-smacked, or as someone said, God-smacked! Isn't that amazing!!!!! Words can't describe how we felt. I had always been disparaging about this sort of thing – but now, wow! We know we have been given a precious gift and time to tell Vic what he means to us.

Sadly from our human point of view, that time proved to be short, only a matter of weeks. Nevertheless, his return to Earth helped the family in their grieving. We assume that whatever further purposes were intended for his brief return, they had also been fulfilled.

Scripture tells us that our times are in God's hands. Nonetheless, some NDErs have argued the point with God. Debbie[1] is typical:

> I know it is Jesus. He had a bright light coming from him.
> He began walking towards me and he said, 'You have more work to do. You have to go back.'
> 'No. I'm not going back there. I don't want to go back there.' And I sat down and argued with him. I told him 'No', I was not going back there.
> He said, 'Yes, you have to go back. You have a lot to do. You have to go back.'
> I stood up and I looked at him, and he just slipped me back into my body.

While still in hospital, Debbie discovered one good reason Jesus had *insisted* that she return – she was pregnant! More than her own life had hung in the balance. 'I was absolutely shocked! I had no idea!' Once again, we see how God's timing is perfect – and how there is a right time to live, and a right time to die. Despite certain medical traumas that followed for Debbie, the baby was perfect and today is a lovely, healthy child.

Guiding the Choice

For some NDErs, the return is automatic without preceding discussion – they simply wake up in the hospital ward or wherever, without prior warning.

In other cases an offer is made – would you like to return to Earth? In these cases, God seems to encourage NDErs to make the choice. The commonest reasons given are that their time has not yet come, and furthermore, there is more for them to achieve on Earth. I have read or heard these reasons hundreds of times. Love of family and responsibility towards them can also be held out to the NDEr as a reason to choose to return.

The experience of Lisa[1] illustrates this process in depth. Lisa was shown her Life Review guided by three angelic beings. Suddenly the scene shifted from the past to future possibilities, dependent on her choices. 'Then I was shown my funeral (a potential future event). I wasn't upset watching my funeral, my kids were not upset; being 3 years old and 6 years old at the time, they didn't really understand what was going on. But then I saw my mother, who was a wreck and had no control. I didn't think she really loved me as much as I saw at my funeral.' Did God allow this glimpse of a theoretical future funeral to improve an ongoing relationship with her mother on her return? That particular funeral scene cannot occur now, as her children are older – so it must have been a 'possibility scenario' only, an alternative that 'collapsed' as she chose to return to Earth to care for them. Similar *visions* of possibilities are relatively common during NDEs, and it can be very difficult to distinguish between potential and actuality.

Perhaps because a glimpse of how things would be at her funeral did not in itself convince Lisa to return to her body at that moment (she was enjoying Paradise too much), a further glimpse into a possible future scene was shown to her:

> Then the three spirit guides, who were angels, showed me my future, and the future of my children. They showed me a hallway and door on the left and a beautiful room fit for a princess. I thought 'that's fine, my children will be well cared for, I don't have anything to worry about',

> but they said 'Oh no, *your* children are over here.' I saw on the other side of the hallway another door, that there was nothing in the room except my two children and stained, filthy underwear. No toys, no dresser.
> Oh no! I am going back to raise my kids!
> I did not see my body; I just slammed into it.
> It was my decision, my will, to live. I had a choice I guess.

Lisa had always been a mother hen fighting for her chicks. Her protective nature influenced her to return. She is another of the 'lucky few' in that her return was accompanied by a physical miracle – she had been told that she would not last the night without a liver transplant because her damaged liver was pumping toxins into her body; this toxicity ceased on her return and her liver rejuvenated itself.

Her mother concludes: 'Lisa is probably a better mother now, knowing how close she came to leaving them (her children).'

It is not only mothers who choose to return of their own volition.

Ian McCormack[6] was given the choice too.

> God stepped back in front of me, and asked me this question. 'Now that you have seen (Paradise) – do you wish to step in or do you wish to return?'
> I thought, 'I don't want to return. I wish to step in. I have no one to go back for and no one has ever loved me, all they've ever done is manipulate me and try to control me...'
> But God didn't move, so I looked back behind me to say 'goodbye, cruel world', and standing behind me in a vision in front of the tunnel was my mother!
> And as soon as I saw her, I knew that there was one person in my life who had shown me love, and that was

my mother, and that she had prayed for me every day and tried to show me that this was the way!

In my mind I thought, 'If I am dead and I did choose to step into Heaven, what would my mother think? Would she know I made it or would she think I went to Hell – because she knew I had no faith?' I realized that it could break her heart and that she would have no reason to believe that God had heard my prayer in the ambulance and forgiven my sins. I thought, 'How can I do that to my mum, it would be so selfish'... and decided I wished to return.

God then spoke to me and said that if I wished to return – I must see things in a new light.

I understood that to mean that I must begin to see through his eyes of Love, Peace, Joy, Forgiveness – from His heavenly perspective, not my temporary earthly perspective.

God Responds to Prayer

Our relational God responds to both prayer and love. These two intangibles from grieving relatives or friends on Earth can sometimes draw an NDEr back – as in these examples quoted by Raymond Moody[7] from interviews:

> 'Joan, I have been over there, over to the beyond, and it is beautiful over there. I want to stay, but I can't as long as you keep praying for me to stay with you. Your prayers are holding me over here. Please don't pray any more.' We did all stop, and shortly after that she died.

And another account:

> As I came back, I opened my eyes, and my sister and my husband saw me. I could see their relief, and tears were

pouring from their eyes. I felt as though I had been called back – magnetised back – through the love of my sister and my husband. Since then, I have believed that other people can draw you back.

Children also report that they have returned because of the anguished prayer of parents. Colton Burpo[8] told his father that 'Jesus came to get me. He said I had to go back because he was answering your prayer.' Many scriptures confirm the dynamic part that prayer plays in life.

Others Guide the Return

Relatives encountered in the afterlife are usually much more succinct than God or angels in their directives to an NDEr to return to Earth.

In Iris Lemov's[9] NDE: 'I saw figures coming towards me who called my name. This man with a white beard told me to go back and said, "Your family needs you; enjoy your life." This beautiful man was my grandfather who'd died two years before I was born.'

Brian Johnson[10] wanted to stay. However, the voice of an unknown lady, perhaps one of the loving ancestors who surrounded him, became insistent that he should return. 'Her voice got louder and louder each time she said it. I really wanted to stay, but they would not let me as they said I still have important things in my life that I have to do, so I agreed to go; when suddenly I woke up gasping for air.'

Re-entry Into the Body

Some record a kind of 'whoosh' when re-entering the body. In PJ's[11] words: 'Then I am suddenly sucked back towards the 2nd storey window, pulled in through the screen in a swoosh, at which point I lose my "spirit" sense and black out. I regain regular consciousness, from where I am lying on the floor.'

The spirit generally appears to re-enter the body more quickly than when it left. Sandy[1] is typical in her observation: 'It was as if someone had flipped a switch. Suddenly I was in my body – no tunnel.'

Re-entry is most commonly through the head.

> NDEr quoted by Raymond Moody[7]: 'I moved through it [tunnel] quickly, back to my body. And as I was being sucked back, it seemed that the suction started from the head, like I went into the head'.

> Julia Ruopp[14] 1941 (written 1963) – 'I returned to the bed on which a body was lying, motionless and limp, while nurses and doctors were working over it. Reluctantly, I entered it through what seemed to be the natural door, the former soft spot at the top of my head, at the same time asking myself, "Why must I return? Do I have to come back?"'

> PMH Atwater[15], who died alone at home, also believes she re-entered through her soft spot: 'There was an audible snap, and I was jerked like an overstretched rubber band into the crumpled, bloody mess on the floor, entering my body through the top of the head, that area that was once my "soft spot" when a baby, and feeling the need to shrink or contract to fit back in. I revived to the reality of blood and pain which I dealt with as best I could.'

Some NDErs have pro-actively tried to re-enter their bodies by sitting or lying down on them, which also appears to be a successful approach.

Feelings reported about the re-embodiment are often of pain and heaviness. Some descriptions are more reflective, though, such as that given by skydiver Mickey Robinson[14].

> The Lord told me that I was coming back to Earth. He did not speak in a language like I am using now, but the knowledge and awareness that I was being sent back just came to me. Immediately, as if someone had strings and was reeling me in like a kite, I began to travel back to the life I had come from.
>
> As I settled into my physical body, I could actually feel my spirit pressing through my flesh. Can you imagine what it would feel like to have the wind blowing through the leaves of a tree? This, as I imagine it, is similar to what I experienced at that time as my spirit meshed into my flesh.
>
> Suddenly, I could see again out of my physical eyes and hear out of my physical ears.

Others wanting to be reunited with their bodies have had problems identifying them. Their body may have been damaged during an accident, fire or explosion, making recognition difficult. But even where there has been no disfigurement, a person has never seen himself or herself in 3D, added to which the image you see in a mirror is reversed from what you look like in reality – so that recognition can be difficult. Dr George Ritchie[2] experienced one of the earliest and best described NDEs of modern times, in 1943 at an army training camp in America: because Ritchie was such a credible witness, his account became an inspiration for Raymond Moody and others to take NDEs seriously. On exiting his body, Ritchie turned around to look at the bed he had just left. A man was lying in that bed!

> I stepped closer in the dim light, and then drew back. He was dead! The slack jaw, the gray skin, was awful.

He did not recognise his own body! 'The thing was impossible,' he recalled. 'I myself had just gotten out of that bed! For a moment I wrestled with the mystery of it. It was too strange to think about – and anyway, I didn't have time.' He wanted to get himself prepared to leave the camp early the next morning, so he dashed out of the room, unaware as yet that he had died and had been viewing his own grotesque body.

The problems of recognition and re-entry can be exacerbated if the body has been moved during the NDE. George Ritchie, wanting to re-enter his body, describes his search:

> I ran from one ward to the next, past room after room of sleeping soldiers, all about my age. I realised how unfamiliar we are with our own faces.
>
> Several times I stopped by a sleeping figure that was exactly as I imagined myself. But the fraternity ring, the Phi Gamma Delta ring, was lacking, and I would speed on.
>
> At last I entered a little room with a single dim light. A sheet had been drawn over the figure on the bed, but the arms lay along the blanket. On the left hand was the ring! I tried to draw back the sheet, but I could not seize it. And now that I had found myself, how could one join two people who were so completely separate?

Raymond Moody[7] provides this striking description by an interviewee.

> Boy, I sure didn't realise that I looked like that! You know, I'm only used to seeing myself in pictures or from the front in a mirror, and both of these look *flat*. But all of a sudden there was I – or my body was, and I could see it. I could definitely see it, full view, from about five feet away. It took me a few moments to recognise myself.

Trauma on Return

All returnees face massive challenges; descriptions of some important ones follow. These challenges affect some more than others. Some even cry out silently for a return to Paradise despite it having been made clear that their work on Earth has not been completed. Gritting their teeth, they struggle on.

Often, the first few days after returning are the worst. Raymond Moody[7] quotes one typical returnee as saying: 'After I came back, I cried off and on for about a week, because I had to live in this world after seeing that one. I didn't want to come back!' Others admit to weeping periodically over many months when remembering God and how wonderful it was in Paradise.

Ankerberg and Weldon[15] summarise possible consequences for both adults and children in these words:

> People who have NDEs need understanding and sympathy because, for many, life becomes more difficult – sometimes even miserable. So many NDErs are having difficulties that researchers are now turning to an examination of this problem and looking for ways to help people with the psychological and other problems resulting from their NDE.

Physical Challenges

These are usually the first to assail the returnee. Even if their revived bodies are undamaged and healthy, they feel confined and boxed in; it may take a while before they feel comfortable again. 'My body is something I put up with. It's the baggage I carry on my trip through life.' Again: 'I felt terrible: heavy, sore, chilled, and extremely sad. I felt as if I was trapped in a large piece of bad meat. I could see out of my eye sockets as if I was wearing a mask and I felt physically burdened by, and separate from, my body. I was well aware of being a separate entity from the body that I was inhabiting.'

For the few who return to a body that has been healed or partially restored in some way, the trauma is not as great. Lillian Oaktree[10] had used two high dose inhalers, one of them steroids, for 20 years to control her asthma. But after her NDE she no longer needed to rely on these drugs. She comments: 'My GP is delighted by my progress, though I haven't told him the change has come about due to healing in Heaven.'

Dean Braxton's[1] return was accompanied with a miracle of healing. Dean had been dead for approaching two hours and even Dr Manuel Iregui[1], who oversaw his care in St Francis' Hospital in Washington, stated that, 'It's a miracle that he's alive. There's no question about it. It is a miracle that he is talking with no brain damage. But this is very exceptional, because he was really, really dead for a long time.'

Dean today is a picture of health, as one can see in video footage of him on the Internet.

We may ask, why don't all returnees find perfectly healed bodies waiting for them back on Earth? Though we don't know, we realise that conditions on Earth are different from those in the afterlife. For example, the hundreds of dead friends and relatives met in Paradise all had spirit bodies which were healed, hale and hearty – the blind could see and amputees had their limbs restored – but we must remember that Paradise is a region entirely under the influence and blessing of God, unlike our fallen Earth or different Prison sections in Hades, where Satan and other spirit entities have a degree of influence.

Living Beyond

Emotional and Psychological Challenges

Crystal McVea[3] has pondered her preference to stay with God in Paradise rather than return to her family – a decision that seemingly flies in the face of her love for her family. Her decision has caused both her and her children some psychological issues.

> Believe me, before this happened I could not understand how it was possible to love anyone or anything more than your own children. But that was before I found myself in the presence of God. Like I said, that changed *everything.* I understood instantly that the love of God is greater and more powerful than any other kind of love. And I didn't only understand it; I felt it and heard it and saw it and tasted it with every fibre of my being. When I was in my spirit form, there was simply no other conceivable option for me but to be with God. I know it sounds funny to say, but not even my babies made me want to return to my human form. I've discussed this with my children, and, honestly, I think it hurts their feelings a bit. Once in a while they like to tease me about it, sort of how they tease me about being late to pick them up at school. 'Gee, thanks a lot, Mom,' they'll say. 'Thanks for *choosing* us.'...

Gradually, Crystal began to feel grateful to be with her family again. They all rushed to be with her and spoilt her. 'I still missed God, but being around my loved ones made me realise again that life is a wonderful gift to be cherished and treasured. It wasn't like a switch being flipped where suddenly I was thrilled to be back. It happened over time.'

Many others do not initially find their return to be emotionally positive. This applies even where they have good, meaningful relationships on Earth. Dr Mary Neal[16] comments on the first few weeks of her return.

> We [the family] spent glorious hours lying together in my hospital bed watching movies and cuddling. Although I adored them and loved the time we spent together, part of me still longed to be with God. This realisation made me feel torn and depressed.

In Mary's case, she had a very hard road ahead physically and emotionally. 'It took me *more than a year* to finally accept that not only had I been sent back to Earth, but that I had work left to do. I was part of a family that I dearly loved, and I finally accepted that I had better get on with my life and make the most of it.'

Might we simply dismiss these psychological problems as arising from weakness of mind? Gabbard and Twemlow[17] have investigated this possibility using a PAL test i.e. 'Profiles of Adaptation to Life.' They found that as a group, the NDE subjects were significantly healthier in their minds than psychiatric inpatients and/or outpatients, and somewhat healthier than college students. Overall, the NDE group represented a very close approximation to the 'average healthy American'.

If these and other studies confirm that NDErs return mentally healthy, from where do their psychological problems derive? One answer is their difficulty re-integrating. This often begins with attitudes expressed towards them of medical professionals in the first hours of return. IANDS has produced a video and teaching kit to help the medical fraternity to recognise and help NDErs, and different articles and books proffer advice. According to *The Handbook of Near-Death Experiences*[19], the top two of 24 most recommended approaches for medical personnel are:

1. Be non-judgmental toward patients as they explain their NDEs.

2. Pay attention to long-term impacts of NDEs on patients and make appropriate referrals to professionals who are familiar with NDEs.

What awaits the NDEr on leaving hospital? Don Piper[19], the Baptist minister, is typical when he writes that his biggest struggle following the experience was adjusting to the difficulties of earthly life, which is imperfect while Heaven (Paradise) is perfect. Many others remain frustrated over the years. Ray[10] writes, 'I have had a very difficult time integrating my NDE experiences into day-to-day life. I was filled with an immense sense of purpose and importance but I cannot seem to reconcile my NDE with living here. I sometimes feel as if I would just want to leave here and go home to be with God – yet I know that suicide is not the answer. I would never burden my loved ones with such a selfish act. I guess that God has some explaining to do when I finally get to go home!'

Atwater[20] summarises these problems: 'Experiencers were not returning with just a renewed zest for life and a more spiritual outlook. They were evidencing specific psychological and physiological differences on a scale never before faced by them. And this was true with child experiencers, as well as with teenagers and adults.'

Writing about child returnees, Cherie Sutherland[4] emphasises that they can find themselves estranged from their peer group and even their family. Academic and sporting performance may nosedive.

> Many children describe feeling estranged from their peer group because they no longer share the same interests. They tend to be indifferent to materialistic and competitive success and status. They have often had an experience of being 'all-knowing' or 'at-one-with-everything' and return with an overwhelming thirst

for knowledge and meaning that can set them apart. As one mother said, 'It's like sending out a six-year-old and getting back a 36-year-old'.

Can returnees be helped professionally with their emotional and psychological issues? Dr Lyn D'Alton[21] observes similarities with people who have been immersed in other cultures, having worked herself with missionaries returning to Australia from overseas service. She observes, 'Many of the difficulties experienced by NDE returnees are the same as others experiencing reverse culture shock/re-entry stress- e.g. soldiers and war veterans, exchange students, business people, religious/aid workers. This is experienced when returning to a place that one expects to be home, but does not feel like it any longer, as they have changed. The shock of seeing 'home' with new eyes is worsened as it is usually unexpected and unanticipated. Naturally, some NDE returnees will have unique "twists" because of involvement with God, angels, deceased family members etc.'

There are approaches found helpful for reverse culture shock that might also be helpful for NDErs — which are perhaps worth trying and monitoring for effectiveness. Other counselling approaches have been proposed for more extreme cases. Some returnees are particularly disoriented and confused, almost in a state of trauma arising from the intensity of their experience. These changes have led some psychologists to propose counselling similar to that given to sufferers of post-traumatic stress disorder.

We await reports on the effectiveness or otherwise of professional counselling with NDErs.

The Love Challenge

It is important to have a quick look at what love is not – because many returnees attempt to practice the wrong kind of love and end up in confusion. Ankerberg[15] comments on an incorrect but popular concept of a soft, unconditional and universal love, that is quite unlike the divine love that was shown to NDErs in Hades. Unfortunately some returnees, often with disturbing results, adopt this inaccurate perception of love. There is nothing like personal experience talking, which PMH Atwater[15] has, besides having interviewed hundreds of other NDErs:

> This kind of love can be more a nightmare than a blessing. It can drive a wedge between people. Let us be very practical about what unconditional love *really* means…. It means you cannot divide or separate people, that you have no expectations, no needs, no wants, no conditions of any sort in loving.

Unsuccessful returnees may also be characterised by a self-absorbed fascination with feelings, 'self-development', a self-indulgent sentimental interpretation of love very different from God's 'tough love', a fascination with what they may perceive to be their new psychic abilities and a focus on whatever else their experience meant for them personally. They consequently have significant difficulties because their understanding and attempts at practising love have been too far from God's demonstration of what love truly is. Weldon and Ankerberg[15] describe a revealing example of this delusion stated by a returnee.

> 'I love my wife and children more than I ever thought I could. I love everyone. My experience taught me real love, unconditional love!'
> This sounds good, but his wife and children did not feel the kind of love he described… He seemed somehow unreachable to them, as if he were 'floating' around somewhere in a world of his own, out of touch with

the reality of what was really going on and what their personal needs were.'

'Floating around somewhere in a world of his own', rather than engaging in the lives of those around, is often a short-term problem while finding one's feet again after experiencing transcendent love during an NDE. But don't be deceived; love that is not energetically serving the lives of others on Earth is not an expression of true, divinely inspired love and does not result in a successful, meaningful outcome.

Relationship Challenges

Most NDErs return with a fresh outlook on life, seeing themselves now as an immortal spirit and soul who is currently residing in an earthly body, with a commission to love others. Dr Kenneth Ring[22] reports that these attitudes transform into positive changes in most returnees' lives in the long term. Nonetheless, in the short term, it can be a rocky road to success. Although the family, friends and work colleagues have remained the same, the returnee has not. Where relationship damage occurs, its fundamental cause is most often a consequence of changes within the NDEr.

Numerous returnees yearn for the love and idyllic life they have seen in Paradise and try to introduce a similar open, innocent approach into the less-than-perfect situations and relationships of Earth. Scripture warns us, for example in Matthew 10:16, Romans 12:2, John 17:6, to be wise regarding the fallen condition of life on Earth and to behave accordingly, yet to be untainted within ourselves of the evil and sin that characterises life here. Universal loving, trusting, warmth and welcoming openness are good, but must be tempered by the divine discernment that Jesus exhorts us to practise on Earth. Atwater[15] observed:

> I am amazed at how many times survivors fall prey to repeated rapes, thefts, lies, cheating, losses of all kinds, fires, floods, financial setbacks, accidents, and to commitment to psychiatric treatment when none is really required. I myself was almost killed a number of times. We walk innocently into dangerous situations because we honestly do not recognise them as dangerous... We trust everyone because we know of no reason not to.

Her observations as a returnee herself, and one who has spoken with hundreds of others, carries significant weight.

Most returnees desire to be a conduit of universal love to others. This can morph into an inability to comprehend boundaries, rules or limits. Sadly, marriages may flounder. Dr Cherie Sutherland's[4] research confirms this. She noted a 'major increase in the number of divorced people following the NDE... almost all ascribed their divorce *primarily* to the after-effects of their NDE.' Atwater in 2008, discussing her results in her article *Near Death States: The Pattern of After-effects,* confirms these startling observations regarding NDEs and divorce:

> With the adult experiencers in my study, the divorce rate was between 75% to 78%. Most of these divorces happened within seven to ten years of the episode. The most common complaints from spouses were: 'I don't know this person any more', or 'This unconditional love nonsense is just an excuse to insult me by flirting with others'.
>
> A common attitude of the experiencer was, 'Since I no longer fit in, I'll move on'.
>
> The general mindset was that significant others were convinced that the experiencer was out of touch with reality, while the experiencer became convinced that the

significant others were slow to move forward and were not interested in making changes.

It was as if the two groups started speaking different languages and could no longer communicate effectively.

How might such a sublime experience as a positive NDE result in such wretched relationship breakdown? Returnees often perceive themselves as equally and fully loving of each and all, openly generous, excited about the potential and wonder of each person they see. Their 'unconditional' way of expressing joy and affection may be viewed as flirtatious disloyalty, and can attract extra-marital attention. This 'openness' can proceed to serial intimate relationships. 'Relationships seem more intense, but only last a short time,' complained one broken returnee.

A typical quote is: 'The love my husband and I shared flew out the window after I found universal love.'

In terms of communication, returnees may find that others are not as accepting and enthusiastic about their experience and its significance as they might suppose, leading to tension – within the family, at work, or socially. A response to this rejection may be to use abstract and grandiose terms to express themselves, or to criticise the attitudes of others. 'I have no problems communicating but have found others cannot accept things as they are. I feel that everyone lives in a fantasy world, and I am the realist outcast,' said one NDEr. While returnees may feel as though they are outcasts, their friends and family in turn can feel excluded by them and even looked down upon.

Another annoying shift can be that they refer to their episode as if it were a type of 'divider', separating their 'former' life from the present one. This can result in listeners feel patronised or 'outside the new me' presented by the NDEr.

Atwater[23] notes, 'Oftentimes survivors become impatient and critical of others, feeling in some way better, and losing in that smugness the ability to understand the weakness and the fear people around them still deal with.' For example, many people still feel uncomfortable talking and thinking about death, even with an NDEr, who conversely no longer fears death and at times wants to talk about it with enthusiasm.

Further difficulties can derive from the importance of living in the moment that distinguishes most returnees. Many become unreliable. They tend to 'flow' with circumstances and become absorbed in situations that interest them, losing a sense of what time it is. Families and workplaces run on routine and schedules. Returnees often are not as concerned as previously with planning ahead or being on time. For example, having been in dimensions where time is different, they may be less regimented about the children doing chores than before the NDE, or neglect household duties because of being easily distracted by other things.

Making social arrangements can seem irrelevant to them when preoccupied with things that have caught their attention. Friends may perceive this behaviour as disinterest in their friendship.

A further problem intrudes. The materialistic goals of many workplaces lose importance and cause returnees' level of motivation to fall off. They can become less competitive, less driven. Careers can be upended and jobs lost. In some cases new and successful careers may be embarked upon, but in others financial hardship is the consequence.

Many NDErs seem otherworldly for a season. This can make them appear 'odd' to family and friends. In fact, criticism and lack of understanding has made some returnees question their own sanity. For most, however, earthly realities impose themselves in a painful process to which they adapt successfully, though a degree of otherworldliness may continue lifelong. Most adapt more quickly than that, but the process nevertheless takes time. Atwater[24] states:

> My research shows that, on the average, it took adults a minimum of seven years to successfully adjust to their near-death experience.
> This timing alters with child experiencers. Children usually compensate for, rather than integrate, unusual or impacting experiences until they are much older.

For parents battling to understand worrying changes in their child following an NDE, Atwater's[24] research results and discussion may prove both informative and helpful.

Spiritual and Religious Challenges

Some studies show that *all* returnees who have met with a Being of Light believe they have had a transformational spiritual or religious experience. However, it appears that fewer NDErs proceed far enough to meet this Being than was originally supposed by the early researchers. Nevertheless, regardless of how extensive their afterlife experiences, most adult returnees indicate that they want to develop spiritually.

Many children on the other hand do not divide their experiences as readily into the religious and non-religious, but simply accept experiences that come along without trying to compartmentalise them. In a study of around 350 NDErs by Dr Peter and Elizabeth Fenwick[25], only 50% of those who had NDEs when they were between 3 and 9 years old reported becoming more religious after the experience, in their childhood perception of the word 'religious'. By 16 or older, this rose significantly to 90%.

Where can this fresh enthusiasm for spiritual understanding and growth be catered for? Returnees search avidly in different directions. Unfortunately, the teaching and preaching in churches can seem trivial, irrelevant or inaccurate after a personal meeting with God. Atwater[26] refers to an NDEr who is the wife of a conservative Christian pastor.

> Since her experience, it has become increasingly difficult for her to attend her husband's church services. 'He's wrong. I know now deep in my heart he's wrong. What he's preaching, that's not the way it is. I feel like he's telling everyone a lie and I don't know what to do about it. I love my husband and I love our children. I don't want to upset him or anyone else. I don't want a divorce or anything like that. But I can't listen anymore. I try to pretend I'm too busy to come.'

Raymond Moody's[27] research led him to conclude that NDErs returned more interested in religion and spiritual matters, but not in the plethora of conflicting groups and denominations. 'They come to realise that religion is not a matter of one "right" group versus several "wrong" groups', which is a common fruit of denominationalism. Rather, they wish to major on the God of Love whom they have met and towards whom all religions should be leading their flocks.'

For example, Dr Cherie Sutherland[7] found that 50% of her NDErs studied were affiliated with Catholic or Protestant churches before the NDE, but only 14% continued in these churches afterwards. Her research concluded that there was a shift 'away from organised religion and church attendance and toward private nonformula prayer, meditation and a general quest for spiritual values.' The research does not give a clear or consistent picture on this point, however. Pim van Lommel noted that the perceived movement amongst Dutch NDErs away from church attendance in Holland could have reflected a prevailing movement away from church affiliation in general. Sabom researched this possibility in America and concluded that in general returnees became more committed to local congregations rather than less so. He found further that a belief in reincarnation and in Eastern, universalist religion is not a direct after-effect of the near-death experience. Penny Sartori discovered something similar for English returnees.

No doubt, each research reflects local realities and perhaps the subjects they have selected. Nevertheless, most reports I have read suggest that the majority of returnees will go wherever they feel their experiences are accepted and can be explained to them.

An important factor appears to be that most returnees are less materialistic than previously. Consequently, the materialistic goals of many churches and New Age groups of the 'God wants you rich and in perfect health' or 'This is our upcoming programme that requires financial support' seem selfish and unimportant after actually meeting with God. Their level of interest and attendance drops off and many search elsewhere for answers.

Not finding the answers or support they need in any one group or religion, scores of returnees become eclectic and incorporate a variety of approaches into what becomes their own personal mix. At heart, although the majority are insecure in this approach, they cannot see a working alternative.

Not realising that a Paradise experience is pre-Judgement, some returnees reassess their previously held beliefs and now feel that God winks at all kinds of misbehaviours, regardless of how damaging they are to others or to themselves, and lays on a happy eternal existence for most of humanity. They may even feel this despite their having seen, during their own Life Review, the harm some behaviours cause on Earth. Consequently, they may adopt a Pollyanna view of harmful and sinful behaviours in their second chance 'to do better' on Earth, and end up in a spiritual and relational morass.

Living Beyond

Thankfully, the successful return of many NDErs who follow God's imperative to love others in the active way he showed love to them during their NDE, demonstrates that religion need not be an ongoing stumbling block. Nonetheless, finding a likeminded group of people with whom to share friendship and fellowship can in itself be a discouraging challenge.

The *Handbook of Near-Death Experiences*[18] has surveyed research and makes an important point:

> It is probably fair to say that NDErs are represented *in every congregation*. As survival of medical and other crises continues, new NDErs will continue to present themselves.

Consequently, all religious leaders should take note and decide how best they can be of service to NDErs. Sympathetic, non-judgemental listening is always a good place to start.

Paranormal Challenges

These are reported in 55% of returnees' lives (IANDS figure). They are generally of less immediate impact than the other changes and do not radically affect lifestyles; consequently they may not be noticed for a while. They are very varied. If not focussed upon, they generally fade away on return.

I believe it to be unwise to be preoccupied by these, as their function is not in my opinion intended for life on Earth. In Hades, the NDEr functioned within certain beyond-normal abilities, such as telepathy, spirit travel, reading the thoughts of others, a new vigour that utilised a novel form of energy, accessing universal knowledge (most of which is forgotten at their return) – and, more rarely, being given 'secret information' that may include visions or glimpses of the future. Consequently, it is not a surprise that on return telepathic communication and perceiving what others are thinking are commonly reported. Precognition or knowing in advance that something is going to happen is reported more rarely, as is an ability to heal others of a variety of physical, mental or emotional conditions. Some report a new internal energy that generates surges along the spine, which may explain unusual effects on external electrical and electronic equipment – such as light bulbs bursting or computers malfunctioning.

However, as far as I can tell, none of these effects have been verified by controlled research.

For some returnees, the outcome is anything but minor and temporary – because they develop an interest in the occult, the paranormal and unbiblical prophecies. I have noticed that this involvement can result in psychological and mental meltdowns, depression, and as an entry point for evil forces. Besides personal danger in this life arising from dabbling in the paranormal, it poses serious spiritual dangers for the afterlife too. It is expressly forbidden in scripture and is unacceptable to God. Amongst other Bible references, Deuteronomy 18:10-12 reads:

> Let no one be found among you who sacrifices their son or daughter in the fire, who practices divination or sorcery, interprets omens, engages in witchcraft, or casts spells, or who is a medium or spiritist, or who consults the dead. Anyone who does these things is detestable to the LORD.

Furthermore, many NDErs appear to be deluded regarding these new abilities, which may be more hopeful than actual. For example, Dannion Brinkley during his NDE claims he was given knowledge about the future. Brinkley subsequently wrote a disastrous but profitable book *Saved by the Light* (1994). He gave supposed future dates for the fulfilment of various fanciful prophecies, not one of which occurred on the prophesied dates, which came and went! Had he made these prophecies during biblical times, he would have been stoned to death for being a false prophet.

To date, I know of no NDEr prophecies that have given specific time frames to have been provably accurate. What are we to make of disastrous prophetic failures? Some will have arisen from charlatans leaping into the market to make coinage from a public fascinated by NDEs. Others may have had hallucinations woven into their NDE because of continuing brain activity or brain activity that begins to 'fire again' during the NDE. Still others may have been confused by drug flashbacks, or have merely been seeking attention.

Counselling sessions biased towards the paranormal can magnify this particular problem. An NDEr's genuinely heightened spirituality may be seized upon and exaggerated by an interviewer or counsellor until the NDEr becomes hopeful that paranormal 'giftings' might be part of their mission back on Earth.

With regard to prophecies, from a Christian point of view, we do well to contrast the truly amazing and proven accuracy of fulfilled biblical prophecy in history with any inaccurate prophetic predictions given by prophets, NDErs or otherwise, in modern times.

Again we look to Jesus, and find that when his close group of chosen disciples spoke with him before he finally ascended heavenwards, they were desperate to know what the future held and asked him (Acts 1:6-8): 'Lord, are you at this time going to restore the Kingdom to Israel?'

He said to them: 'It is not for you to know the times or dates the Father has set by his own authority. But you will receive power when the Holy Spirit comes on you; and you will be my witnesses in Jerusalem, and in all Judea and Samaria, and to the ends of the Earth.'

In other words, disciples should get on with the work of building the Kingdom of God on the Earth and leave the future in the hands of God the Father. I would hesitate to believe any returnee claiming to have been given more detailed knowledge of mankind's future than that already mentioned in scripture.

Having said that, God does occasionally prepare an individual for upcoming events that will be traumatic for him or her – as he did with NDEr Mary Neal[16] being given advance knowledge of the future death of her son. A number of other returnees have been given similar personal information to prepare them for difficulties ahead. Indeed, this occurrence, though rare, is not exclusive to the NDErs of the world.

Millions of NDErs have successfully overcome the challenges they have faced on return to Earth, and their lives have been immeasurably enriched by their afterlife experiences as a consequence. How they have achieved this is the subject of the following chapter.

14

Succeeding as a Returnee

There is one common element in all near-death experiences: they transform the people who have had them.
—(IANDS)

The International Association for Near Death Studies (IANDS) has carried out an analysis of long-range investigations of NDEs done by themselves and others, and reports on their website that 80% of NDErs claimed that their lives were forever changed by what happened to them.

80% means around 13 million transformed adults in America alone, not counting transformed children, plus multiplied millions more around the globe. And the changes, as they see it, are overwhelmingly for the better, in particular if the challenges described in the previous chapter are overcome successfully.

Positive Changes According to the NDErs

Most NDErs report their NDE to be life-changing for the better. 'It's like one life ended and a new one began,' is a typical statement. Raymond Moody[1] quotes a response he came across:

> Since I died, all of a sudden, right after my experience, I started wondering whether I had been doing the things I had done because they were good, or because they were good *for me*...

> I try to do things that have more meaning, and that make my mind and soul feel better. And I try not to be biased, and not to judge people. I want to do things because they are good [of themselves], not because they are good for me.
>
> And it seems that the understanding I have of things now is so much better. I feel like this is because of what happened to me, because of the places I went and the things I saw in this experience.

The cardiologist Maurice Rawlings[2] also quotes a patient:

> I always thought about social status and wealth symbols as the most important things in life, until life was suddenly taken from me. Now I know that none of these are important. Only the love you show others will endure or be remembered. The material things won't count.

Here are some further short descriptions by returnees themselves, describing how the NDE has impacted them.

> Christi-Ann[3]: 'I was given a second chance, and now I see the glass as half full and not as half empty.'

> Teresa[3]: 'This experience has changed my life tremendously. It's changed my perspective of people and how I look at them. I'm far more tolerant of things in my life now.'

> Lisa[3] found herself to be less intense about things. Today she 'stops and smells the roses'.

> Julie[3] said that before her NDE: 'I just didn't know who I would be if I wasn't working.' After her NDE, she has

found life to be more than her career, and has come to embrace it much more widely.

Crystal McVea[4]: 'I also stopped being so attached to my possessions. I'd always been very sentimental about objects that meant something to me, but after I died I no longer cared much about material things.'

In similar vein, even though only 16 years old, Mike[3] who died at school, said he had set his heart on material things such as a brand new 'cool' car that would 'wow' the other kids. But following his NDE, *people* rather than *things* became much more important to him.

Linda,[3] who was wealthy: 'Life is so precious, and I changed my attitude. While in that MRI tunnel with my [dead] son, I did not have diamonds, I did not have my cars, nor my houses, but what I did have was the *love* of my family: my daughter outside the door, my son Michael praying on his knees in the hallway, my son Scotty cradling me in his arms – that's what we leave with, love's the *only* thing we take with us.'

Scripture confirms Linda's conclusion that love accompanies us into the next phase of existence, while of course material things are left behind.

Scripture supports this lack of materialism found in returnees. 'Do not store up for yourselves treasures on Earth, where moths and vermin destroy, and where thieves break in and steal. But store up for yourselves treasures in Heaven' (Matthew 6:19, 20).

Enduring Changes

A few of the major positive changes resulting from NDEs are listed below, and though each change contains a quote from just one returnee, it reflects hundreds of similar statements on the same point.

No Further Fear Of Death.

'But when it comes to my time,' says Julie[13], 'I am *so* ready. There is a beyond – that beyond is a very peaceful place, something we can all look forward to.'

An Inner Peace.

Jim[2], who saved his brother from a collapsed warehouse, observes regarding his brother: 'He has found peace. I know that. He definitely found peace, and it still resonates in him now. Before this (his NDE) it was "work, work, work – get the money, get the money", but money is nothing unless you have peace.' His brother still runs his construction company successfully, but an inner peace characterises all he does.

Psychological Changes.

Some are very positive about their new insights. Lillian Oaktree[5] is one.

'I just sat there with a renewed inner calm,' she recalls. 'I'd never felt so good in my entire life. It was like I'd been given a new insight into life – and death. Up to then I'd worried about everything from paying bills to upsetting people. I was one of life's natural worriers. I'd always been like that, even as a kid. I blame my mother for telling me her worries. And the older I got, the more I worried. I had this tense feeling hanging over me, like a black cloud. I found it impossible to relax, which I'm sure contributed to me developing asthma. But it had lifted; it truly was a life-changing experience. My personality altered overnight. It's like someone had sucked all the tension out of me. At last I felt at peace.'

She concludes her description on a positive note of forgiveness that would not have happened had she not met her parents again in Paradise.

The biggest transformation has been deep within me. I've forgiven my mum for heaping her worries on me, and my father for leaving me. And I now know there's no need to fear anything in life – including death. Our souls really do live on.

Absolute Belief In Life After Death.

Darlene[3] puts it this way: 'There is no death. There is only the ending of this lifetime. I will not die, neither will you. We do not die.' Almost all NDErs agree.

An associated benefit is that afterlife experiences can comfort returnees during a time of trauma. Here is NDEr Jeanette Atkinson's[5] response on losing a child.

My daughter Rachael died of malignant melanoma 19 months ago when she was 17.

Losing a child is the worst possible thing that could ever happen to a parent, but I suppose that in some way, the experience I have had myself affords me some comfort. If the journey Rachael went on was even half as wonderful as mine, I know she would have been a very happy girl, and at total peace.

Returnees often make effective grief counsellors.

A Sense Of Purpose.

This incorporates things that returnees feel they should accomplish on Earth before they return to Paradise. For example, Lucas[3] is an advocate against drinking and driving, following the shocking accident that almost took his life permanently. Returnees are prominent in a wide variety of community work. They are also attracted to the 'helping professions', such as teaching, nursing, social work and a variety of medical fields.

New Priorities.

There is emphasis on the importance of the spirit and soul over trivial issues such as good looks or bodily wellbeing. Moody[1] quotes one returnee: 'The body had been my main interest, and what was going on in my mind, well, it was just going on, and that's all. But after this happened, my mind was the main point of attraction and the body was second – it was only something to encase my mind.'

A Desire To Tell Others About Their Experiences.

In modern times this has become more socially acceptable, but even now scepticism, disinterest or hurtful comments can discourage the NDEr. 'They think I'm lying! Or they think I'm crazy!' decided Crystal McVea[9] when silence and disinterest met her first attempt to tell her story at a meeting. 'My face turned beetroot red, and I sat there feeling utterly embarrassed and mortified. I wanted to jump up and say, "You're all missing the point. Don't you know why we're here?" I felt myself withdrawing deeper and deeper into my shell.'

She soon stopped telling anyone. 'I didn't know if I could handle another eye roll or another look of indifference. Inside, I yearned to talk about God, but doing it in public made me feel like an idiot. So I shut down and didn't tell anyone for several long months. The greatest thing that ever happened to me got packed away in mothballs.'

However, she has since gained confidence, has written a book, and speaks publicly about her experiences. So do many other returnees.

A surprising number return believing that 'the End Times are starting' and that they have a responsibility to tell others this fact.

A Fresh Emphasis On Loving Others.

Kat[3]: 'We need to tell those people we love how much we love them.'

Seeing Themselves As Eternal Spiritual Beings.

Dean Braxton[3] expresses this: 'You leave your body and your body dies, but your spirit never dies. The real you never dies.'

This emphasis on finding themselves to be primarily spiritual beings has long-term ramifications for most returnees. The majority want to develop spiritual aspects of their lives and a variety of paths may be attempted. We should look at these more deeply because their outcomes are often not clear-cut. As we saw in the previous chapter, some appear to prove positive, but others result in confusion for the returnee.

Ivan Rudolph

Classifying Long Term Religious Changes

1. New Spirituality – Formal Religion.

Some returnees, but by no means the majority, convert to Christianity (mostly) or some other form of organised, formal religion. This is for the Western world; there are too few examples to make any general statements about the non-Western world.

Howard Storm[6] is typical of many who return. He believes the core of what he learnt was the importance of love and peaceful unity among people, whom he says are 'all loved by God'. His emphasis is on 'unity' of spirit rather than an imposed authoritarian 'uniformity', and an interconnectedness of humanity that is commonly remarked upon by returnees. He constantly emphasises the importance of caring for others while seeking spiritual truths and is absolutely against religious conflict. Howard converted from atheism to Christianity and became a minister in a structured Christian denomination until he retired after an influential ministry.

J Isamu Yamamoto[7] quotes the example of an active homosexual, Dan, who died during his treatment for an STD. 'He met a brilliant light – but he knew that the source of the light was Jesus Christ. He heard a voice from the light that said, "It is not time to come into My Father's Kingdom. You have not lived as I intended. Go back and glorify me."' Jesus did not reject Dan but gave him a redirection for his return, the young man having already battled an STD and lost. Jesus' advice was loving but also practical. Dan converted to being a follower of this Christ he had met – left his former lifestyle – and joined a strong and supportive Christian community.

Yamamoto had been sceptical on hearing Dan's account and checked it out carefully. He found that, 'To this day, he glorifies God for giving him a new chance to live his life in accordance with biblical teaching.' In a follow-up article, he discovered Dan to be still an ardent follower of Jesus.

2. New Spirituality – Informal Religion.

Returnees seek answers in many directions and may adopt a variety of practices en route. To what extent is their new spirituality successful?

For many, these global changes in spiritual theory and practice result in a greater level of personal satisfaction and achievement in their lives. For others, their return is marked by failure, confusion, dissatisfaction, depression and disastrous relationships.

On reviewing hundreds of examples, I believe their success or failure depends primarily on the degree that divine love has become incorporated into their lives. Not a fluffy, self-interested version of love, which can lead to consequences ranging from dissatisfying to disastrous, but a strong love *centred in others* as shown to them by God the Father or Jesus during their NDEs. Those whose NDEs did not develop to a point of interaction with God can learn from those whose did – as might we all.

Love is the Goal

Whether their spiritual searching proves successful or not, regardless of cultural or religious background almost all NDErs return with an enhanced understanding that love is vital to living a meaningful life on Earth.

Their greatest challenge becomes to practise on Earth the principles of the divine love they came across in the afterlife. Moody[1] quotes a typical NDEr: 'He felt that the question that the Being was asking him was whether he was able to love others... He now feels that it is his commission while on Earth to try to learn to be able to do so.'

God's Love

God illustrates the true nature of love during his conversations with NDErs. Consider his discussion with Mary Jo Rapini[8]:

> He spoke through all of my senses. He called me by name and told me I could not stay.
>
> I protested. I told him all of my services on Earth (working 24/7, not much money for my work, a good wife, a good mother). I did not want to leave this place!
>
> Then God asked me, 'Let me ask you one question; have you ever loved another person the way you have been loved here?'
>
> The love I had received in that time was so overpowering, I had never felt anything like it, so I answered God honestly. I said, 'No, it is impossible, I am just a human, you are God.'
>
> He gave me the illusion of a sweet protective chuckle. He then said, 'Mary, you can do better.'

What are these features of 'the way you have been loved here'? We learn from the many NDErs who have interacted with God, especially after a rescue from the Prison or during an interview based around the Life Review:

1. Love serves others.
2. Love focuses on the needs of the beloved.
3. Love challenges.
4. Love guides.
5. Love is expressed.
6. Love takes a deep interest in others – all others.
7. Love plans ahead.
8. Love instructs.
9. Love is hugely empathetic.

10. Love rescues.
11. Love answers questions.
12. Love gives guidance and hope.
13. Love is supportive.
14. Love is not prejudiced.

God no doubt realises that the rubber hits the road when returnees try to practise this style of divine love in a harsh, uncomprehending world, but a world that nevertheless provides possibilities for personal growth that will not be available later. For example, loving one's enemies is the highest form of love, but is only possible on Earth because we will not have enemies later on in Heaven.

God knew that learning to love on Earth would be tough. Therefore Jesus came into the world to demonstrate how love can be practised even in the face of fierce opposition. Jesus did so successfully, but at great personal cost, while we can love in similar vein even though less effectively. Nevertheless, because love is eternal, whatever we learn becomes part of our character for eternity, so is extraordinarily beneficial for us and for others.

In addition to having the example of Jesus to guide them, the Holy Spirit on Earth can provide reurnees with ongoing help and support. Since the day of Pentecost almost two thousand years ago, the Holy Spirit has been made available to anyone on Earth because he has been 'poured out on all people' (Acts 2:17; Joel 2:28). How to access his guidance, teaching, advocacy and power is beyond the scope of this book, but much has been written on that subject. One of the qualities he grows in the lives of those who cooperate with him is that of divine love (Galatians 5:22).

Love of Others

RaNelle Wallace[9] was given this insight during her NDE: 'Love isn't simply a word or an emotion; Love is a power that gives action to all around it. Love is the power of life.'

God's kind of love is personal and active in the lives of others. IANDS reports that over 80% of surveyed NDErs expressed a strong increase in their concern for others. This included accepting and forgiving others rather than being critical of them.

Crystal McVea[4] zeroed in on God's requirement to forgive others, to seek forgiveness, and to put relationships right.

> After I got past being upset with everyone I felt had dragged me back from Heaven, I realised all the grudges and grievances that had cluttered my soul for so long had disappeared! It was like God wiped the slate completely clean. And the big stuff – the resentments I'd lived with for so many years, just melted away...
>
> I don't know, I just felt liberated from all the baggage I'd carried my whole life. I asked Virgil's mother to forgive me for pushing her away. I asked Virgil to forgive me for making him choose between his family and me. I asked my brother to forgive me for not paying enough attention to him when we were young, and I asked my mother to forgive me for always making her the target of my anger. I even called my father in Illinois and asked him to forgive me too.
>
> 'Oh no, you don't need to apologise for anything,' he said.
>
> 'But I do,' I told him. 'I need you to forgive me for being so hard on you.'

In summary, NDErs find that the best way to regain balance in life is to obey the love principles they have learnt characterises God; not love of self, but an active love of others. Those who find ways to contribute love to the lives of others reorientate quickly, as I observed in the NDErs I spoke to in the early days – Denis Cooper helping dysfunctional people in his farming community, Rhoda Fryer with her teaching and setting up fellowship groups,

Living Beyond

Bob Bosworth with his outstanding missionary work helping hundreds, and so on.

Applying God's Love

Divine love has many practical, action-packed features, some of which can be seen in 1Corinthians 13.

Whole courses may need to be designed for returnees to help them to apply divine love in a way that fulfils their strong motivation to do so.

Jesus provides our best example of how to serve others, which he did throughout his earthly ministry. This incident occurred shortly before he died, as described in John Chapter 13:

Jesus Washes His Disciples' Feet

¹It was just before the Passover Festival. Jesus knew that the hour had come for him to leave this world and go to the Father. Having loved his own who were in the world, he loved them to the end.

³ Jesus knew that the Father had put all things under his power, and that he had come from God and was returning to God; ⁴ so he got up from the meal, took off his outer clothing, and wrapped a towel around his waist. ⁵ After that, he poured water into a basin and began to wash his disciples' feet, drying them with the towel that was wrapped around him...

¹² When he had finished washing their feet, he put on his clothes and returned to his place. 'Do you understand what I have done for you?' he asked them. ¹³ 'You call me 'Teacher' and 'Lord,' and rightly so, for that is what I am. ¹⁴ Now that I, your Lord and Teacher, have washed your feet, you also should wash one another's feet. ¹⁵ I have set you an example that you should do as I have done for you. ¹⁶

Very truly I tell you, no servant is greater than his master, nor is a messenger greater than the one who sent him. [17] Now that you know these things, you will be blessed *if you do them.*'

In practice, start serving those closest to you and be prepared to prioritise their needs above your own. How can you add value to the lives of your husband or wife, children, parents, friends? How can you serve them, asking nothing in return? You can ask God to show you other people to love and serve, in your personal capacity or through an established charity or service group. Then get involved, but without robbing of your love those whom God has already put into your life.

It is never too late to get started serving others. For example, Darlene[3] suffered an emotional and spiritual breakdown that lasted for several years after her NDE. She changed her tack, and instead of a self-indulgent preoccupation with who she was, she became involved in helping terminally ill AIDS patients. This radical change of focus, in addition to helping those patients, has helped Darlene to recover and discover who she really is.

Love Grows

Relationships are always the anvil on which love is shaped. Loving relationships on Earth, primarily family ones, are thereby the supreme training ground for developing love – for all of us. And loving family relationships appear to continue into Paradise! God certainly regards them highly, himself a father who relates lovingly with his son Jesus and with all his adopted children.

Encouragingly, many family relationships are enhanced by the NDE experience. For example, Terese[3] says her relationship with husband Ron has deepened as a consequence, and he nods in agreement.

Living Beyond

Developing true love, however, never comes easily and entails dedication. Consider the experiences of Mary Beth Willi[10], who negotiated the worst threats to her family relationships through prayer and applying love. As with us all, the challenges of practising love in daily life continue for her.

> I almost lost my husband. I was a completely different person after the NDE and he didn't know what to do with me.
>
> After 6 months apart, a retreat and counselling, we have an amazing relationship now. Despite the fact that he doesn't believe me, he is a scientific personality and needs proof, he celebrates the person I have become.
>
> I made huge changes and amends with my kids...
>
> I lost most of my friends. It is difficult for me to be around negative people and they couldn't stand me anymore anyway. On the upside, my new friendships are amazing.
>
> Despite the fact that my relationship with my parents will never be fixed, I was able to forgive them – and it doesn't eat at me anymore.

One Example of a Successful Return – Dr George Ritchie[11]

Since Dr Ritchie's NDE predated modern reports, he was not influenced by popular concepts regarding NDEs. His writings are very Christ-centred, as his personal guide in the afterlife was Jesus, so this is understandable.

Similar to very many NDErs, he was traumatised at having to return to Earth. 'The contrast between the love of Jesus and the world in which I found myself having to go on living made the year following my illness the most difficult of my life.'

Why had he returned to life when he had not wanted to? He felt he needed to know. He began by researching his own death in the hospital, viewing his chart that read: 'Pvt. George Ritchie, died December 20 1943, double lobar pneumonia.'

Then he spoke to the doctor who had signed the report. 'My return to life, he told me, without brain damage or other lasting effect, was the most baffling circumstance of his career.' (*Guideposts Magazine* in 1963 investigated and obtained affidavits from both the Army doctor, Dr Donald G. Francy, and the attending nurse that Private Ritchie was pronounced dead on the morning of December 20, 1943.)

Following his NDE, George Ritchie was discharged from army camp to go to medical school. En route he visited his stepmother again, whom he had disliked. But something had changed inside George, and he no longer resented her. He saw her not in her hated role as stepmother, but as a brave and caring woman with issues of her own. 'I recalled my teenage withdrawal, my sulks and hostility, but now I was seeing the heartache they had caused to the loving woman sitting in front of me... Even as I talked about the absolute acceptance I had encountered in him (Jesus), a brand new ability to accept mother for herself was born in me.'

God had given Ritchie a fresh potential to incorporate that love he had experienced in Jesus into his own life when dealing with others. As he reflected on his NDE, forgiveness and a new caring for others developed and became his trademark. To love others actively at their point of need became his goal. But as with many other NDErs, he found good intentions needed to be worked at to become reality.

After a year, he assessed his progress. He was failing!

> You'd expect, I told myself, that anyone who had had an experience like mine, anyone who had glimpsed even dimly the love behind the Universe would no longer get upset by external things that happened.
>
> But I was. Terribly. I was riled by the blustering sergeant sitting three seats ahead of me now. I was

> bothered when the men in the 123rd, mostly Northerners from big cities, made fun of my Southern accent and small town ideas. Instead of being able, now, to shrug such things off, I found them bothering me.

During active duty, he discovered something else about himself.

> About the prospect of being torpedoed and having to take lifeboats in that icy gale, I was as terrified as the next guy. The mechanics of dying, the pain and panic, were as frightening to me as they had ever been. But as for death itself, I not only felt no fear of it, I found myself wishing it would happen! Then I would be with him [Jesus].

It was while patching up wounded and sometimes dying soldiers that Ritchie learned to look for that image of God in them that each person carries. He put aside his self-pity, his self-incrimination, and focused compassionately on *their* problems instead.

He also learnt to cultivate friendships with spiritual Christians who could understand him, teach him, and pray for him. One of these men, a Pole who had suffered terrible deprivation in a concentration camp, taught him a profound lesson about hatred and forgiveness.

> 'When the Germans reached our street, they lined everyone against a wall and opened up with machine guns. I begged to be allowed to die with my family, but because I spoke German they put me in a work group.'
>
> He paused, perhaps seeing again his wife and five children.
>
> 'I had to decide there and then,' he continued, 'whether to let myself hate the soldiers who had done this. It was an easy decision, really. I was a lawyer. In my practice I had seen too often what hate could do to people's minds and

bodies. Hate had just killed the six people who mattered most to me in the world. I decided then that I would spend the rest of my life – whether a few days or many years – loving every person I came in contact with.'

Ritchie imported these life-changing lessons from the Second World War into his civilian life. And years later, in 1963, Guidepost Magazine investigated Ritchie's NDE and aftermath:

> Probably as remarkable as the story itself is the transformation it caused in Dr Ritchie's life – a transformation that changed him from an indifferent Christian into a man whose life is centred in Christ. For 18 years he has been active in youth work in Richmond, Virginia, and in 1957 he founded the Christian Youth Corps of America, for the purpose of helping to develop Christian character in our young people. Dr Ritchie's vision is 'a world run by men who are run by God.'

More recently, in 1978, Raymond Moody[12] indicated that Ritchie had achieved success in his determination to love others: 'Unfortunately, only those of us who know him as friend can truly sense the depth of kindness, understanding, and loving concern for others which characterise this remarkable man.'

Ritchie became Head of Psychiatry at Northeast Alabama Regional Medical Centre. He died in 2007 age 84 years.

***'Death is nothing more than a doorway,
something you walk through' –
Dr George Ritchie.***

15

The Global NDE

An NDE is designed to take into account each person's individual needs, beliefs, background and culture.

Our family lived in the lovely African country Malawi during the early 1980s. Our African gardener, John, was a cheerful young man whom we all liked. One day he told me about his experience of death. John explained how he had died from a heart attack, and found himself in a beautiful garden, 'Not like this one,' he said, waving his hand to indicate our garden, 'This one rubbish.'

I was amused at this disparaging description of our garden, considering that to maintain and help develop it was his responsibility.

He continued: 'The garden when I died, very good. Green... flowers... water come up like this one,' and he used his hands to show water spouting up and falling in a fountain. From my questioning, John had never actually seen a decorative water fountain. I probed further. His descriptions of Paradise dovetailed with those I had heard from Westerners, despite the disparity between our cultures.

But do all people who die experience similar NDEs, regardless of race, religion or culture? Are they a global phenomenon? This is a fascinating question, but unfortunately research into non-Western NDEs is sparse and conclusions must therefore be conjectural. Sample sizes have been too small. I have read accounts of NDEs based on Guam, sample size of four, and Hawaii, sample size of one, and Australian Aborigines, sample size also one – and that one taken from a legend! The Australian Aborigines were generalised as not experiencing Life Reviews. Meanwhile an Aborigine who has described his NDE at a number of public meetings recently states that he could not stop watching his Life Review, although he had desperately wanted to! Besides a Life Review, his NDE shares other features with classic Western ones, such as seeing his body during the OBE stage, and an unpleasant Prison experience, before being rescued by Jesus when he called out desperately for help.

Certain organisations that have been recording NDEs over some years, such as Celestial Travellers[1], which leans towards a New Age interpretation, have made generalisations that may help to guide future research:

> One most extraordinary aspect of NDEs is that the underlying pattern seems unaffected by a person's culture or belief system, religion, race, education, or any other known variable, although the way in which the NDE is described varies according to the person's background and vocabulary. There is no evidence that the type of experience is related to whether the person is conventionally religious or not, or has lived a "good" or "bad" life according to his/her society's standards (although an NDE usually affects strongly how life is lived afterwards).

IANDS[2], who have thousands of NDE records, makes their own analysis.

> Similarities to Western NDEs are: the belief that this is the afterlife, a profound sense of peace, being in an otherworldly realm, meeting deceased relatives, meeting spiritual or religious figures (usually in keeping with one's cultural background), and to a lesser extent experiencing

some type of Life Review. The tunnel sensation was rarely reported in non-Western cultures.

In addition to small sample sizes, there are further problems in conducting international research. One is that of obtaining information from people of another culture and perhaps language from the researcher. For example, the IANDS summary above states that the tunnel sensation was rarely reported in non-Western cultures. More recently, J Steve Miller[3] has investigated this claim and found that in his sample, tunnels were reported more frequently, by a small margin, in Indian accounts than in Western ones. He suggests that tunnels may not have been asked about clearly enough in earlier international studies, or that the NDEr had not comprehended their significance to the research. Miller also disputes two further differences of degree claimed in earlier studies – that the presentation of Life Reviews was often by reading from a book, and that the manner in which the return was conducted was curt. In his investigations, he found no essential differences at all.

Much more extensive and confirmatory research is obviously needed. Miller's conclusion, however, is worth reflecting upon.

> So does the (NDE) pattern break down across cultures? Not in my opinion. As in western NDEs, some experienced only a few of the elements, while others reported a much deeper experience.

He also reports that similar changes occur in the lives of returnees across the world. Love is given priority. 'I was amazed that even those who experienced only a brief NDE were typically motivated to change their lives – specifically to love, serve and help people.'

Notwithstanding IANDS, Celestial Travellers and researchers such as Moody and Sabom, who tended to concentrate on similarities between NDEs, there are also significant individual differences. Some of these are birthed perhaps in cultural and religious influences and descriptions. Dr David San Filippo[4] observes:

> Near-death experiencers report that there are not appropriate words to accurately describe their near-death experiences. They therefore interpret the experience using words, phrases and metaphors that reflect their religious-cultural backgrounds and experiences.

Some differences are certainly birthed in language difficulties, but in my opinion others derive from how God always deals with us as individuals. Consequently, the experiences in the spirit world are personalised and vary to an appropriate degree. Culture and religion have had an influence on the individual's development, and thereby on the nature of the NDE planned for him or her, together with an awareness of the situation they will return to on Earth. We need always to keep alert to the NDE being a learning experience for one individual within which the Transfer Principle applies. Consequently, it would not be helpful for a Tibetan Buddhist, for example, to meet with people from another culture or religion in unfamiliar surroundings speaking another language. Instead, spirit beings or relatives meet the NDEr in reasonably familiar surroundings and communicate in such a way that they are immediately understood.

NDEs in Different Religions

In practice, religion and culture are difficult to separate in most non-Western studies, so I will not attempt to.

Many view life after death as the exclusive province of religion. Should adherents of different religions expect NDEs to be similar to one another, based on the teachings of their particular religion?

A member of the Baha'i religion, Farnaz Masumian[5], conducted a search for common NDE elements across major religions. She states that OBEs, a spirit body, elements of a Life Review, seeing God as a Being of Light, meeting deceased relatives and the importance of love are found in the theory and texts of the major religions. Despite this, most religions nowadays reject or look with suspicion on accounts of NDEs. Consider PMH Atwater's[6] statement based on her years of research:

> In seeking stories from near-death experiencers, bear in mind that today, more than in the past, the various religious groups tend to be rather protective of their faith's dogma. For instance: in the Muslim faith, visions and experiences like near-death are considered blasphemy. Even if a Muslim had such an experience (which they do), nine chances out of ten, he or she would never admit to such a thing – usually out of fear. I never encountered any problem with Muslims during most of my research fieldwork, *but I do now*. They clam up when I broach the topic.

A similar dearth of modern NDE material pertains to Hindu, Buddhist and other religions, for similar reasons.

The problem is not solely with religious leadership, but also with the expectation of the local society for people to follow tight cultural norms. They do not readily accept anything out of the ordinary. If you have lived and worked within other cultures, you may have seen the powerful influence of following 'tradition' and not 'rocking the boat'. If NDErs who live in influential cultures claim to have had afterlife experiences, they may be looked upon with mistrust or even hostility, and perhaps in addition become suspected of grabbing at status. Many returnees save themselves social discomfort by saying nothing.

Nevertheless, my hope is that there will be increasing worldwide recognition of the importance of NDEs. As more religious leaders have them, it will become increasingly difficult for those religions to continue to discount or ignore them. A consequence could be that religious and cultural restraints could weaken; testimonies may then flood in by the thousand. A reliable worldwide analysis could then begin. Time will tell.

Meanwhile, for interest, let's look at a small number of NDEs pertaining to followers of some non-Western religions.

Hindu NDEs

Padma[7] remained a Hindu for a while following her afterlife experience, but is now a Tibetan Buddhist because she feels it is more in tune with what happened to her. Here is her experience after falling from the third floor directly onto the concrete below and being rushed to hospital:

> As I lay in bed, with doctors and nurses administering emergency help, all of a sudden I was on the ceiling looking down at my twisted and mangled body. I saw the doctors cutting my clothes off hurriedly. I saw them put traction on my waist. I saw what the traction looked like. It was a contraption made of thick heavy metal rods going down my sides from my waist. At the level of my feet heavy chains hung suspended by two big metal balls. Great compassion and sorrow arose from seeing myself in that terrible position.
>
> Next thing I knew, I was being pulled with a force like a hurricane or tornado and was trying to hang on to

the ceiling with my nails, both with my feet and hands. I was being pulled towards the wall facing me, and when I came close to there, I saw this most beautiful, rotating light, like that of the Universe, in fact it moved like the Universe. It had life and knowledge and it felt like a loving parent beckoning me. Coming close to it gave me the most warm, loving feeling.

In line with other returnees regardless of culture or religion, Padma emphasises her changed attitudes towards both appreciating life on Earth as a wonderful gift to be cherished, and also towards loving others. 'I have been left with a feeling of great loving-kindness, compassion, and a need to never give up on anyone. I try to do whatever I can within my own limitations to help people. I can put myself in another's shoes and feel their anguish and feel the need to protect them.'

Here is a shortened account of Mahesh Chavda's[8] experiences. A devout Hindu as a youth, he visited the Hindu temple three times a week to burn incense, bow to the images and talk to the priests. Disillusioned by the hypocrisy he saw in certain priests, he walked away from Hinduism and began to read a Bible he had been given by a visitor to the family home. Late one night he decided to turn his back on the Bible and the Jesus portrayed in it.

> "No more," I said to myself. "Enough is enough. I am never going to think about Jesus Christ again. I am never going to read this book again. My mind is made up"
>
> And that was that. Or so I thought.
>
> The next thing I knew, I *heard* my head hit the desk. I mean I literally heard it, as if it were happening to someone else. *Bang.* I seemed to be in a sort of half-sleep, no longer fully awake and in control, but aware of what

was going on. I remember hearing the noise and thinking to myself "That's my head, hitting the desk."

An OBE followed, moving into what might have been a vision, or even a deeper NDE.

> I immediately found myself in a strange and wonderful place. My body was still there at the desk, but in my spirit I was somewhere different, somewhere wonderful, somewhere I had never been before.

Then Mahesh describes what he experienced, including grass as thick as a blanket, colours more vivid than any he had ever seen, music that he experienced more than felt.

> I felt I was *home*. This was where I wanted to be, where I was *supposed* to be. This was why I had been created.

Then he became aware of a brilliant white light coming toward him. Within that light was a man. He sensed immediately that this was Jesus – even though he had not previously seen any art depicting him. And though he looked like an ordinary man and walked like an ordinary man, he was so brilliant Mahesh could hardly bear to look at him.

> As he came closer to me, I could see that he was smiling. It was the same kind of smile you see on the face of a mother or father when they pick up their little baby, a smile of utter love and delight.
> Then, as I stood there gazing into his eyes, he stretched out his hand and placed it on my shoulder and said to me simply, 'My little brother.'

This interaction and the salutation as 'My little brother' affected Mahesh deeply, and became a turning point in his life. He reassessed his belief system and in time became a Christian minister.

Certain Hindu NDE reports originating in India are similar to those reported in the West. Others employ radically different language and concepts, such as 'yamatoots' being sent to fetch the spirit of the departed instead of the 'guides' or even 'angels' described in some Western NDEs. This could be the use of different and culturally familiar terminology to describe what may be similar experiences.

Perhaps as more accounts come to hand, greater clarity regarding similarities and differences between the Hindu NDE experience and that of others will become apparent.

Buddhist NDEs

Within Buddhism, as is the problem for researchers dealing with all the major religions, there are different groups holding differing beliefs and teachings about the afterlife. Raymond Moody in *Life After Life* devotes several pages to startling similarities between the NDEs he studied and the model of the afterlife described by Tibetan Buddhism in the Tibetan Book of the Dead. There *are* extraordinary similarities, and that is perhaps in part what attracted the previously mentioned Hindu lady, Padma, to become a Tibetan Buddhist, but what Moody did not do is point out the large number of *differences* that also exist. In my own readings, I discovered many significant statements at odds with the classic NDE.

With all this confusion, we can sympathise with Susan Onizuka[9], a Buddhist of Japanese ancestry, when she writes:

'According to Buddhist beliefs/interpretations, you cannot truly be a Buddhist if you believe in God, which I did not until my NDE… The light was so incredibly bright that I was certain it would blind anyone gazing upon it, but instead it gave me the greatest joy and feeling of intense love that I can barely describe it properly.' Alongside this encounter with God, Susan experienced other standard NDE features such as telepathic communication and a Life Review, which she describes in these words. 'Everything I had done, good or bad, seemed to happen all again all at the same time. My entire life was experienced again, but with an added dimension, I experienced the emotions and outcomes of everyone (pets included) that my actions had created, good or bad.' Her NDE also featured rapid travel. When told she had to return because it was 'not your time', she argued that she preferred to stay: 'No way. I'm here and I'm staying!' Despite her arguments, she was swiftly returned to her body.

Susan Onizuka's descriptions would fit many a classic Western NDE.

Because the concept of God was totally outside Susan Onizuka's personal Buddhist belief system, she could not integrate her NDE into her pre-existing faith. Her resulting bewilderment is obvious and sad. (Author's note: many Buddhists do believe in God).

The terminology used in Buddhist descriptions can sound 'cute' to Westerners, because of the different expressions used in their culture. Here is an example of non-recognition of the body left behind during an OBE. Shibani[10], a Buddhist in India, fell out of a bus in 1990 and died as his head struck the ground. 'Next instant I saw myself standing next to my own body, and the first thought that came to me while I looked at my body lying on the ground was, "Thank Goodness I did not fall; that is someone else lying there"… During the time that I was watching my own body, I distinctly remember feeling joy at not being the one hurt! Having complete disorientation from my own body, I did not recognize my own body, nor identified myself as being the one. Watching the other body lying on the ground, I did not feel any pain, or other feeling, apart from feeling happy at not being hurt.'

Of course, many Buddhists are themselves Westerners. I was talking to a Dutch lady recently in a small meeting who was one of three seniors (the only Buddhist) who claimed to have had an NDE. While two others freely told us about their classic NDE experiences, she would talk to me only privately after the meeting. Because of an unusual medical condition, she says she has experienced a number of OBEs while undergoing operations over the years, during which she has seen things she could not have seen had her consciousness remained in her brain on the operating table. Although she finds these experiences confusing, she assured me that the OBEs have had one very positive consequence for her – she no longer fears death.

Muslim NDEs

As explained earlier, accounts of Muslim NDEs have dried up. There will I am convinced be millions of Muslims around the world who have had NDEs but are not saying so. I have selected a few anecdotes of interest from amongst those I have read.

Wan I[11] was a 15-year-old Muslim domiciled in Malaysia at the time of his NDE in 1995. We pick up his account from the time that his spirit left his body.

> For a few seconds, I saw myself from above, lying on the floor. I saw uncle Muharram on my left and my dad on my right, my mother near the sofa looking worried, but I kept on floating upwards and away. For a brief second I saw the rooftop of my house. I saw the housing area where I lived from above, and as I got higher I could see some night clouds in the sky. I felt sad leaving my parents and

> my family, of leaving this world, as I knew that I might never come back.
>
> As I turned to face the direction to which I was being pulled, the moment I turned around, there was a bright blinding light – I expected to see the moon. But at that precise moment as I faced towards the direction I was floating or being pulled towards, it felt like an instantaneous 'vacuum', as if I was being sucked at incredible speed towards that light.
>
> It felt like a tunnel with a light at the end of it. I felt as if I was in outer space being sucked like a vacuum racing towards the light at the end as I could make out the dots like stars around me while rushing towards that light. The only way to describe the feeling was almost like riding a motorcycle at breakneck speeds without your helmet on, or skydiving with the wind blowing hard against you, that feeling of tremendous speed where you're helpless to do anything about it, as you have no control.

He added later that 'It felt almost as if my field of vision was like 360 degrees as I could see everything, but I couldn't control where I was going, which was towards the light.' Movement like this without control often causes fear, but another concern dominated his thinking just at that moment.

> I felt so afraid, as I thought that I might go to Hell for some of the things I've done.
>
> I've only 'heard' them talk about it [Hell], but this time I realized I might be GOING there! Worst of all, so many thoughts were happening at the same moment as I also thought how young I was. I haven't felt what it was like to fall in love, I haven't gotten married yet, I wouldn't see my family again or my friends and I haven't had the

chance to experience so many things in my life; all these sad thoughts occurring at once made me sad.

But as I grew closer to the light and felt its shine, a sudden cool and calmness came over me. For the light made me feel peaceful all of a sudden as I grew closer. It was a kind of peace and calm which I've never felt in my entire lifetime, even until this very day.

From afar, as I grew closer to the light, I could see almost like figures in the light, like heads, people all dressed in white, as if it were some sort of congregation or a crowd. The more I came closer, the more I felt like 'staying' and my sadness and fears disappeared. It felt like that comfort feeling of 'home'.

Elsewhere, he states that this feeling of peace was like the joy of a child.

My mind began to change with that overwhelming feeling of peace, comfort and calm, a sort of happiness I've never felt – when getting closer to the light. The peace and comfort felt like being embraced or hugged by a lover, and the calmness felt like the feeling of lying in your lover's embrace after making love to someone special. The safety feeling it gave was almost that soft, safe and comfort feeling that we got when we were just a child being embraced and carried around in our parents' arms.

As I finally arrived or hit the light, for a few seconds I saw a young man – he seemed around 17 to 20's. He looked a bit familiar and smiled at me as if he 'knew' me. He raised his hand to signal me to stop – and at that precise moment I started breathing again.

I awoke, which felt as if I had been holding my breath underwater far too long. Slowly my physical consciousness came back to me.

Since his return, Wan believes that there definitely is a God and that there is a life after death, and angels. His experience has removed all fear of death from him.

The youthful figure in the light that Wan saw turned out to be his late grandfather, who Wan recognised later when looking through old pictures in his grandmother's photograph album. 'I could not recognise him as I've only known him as the way he looked when he was around his 70's, but the picture of my grandpa in his late 20s looked exactly like the young man whom I met in the light who had smiled at me.' Once again we see the goodness of God, sending a loving relative to meet Wan in order to send him back to Earth.

Please note that Wan has remained a Muslim, but his focus has changed, becoming more determined to obey God and also to do good for others. 'Today I try not to be racially or even religiously biased, even though I do very much believe in my own faith, but I believe that doing good to one another as human beings is much more important as this is what God wants...'

Khadija[12] had an accident falling from a horse while working with a film crew in Egypt.

> The next thing I remember was saying 'I cannot breathe...' And then darkness. I was high above my body looking down when I next became aware. There were people around me. I did not care to return and turned around. At this time, I seemed so light and happy and could actually look down at the Sphinx below! I then saw another level of existence opening up. There were many beings who had come to meet me. I was told that I could either come or go back, but that I would suffer great pain if I did. I remember making a choice, as I thought there was something else I needed to accomplish in this life.

Khadija has a charming non-Western way of unfolding what others have described as the spirit leaving the body while the inactive brain remains behind: 'I have come to believe that we are NOT the body. Especially the brain. I see it as sort of a radio receiver that can be broken and unable to respond. I clearly wanted to talk to my friends when they were hysterical and crying, to tell them I was OK, but the brain was not functioning. I clearly remember being annoyed with it and knew it was like a sort of machine that was malfunctioning. I felt separate from the body – totally! I could not get it to work, or even move my fingers to tell them I was not dead!' It is interesting that Western theorists Pim van Lommel, Simon Berkovich and Chris Carter have conjectured that the brain acts as a receiver for the mind and not vice-versa, as is most commonly supposed. Khadija's impressions would fit this new model. NDEs would suggest consciousness can act as an alternative storage unit, because consciousness functions outside the brain and stores vivid and precise memories during afterlife experiences.

Khadija did not progress as far as a Life Review, but other Muslims have done so. Some use great brevity to state what has happened to them. For example, Sameer[13] (a Muslim in Israel) describes his Life Review as: 'I also saw all my past life since my breast feeding till now.' That is his total description! Others give more detail, such as Muhammad F[14] (a Muslim in Egypt) whose Life Review occurred during a car accident.

> During this I remembered everything with all the details and very accurately, since my birth till the time of accident. I remembered all the people I knew, even the ones whom I met once or twice. I remembered all the events, the important and non-important ones when my age is less than a year. I remembered it with all its details. The past was in front of me and I saw it as a cinema show in just 15 minutes.

A 2009 study by Iranians of local Muslim NDEs concluded that while the sample was too small (ten men and nine women] to draw definite conclusions: 'Our informal assessment was that both the contents and after-effects of the Muslim NDEs were quite similar to those of Westerners. We concluded that NDEs are not particularly rare in Muslim groups and that their similarity to Western NDEs suggests they may be a cross-culturally universal and transpersonal phenomenon.' Dr Scott Young of the Florida Mental Health Institute acted as the Western analyst for this interesting research, but the researchers themselves remain incognito for obvious reasons.

Dr Nasir Siddiki[15], claims his own life was saved when critically ill through a deathbed vision of Jesus Christ, and thereafter he became a Christian. Several years later, he received a phone call from London that his brother Asif, an ardent Muslim, had died. Nasir lived in the USA, and he and his wife agonised in prayer for hours, during which time a sheet that was covering the brother's face in the London hospital morgue moved and attracted attention. Nasir flew to the UK to be with his brother, who by now had been declared alive but in a coma.

Nasir prayed and sat with Asif, who subsequently revived and described the frightening NDE he had experienced, beginning with an OBE during which he watched doctors trying to restart his heart before covering his face with a sheet and wheeling his body into an elevator and down to the morgue in the basement. Meanwhile, in his spirit body, Asif had experienced the sensation of falling into a very dark space inhabited by demons – his eyes grew large as he spoke to Nasir about this and he did not want to talk further. During this terrifying NDE, he had looked up and seen a cross with a figure hanging on it.

'You saw Jesus on the cross?' Nasir asked incredulously.

'No. No. I saw myself hanging on the cross.' It had been a confronting vision! 'It was the most horrific thing I had ever seen. I never want to see it again.'

Immediately Nasir perceived the significance of the vision. 'Asif, you deserved to be on that cross, because the wages of sin [what you earn from wrongdoing] is death, as the Bible teaches.' He explained that the sins we have committed may result in eternal spiritual death unless we ask Jesus to substitute for us. That mysterious substitution then sets a man or woman free from future punishment, because Jesus has served their death sentence already for them.

Asif understood. He and Nasir prayed and Asif accepted Christ's forgiveness.

There are accounts of professing Christians who have converted to Islam in their search for a deeper knowledge of God. A prominent convert was Mark Hanson[16] (now Hamza Yusuf), who aged 17 in 1977 experienced an NDE during a car crash. He does not go into details. While he does not report a 'deep' NDE, his experience showed him there was an afterlife and that he should investigate what religions taught about it. He found Islam to have a more detailed theology of the afterlife than did Christianity, and after intense study he converted. Now he is very influential. In fact in 2009 he was ranked[17] as 'the Western world's most influential Islamic scholar'. Nevertheless, as one would expect of an NDEr who has understood that God is more interested in love than in hate and terrorism, he has aligned himself strongly against Muslim fanaticism. He described the 9/11 attacks as 'an act of mass murder, pure and simple'. Condemning the attacks, he expressed the opinion that 'Islam was hijacked on that plane as an innocent victim'.

Jewish NDEs

These tend to be similar to the 'regular' NDEs as recorded by others, but with a couple of differences that are peculiarly Jewish. They tend to be more questioning and confrontational than many others.

Some Jews report being confused by the Being of Light, and uncertain as to the identity of other spiritual beings they meet as well.

Beverly Brodsky[18] described her encounter: 'I was joined by a radiant being bathed in a shimmering white glow... I felt a reverent awe when I turned to him; this was no ordinary angel or spirit, but he had been sent to deliver me. Such love and gentleness emanated from his being that I felt that I was in the presence of the Messiah.' The Messiah! The one for whom the Jews have waited so long, to rescue them from oppression! But elsewhere she described this being as an angel. In April 2014, as a kind answer to my 'please explain', she wrote: 'I don't call him the Messiah any more. It just confuses people. I believe he was an archangel.'

So far so good, but later in her NDE she met with God the Father: 'I immediately lashed out at him with all the questions I had ever wondered about; all the injustices I had seen in the physical world. I don't know if I did this deliberately, but I discovered that God knows all your thoughts immediately and responds telepathically. My mind was naked; in fact, I became pure mind. The ethereal body which I had travelled in through the tunnel seemed to be no more; it was just my personal intelligence *confronting* that Universal Mind, which clothed itself in a glorious, living light that was more felt than seen, since no eye could absorb its splendour.'

Beverly goes on to describe the nature of their interchange: 'I don't recall the exact content of our discussion; in the process of return, the insights that came so clearly and fully in Heaven were not brought back with me to Earth. I'm sure that I asked the question that had been plaguing me since childhood about the sufferings of my people. I do remember this: there was a reason for everything that happened, no matter how awful it appeared in the physical realm.'

Dr Rene Hope Turner[19], another Jewish lady, who died after a dreadful car accident that smashed up her head and face, described meeting her Guide whom most Christians would at once assume to be Jesus, but who did not identify himself as such, nor did he indicate that he was her expected Jewish Messiah: 'I arrived in an explosion of glorious light into a room with insubstantial walls, standing before a man about in his thirties, about six feet tall, reddish brown shoulder length hair and an incredibly neat, short beard and moustache. He wore a simple white robe. Light seemed to emanate from him and I felt he had great age and wisdom. He welcomed me with great love, tranquillity, and peace indescribable – no words. I felt within myself, "I can sit at your feet forever and be content," which struck me as a strange thing for me to think/say/feel. I became fascinated by the fabric of his robe, trying to figure out how light could be woven!'

The rest of her NDE illustrates similarities to others. For example, here is her Life Review, through which her Guide led her:

> He stood beside me and directed me to look to my left, where I was replaying my life's less complimentary moments. I relived those moments and felt not only what I had done but also the hurt I had caused. Some of the things I would have never imagined could have caused pain. I was surprised that some things I may have worried about, like shoplifting a chocolate as a child, were not there, whilst casual remarks, which caused hurt unknown to me at the time, were counted. When I became burdened with guilt, I was directed to other events that gave joy to others, although I felt unworthy. It seemed the balance was in my favour. I received great love.

Her subsequent meeting with her beloved grandfather was also fairly typical, as was the instruction to return and the warnings she received about problems she would experience.

There coming towards me was my grandfather. He looked younger than I remembered and was without his harelip or cleft pallet, but (was)undoubtedly my grandfather. We hugged. He spoke to me and welcomed me. I was moved to forgive him for dying when I was 14 and making me break my promise to become a doctor to find a cure for his heart condition. Until that moment, I had not realized I had been angry with him!

Granddad told me that grandma was coming soon and he was looking forward to her arrival. I inquired why she was coming soon as she had been travelling from her home in Manchester to New Zealand to Miami for continual summer for a number of years. Granddad told me she had cancer of the bowel and was coming soon. Granddad seemed to have no grasp of time when I pressed for how soon. [Grandma was diagnosed three months later and died in August. I upset my mother by telling her about it when I regained consciousness.]

The Person who first welcomed me came and placed his hand on my shoulder and turned me towards him. He said, 'You must return. You have a task to perform.'

I wanted to argue. I wanted to stay.

Rene awoke in hospital, and a painful recovery process began. 'I was for two years angry at God for sending me back in such torment with a task to do with no clues or instructions – only one thing: a clear message I have no idea how to pass on, which is:

"It is time to live according to your beliefs, whatever they may be – to put your house in order – for the end times are upon us!"

It took me five years as a zombie before I was able to rehabilitate myself. I have gainful employment, formed the Head Injury Society of New Zealand in 1987, and am paraded as the example of how well it is possible to recover from acquired brain damage. I still don't know my task – still have pain, anosmia, diplopia, etc.'

Despite the brain injury, her NDE remains clear in her memory. 'The memory of the NDE is more real than what I did yesterday. Salom... *Rene Turner.*'

Many Jewish people have become secular atheists on Earth, and are shocked when their spirit rises out of the body at death. Barbara Harris Whitfield[20] recalls: "I suddenly realized that what I had believed in the past might not be real. Maybe my belief systems were really messed up. Maybe this was real and everything else had been an illusion."

Barbara had a very positive afterlife experience. She was eased into it by having a wonderful interaction with her dead grandmother, whom she had always loved very much. Her Life Review later on taught her a great deal about herself, her parents and others in her life. God walked her through it. "I realise now that without this God force holding me, I wouldn't have had the strength to experience what I am explaining to you."

Barbara's Life Review included many painful memories, but enabled a radical course-correction in her life once she had returned to her body. Materialism went out of the window; to love and help people became her passion. She forgave those who had bruised her emotionally and became involved with helping hospital patients who were dying. She researched NDEs and trained as a therapist who practises in Atlanta, Georgia. She has written a number of books about NDEs and helps struggling returnees through her work with IANDS.

Religious Founders in NDEs.

If a figure is seen within the radiant light encountered during an NDE, some NDErs make an assumption about who that figure is. However, this person hardly ever identifies himself. On the rare occasions he does, it is interesting that the Being of Light does not seem to identify himself as Brahma, Shiva, Buddha, Krishna, Vishnu, Mohammad, Allah, Matreya – or any of the other religious gods or spiritual leaders that people follow. He has however identified himself to a growing number of NDErs as Jesus – usually to those who are Christians already, but also to unbelievers.

This is perhaps the most startling fact of all about NDEs, that only one founder of a world religion seems to make an identifiable appearance – Jesus Christ.

Lest the statement above sounds like my Christian bias, let's hear from David Sunfellow[21], who heads up the NHNE research site and appears to me to lean towards a New Age interpretation of NDEs. He summarises his observations regarding Jesus:

> It is only a matter of time before you start to notice something quite remarkable: 'Hey, there sure are a lot of parallels between what Jesus said and did and what a growing number of NDErs are reporting today.' There are, in fact, so many common threads that I personally believe there is no other spiritual leader, teacher, master that embodies the core elements of NDEs more fully than Jesus.

With over 4000 NDE reports published on the Internet, the Near-Death Experience Research Foundation (NDERF) website is another rich resource for probing important questions. Jody Long, who maintains its website, has investigated the known identities of persons met in the afterlife. She found that Jesus Christ was most commonly encountered. Apart from Jesus, no other founder of a religion was reported. NDERF is not a Christian website, so these results must assume unbiased credibility. (NDERF state on their webpage[22]: 'We do not allow proselytizing. We welcome and encourage all people of all backgrounds, nationalities, countries, and religions to read and participate on the website.')

A little perplexed by this, I wrote the following in April 2014 to Dr Jeffrey Long as the founder of NDERF:

> I (Ivan) have read in several books the principle that during an NDE the NDEr may see religious figures from their own religion e.g. Islamists see Mohammed, Buddhists see Buddha etc. I have skirted your web page accounts and those of IANDS without finding any of these accounts in the thousands of reports. So is this a theory without experiential support, or can you direct me to what you believe are valid confirmatory accounts, please?

Dr Long kindly responded:

> I am aware of those who have written that non-Christian NDErs see religious figures from their own religion, but those who wrote that generally gave no examples to support this. Jesus makes a regular appearance in NDEs. I have over 100 NDEs that encountered or were aware of Jesus in their experiences.

And so, for the present, I must reject the model that claims people see in the Figure of Light whoever it is that they suppose to be their religion's founder – that Buddhists will see Buddha etc. Exceptions may be found amongst pre-NDErs, whose dreams and visions are certainly culturally and religiously influenced, and whose hallucinations may include any number of religious symbols or beings, as described in Chapter 3. My supposition is that the Figure of Light is encountered too deeply in the *genuine* spirit world to give rise to the inaccurate or hallucinatory.

I believe the inaccurate view regarding the appearance of religious leaders in NDEs has arisen because of misidentification by the NDEr, or through fluffy New Age and paranormal hopes that all religions are equal and simply different ways to approach God. The evidence from reported NDEs does not support the New Age view.

For interest, I looked further at the only NDE that I could find after prolonged searching that claimed all religions see their own leader. I applied internal and external tests for being a reliable witness to that claimant, who failed dismally in both dimensions. His account is almost certainly false. Consequently, until a number of reliable witnesses begin saying the same thing, I must discount that hypothesis.

Because Jesus is the only founder of a religion identified to make an appearance during NDEs, and because he has been reported to do so by a wide spectrum of NDErs of differing beliefs, it is prudent to consider his interactions with NDErs in more detail.

Fortunately, most children have not been prejudiced against Jesus from a young age, so we can take heart from research into what they say they have experienced. PMH Atwater[23] notes that pictures of the 'holy one' seen in the afterlife demonstrate a strange consistency amongst children of mixed cultures, indicating his reality to them even when words cannot be found by the young children to describe him.

> It is striking that child experiencers of near-death states tend not to mix up racial skin tones, as do adults. Example: most Western children that I am aware of **see Jesus** as light brown, not white. It is the adults who sometimes see Jesus as white-skinned. Where this situation gets

fascinating is when you invite experiencers to draw the high holy one/religious figure who visited them. To a person, you cannot tell the difference between a drawing from someone in the State of Wyoming from one done in Thailand or Israel or Russia or China or Nigeria. Patterning holds; differences in patterning only concern a few details of dress and behaviour. That's it.

This 'holy one' looks to me like Jesus in pictures I have seen, and a number of children have identified him to be so later when looking at pictures in Bibles or elsewhere, which pictures, however stylised, generally try to depict the robes and the beards of first century Jewish men.

Jesus in NDEs

Here are brief extracts from just a small sample of the NDEs that record an encounter with Jesus. I have not tried to discover the religious beliefs of the NDErs who have related these encounters; my emphasis has now shifted to 'who is this Jesus who appears in NDEs?'

Jesus seems to change his representation of himself such that he appears to NDErs in a way that does not frighten them. This puts new arrivals at ease and allows them to relax quickly while being with him. Descriptions sometimes go beyond the physical presentation to the mysterious nature of Jesus, as in this one given by Dr Mary Neal[24].

> His hair was long. His features were indistinct. I don't know how to describe this, but my impression of his appearance was that of love (yes, I realise we don't typically 'see' love, but as I said, I don't know how to describe this phenomenon of 'seeing' something we would

normally 'feel'). He conveyed the impression of complete love, compassion, kindness, and infinite patience.

Each of the following examples of Jesus in NDEs illustrates something different about him.

Susan[25] was an anorexic who had kidney failure:

> Then Grandma asked me if I wanted to go and see Jesus. I literally screamed, "YES!!!"
> The second I saw him I started to cry. I could feel his compassion for me. He comforted me as I told him how people on Earth had wronged me because of my condition and how I had suffered with anorexia. He was so, so kind. He told me that he knew all of that and that it was going to be all right.
> I asked him if he promised and he said, 'Yes.'
> I told him something that maybe I shouldn't have. I said to him, 'You are a very handsome man.'
> He just laughed. Then I laughed. It was such a great time.
> I noted his appearance. He was about 5'9" and probably weighed about 150 pounds. He was slim, with dark brown hair and brown eyes.
> There were so many people around him; but, and this is what touches me so much, I was able to go right to him and talk to him. It's not like it would be here. You can't just go up to someone that important and talk to them. But with Jesus you can.
> He then told me to go back and tell everyone what I had seen. I said I would (but didn't, for some years). Then he hugged me. It felt like a million volts of electricity going through my body from his hug, I couldn't stand up because of the intense power I felt coming from him.

Susan's return was accompanied by a healing – she began eating normally right away, and further tests showed that her kidneys had been healed:

> Now, nine years later, I went from weighing 64 to 135 pounds. I have never had any kidney problems or any other kind of health problems that anorexia can cause. I am fine. I am healthy.

Lynn[26] was just 13 years old:

> I knew this light was Christ. I leaned against it for one moment and then asked my question. 'Dear Jesus, is it true that you gave me this heart condition so that I would have a cross to carry like you did?' Sister Agnes, my sixth-grade teacher, had told me that my heart condition was my cross to bear from Christ.
>
> I heard the voice of Christ vibrate through me as he said, 'No, this heart condition of yours is not a cross from me for you to bear. This heart condition is a challenge to help you grow and stay compassionate. Now, go back.'
>
> As I walked back, my grandmother told me that my father was going to leave my mother and that I would be my mother's strength.

Sadly, her father did leave her mother as Lynn had been forewarned during her NDE, but she had been prepared for the trauma and challenges. She proved to be sufficiently compassionate to fulfil this demanding mission for one so young.

Vavita Jones[27] was feeling devastated by her Life Review:

> Then Jesus' hand touched me, and I was able to get back on my feet because I had previously had no strength.

Taking me by the hand, he led me to the side of a main arena. He looked into my eyes, into my soul, and I knew he knew and understood everything I felt. When he looked into me, it was with more love than I ever thought possible for anyone to know. He smiled, one look letting me know everything would be all right.

With this reassuring look he led me to one side. He stepped away from me and went alone into the light. Where Christ's light ended and God the Father's began, I cannot say. They both gave off light and their light was the same light. I will never forget this as long as I live.

When Christ had stepped away from me, he turned sideways and stretched out his arms as a bridge. One arm extended to me, and one to the Father. His arms were extended as if they were making a cross and a bridge to cross over. It was like a visual representation of the scripture: 'For there is one God and one mediator between God and men, the man Christ Jesus, who gave himself as a ransom for all' (1 Tim. 2:5-6). God is on one side, and all people are on the other side: Jesus himself is between human beings and his Father to bring them to him.

Vavita had a problem with insecurity, especially after her Life Review. What would they decide about her? She listened carefully as Jesus and Father God communed over her case.

Jesus said, 'My blood is sufficient. She's mine.'

When he said that, all the doubts about my unworthiness disappeared. I jumped up and down, shouting and rejoicing. I have never been so happy in all my life! The kind of love I felt is beyond explanation. I kept saying, 'Oh, my God. Oh, my God. This is my mediator. This is my advocate.' Just as I had read in the Bible.

Jesus came back to where I was and looked at me again with comforting love. We rejoiced together.

He went on teaching me and talking to me a lot, but I don't recall the details. Now being so free and so loved, I never wanted to leave his side. I told him so, but a look in his eyes told me I had to return.

I asked, 'Must I really leave?'

He looked at me with tenderness and said, 'Yes, because there is a work I have for you to do.'

Vicki Umipeg[28], the blind lady we met in an earlier chapter, was one of those who met with Jesus during her NDE.

He greeted her tenderly.

He communicated telepathically to her: 'Isn't it wonderful? Everything is beautiful here, and it fits together. And you'll find that. But you can't stay here now. It's not your time to be here yet and you have to go back.'

Vicki objected, 'No, I want to stay with you!'

Vicki, being blind, had never seen a picture of Jesus, so her description is especially interesting.

> I was real close to him. He actually hugged me. He embraced me, and I was very close to him. And I felt his beard and his hair. His hair wasn't curly, but a bit coarse, dropping well below his shoulders.

And his eyes? What did they look like?

> They were piercing eyes. It was like they permeated every part of me, but not in a mean way. It was like you couldn't lie about anything, and he just looked everywhere and could see everything. And his beard had very bright lights in it. It was like lights came out of it. He had nothing on

his feet. He had this kind of robe on that didn't come all the way down to his feet.

Jesus reassured Vicki that she would come back, but that for now she had to return to Earth, 'and learn, and teach more about loving and forgiving'. In addition, she should speak to people to 'let them know of this day and tell them that I AM'. [This is his identification with the eternal divinity – as in John 8:58 – 'Before Abraham was born, I AM'.]

Vicki did not want to return, but Jesus sweetened the pill by telling her she needed to go back to have her children, something Vicki desperately wanted.

Before sending Vicki back, Jesus led her through her *visual* Life Review gently, starting with her birth. At last she could *see* all the meaningful people in her life!

Since her return, Vicki has had the joy of mothering three children of her own. She is still blind, but only physically.

Howard Storm[29] called out to Jesus to rescue him from the Prison section of Hades, at which point a brilliant light appeared, within which he saw Jesus. His description of him was almost ecstatic and zeroed in on his eternal qualities:

> He was King of Kings, Lord of Lords, Christ Jesus the Saviour. Jesus does love me, I thought. I experienced love in such intensity that nothing I had ever known before was comparable. His love was greater than all human love put together...
>
> He was indescribably wonderful: goodness, power, knowledge, and love. He was more loving than one can begin to imagine or describe.

Dr Gerard Landry[27] is an anaesthesiologist and Christian. He had a fairly typical interaction with Jesus during his NDE. Jesus greeted him using his nickname 'Gerry' and told him he must return, giving him the inspiring news that he would be out of hospital in a week [he was].

Jesus left Gerry with an unusual final exhortation: 'I want you to read the Gospel of John, the first two letters of John, and all of Revelation.'

'Lord,' I said, 'why do you want me to do this?'

He said, 'John is my friend. He knows all about *my love.*'

This is a good report to end with, because of Jesus' emphasis – that Gerry should return to Earth to learn more about love. As we have seen, this is the most commonly reported instruction given to NDErs, whether or not they are of any religious persuasion.

The Book of Revelation that Jesus wanted Dr Landry to read describes more than God's love; it gives fleeting glimpses of the future too, including visions of life in Heaven.

> After this I looked, and there before me was a great multitude that no one could count, from *every* nation, tribe, people and language, standing before the throne (Revelation 7:9).

Every tribe, people and language will be represented in Heaven! If the Bible is to be taken as meaning precisely that, then there must be an aspect of Judgement based on more than a conscious allegiance given to Jesus Christ as a personal saviour while on Earth, because many tribes and peoples passed into history without ever hearing about him. For example, great civilisations came and went in South America without ever hearing about Christ because the gospel only arrived in the 1500s – and the situation is similar for all of the continents. A selection process for

Heaven that explains thoroughly how God will accomplish this is probably beyond the scope of human religious analysis. I like the way the apologist Glenn Miller[30] describes this dilemma when considering biblical verses that promise a wide, international composition for Heaven's future population:

> So, whatever theory we come up with HAS TO ACCOUNT for a membership in heaven from every major group in history!
> Notice that although I may not be able to come up with an explanation as to HOW this occurs, at least God points out that the extent of His work is not as limited as the objections might contend.

And so, how will God judge people on Judgement Day? Thankfully, we can leave that to him, knowing that as a loving and fair but holy God his judgements will be just and appropriate. NDEs are an intermediate state right now, between our deaths and resurrection, and can tell us nothing about the Judgement Day to come.

Jesus' appearance to non-Christians in some NDEs, including to some who were trapped in the Prison section, and even to certain atheists, illustrates that he does not concern himself exclusively with Christians and Christianity; he is concerned with all people, just as he was when he walked on this planet. Most major religions recognise that Jesus on Earth was an inspired and holy person. Seeing that we live in an era of increasing availability of knowledge, it is time now for all people to read about Jesus and his teachings, and investigate his claims to be the saviour of the world.

Does that mean God is at work in this world for the benefit of all people? Of course. We are assured that after Jesus returned to Heaven, that God's spirit was poured out on *'all'* people' (Acts 2:17), denoting all persons on Earth. It is beyond the scope of this book to discuss this exciting fact further, excepting to note that the commonalities in NDEs indicate that God is involved, albeit to a greater or lesser extent, in *all* of our lives, regardless of our race, culture or creed.

Certainly one significant overall intention God has in returning NDErs to Earth is to learn to love and appreciate others, whatever their nationality or religion, and thereby to adopt a more global perspective. On a deeper level, we are all made in the image of God and each person alive carries some of that image regardless of religious beliefs. Therefore loving others brings God himself into clearer focus. John, the "apostle of love", expressed it like this, "whoever does not love their brother and sister, whom they have seen, cannot love God, whom they have not seen" (1John 4:20). By loving people we learn to perceive and to love God more deeply.

But that is not the end of the story. Christians are people who are putting their faith in Jesus Christ and thankfully have escaped the everlasting repercussions arising from their sinfulness at the final Judgement of mankind. How? By each one personally accepting Christ's substitutionary death on their behalf. Consequently, because their sins have been fully paid for, they can live in a personal relationship with God while still on Earth – and subsequently forevermore.

Does forgiveness automatically make Christians better than other people while on Earth? Of course not, although God's spirit is always trying to help us to be better than we were before conversion. Frankly, a loving Hindu, Buddhist, Jew, Sikh, Muslim or atheist may live a superior life and be a better person than a selfish Christian. Nevertheless, Christians do have access to something that other religions or philosophies seem to me to lack: which is an assurance regarding their salvation from the eternal consequences of their sins, and thereby an assurance too of an eternal future with God.

Christians believe this from many biblical teachings, for example they trust and depend on Jesus' promise in John 5:24:

> Very truly I tell you, whoever hears my word and believes him who sent me has eternal life and will not be judged, but has crossed over from death to life.

One thing I am convinced of from the Bible, and have seen consistently affirmed in my study of NDEs, is this: The death of our bodies on Earth is not the end of us!

Through Jesus, and after the final Judgement, certain people from every race and ethnic group on Earth will somehow populate Heaven. They will be enjoying that wonderful place, learning about God and each other, and enjoying one another's company.

God would love you to be there.

Website

Please visit my website. My web address is www.ivanrudolph.com

You will find there details of my next unique book which has the unusual title:

THE EVOLUTION OF CREATION

NEAR DEATH EXPERIENCES ENTER THE DEBATE!

Appendix
Statistics, Research and Support

I will begin by addressing the question, 'just how many people have had NDEs?' I begin here because this has been the question most asked of me, and happily happens to be one of the very few statistics regarding NDEs that I consider pretty reliable.

International NDE Frequencies

What proportions of the populations of different nations have had NDEs?

A well-respected Gallup poll[1] in the USA in 1982 indicated approximately 11.5 million adult Americans had had an NDE – about 5% of the total population at that time. The number of child NDEs was not sampled, but other researches indicate would be significant and raise the total well above 5%. This percentage is consistent with an examination of an elderly population (Olson[2] and Dulaney, 1993) and is also fairly consistent with Linzmeier[3], 2001, who arrived at an overall incidence rate of 7.5 percent with incidence being higher in those 55 or older – 'elderly people have been around longer and have had more chances to have an NDE'! Taking 5% as the lowest and most conservative figure for America, those statistics would translate to a minimum of 16 million adult Americans alive today having experienced an NDE.

Let us assume figures are a little lower across the rest of the world, on the basis that resuscitation techniques are not as well developed throughout. There may none-the-less be as many as 350 million NDErs alive today with many thousands of new NDEs being added daily. This figure for the world assumes 5% of the adult population have experienced an NDE, but research in Germany[4] in 2001 for example indicated perhaps only 4% of their adult population had had this experience: the statistics put out by the International Association for Near Death Studies (IANDS)[5] has 4% as their lowest margin (Germany), and up to 15% for some populations – so 5% is a conservative figure, especially when the NDEs of children are included.

I live in Australia and wondered how many NDErs might be in our population. I found that in 2005, Perera[6] conducted a telephone survey of a representative sample of the Australian population, as part of the Roy Morgan Catibus Survey, and concluded that 8.9% of the population had experienced an NDE, which indicates 2 million or so living Australians have had this experience. Little co-ordinated help or guidance is available for this significant number of Australian NDErs.

Some researchers have used the chi-square analysis on NDE accounts. They report without exception that the similarity in the accounts could not have happened as a result of chance, but are consistent phenomena. Individuals regardless of age, gender, race, religion or national origin have reported similar experiences during their NDEs.

Happily, statistics indicate that people are becoming less fearful of death. For example, Kenneth Ring[7] quotes a research that suggests that more than 80% of readers about NDEs who have not had one themselves, none-the-less have had their own fear of death diminished. This is most encouraging!

Even being exposed to many NDEs accounts can be influential. Raymond Moody[8], ever cautious and sceptical, admitted in his 2012 autobiography that he had found the evidence gathered over many years to be overwhelming, and that he was now "brazen" in voicing his conviction that both God and an afterlife exist.

Discussion of Some Statistics

I consider the Gallup Poll[1] as used in America to be a valid gathering of statistics, particularly as later researches in the USA and around the world published similar figures, although generally a little higher.

However, not all statistics in my opinion are as valid. The statistics and tables of information about NDEs often suffer from a fatal flaw – they take no account of the afterlife *venue* where the information is drawn from. Each venue has its own features, conditions, rules, laws, science and personnel, so comparisons and statistics should be taken within one venue – or at least specify which venues are being considered. Otherwise it is similar to relating statistics for road accidents in India, one venue, to rainfall affecting motoring in London, a second venue. The events are not interconnected; they are taking place at very different venues, as are aspects of NDEs that have often been lumped together.

It is also significant that researchers have not taken account of the different *stages* of the NDEs before making some comparisons, and so they are often comparing disparate situations. For example, during a pre-NDE hallucinations are common and what is reported should not be lumped together with other stages, especially given that the scientific method can investigate that one but not those beyond it. Each stage is best looked at separately.

Statistical Bias

In our discussion of the reliability of NDE statistics, issues of bias have to be addressed. Questions have been raised in this regard.

Cardiologist and resuscitation expert Dr Maurice Rawlings[9], now deceased, was troubled by what he considered to be unwarranted bias. He claimed to have offered details of unpleasant experiences in NDEs from his own case files to prominent researchers in this field. To his shock, they all rejected his offer. Rawlings assumed this was because his examples did not fit the patterns or conclusions already published – he mentioned critically Raymond Moody, Elizabeth Kubler-Ross, Kenneth Ring, Melvin Morse and other prominent writers by name, and was not sued for libel or defamation. If true, his contentions would suggest that the field of investigation has been curtailed by philosophy, whereas researchers should rather have been pursuing objective analysis of information.

Statistics for Unpleasant NDEs

What proportion of NDEs incorporate unpleasant experiences? At present, the estimates are very wobbly, in part because of bias, but also because of psychological factors within a person, by which traumatic events may be put into 'deep storage' in the subconscious mind to enable a returnee to resume normal life.

Consequently, depending on the approach taken, there are three broad groupings by which a search for statistics is done for this intriguing piece of information.

Group 1. Dr Maurice Rawlings[10], who would wait to speak to a reviving patient with notebook and pencil in hand to record what he was told, suggests up to 50% of NDErs have had unpleasant experiences. He notes:

> The truth remains that the negative reports are there (i.e. on the lips of the survivors), but the observer has to be on the scene to capture them before they are swept away into painless areas of the memory.

Other researchers support his high figures for unpleasant NDEs – for example Dr Charles Garfield[11] wrote: 'Almost as many of the dying patients interviewed reported negative visions (demons and so forth), as reported blissful experiences.'

Group 2. Other very good researchers in the past, including Barbara Rommer[12] and PMH Atwater[13], suggest much lower figures for unpleasant NDEs – Rommer around 19% of 300 interviewees and Atwater 15% of an even greater number of NDErs. Atwater had the lowest percentage, but had to depend on later interviews than those conducted by the physicians Rawlings, Garfield and Rommer. By the time she interviewed patients, perhaps the psychological suppression of unpleasant memories may have come more prominently into play.

Both Rommer and Atwater depended on interviews, but interviewees can avoid owning up to an unpleasant NDE. Researcher Nancy Bush[14] comments that 'People who have had a terrible NDE are notoriously reluctant to talk. In my own experience, they make contact but do not answer call backs; they cancel appointments; they disappear.'

This reluctance to talk can stem from a variety of reasons:

- Hoping the distressing experience will just go away, or fade like a bad dream, if not spoken about.
- Wanting to avoid the anguish that occurs when they talk about the experience.
- Feeling ashamed for having had an upsetting experience when so many other people have reported pleasurable experiences. They feel that having had an unpleasant NDE might reflect badly on their character.
- Being afraid that others will judge them as drug addicts, delusional or crazy.

- Family pressure – not to let the world know that the NDEr may have lived a life unacceptable to God.
- Fear of being ostracised.

Fear of being ostracised applied also to researchers who reported unpleasant NDEs, because the popular assumption at the time when most of this researching was done was that almost all NDEs were pleasant ones; thus researchers concentrated on these and ignored the unpleasant ones. In fact their line of questioning was designed to be cheerful and upbeat to the extent that it was unlikely to elicit disturbing testimony. The prestigious Bruce Greyson[15] admits that in those early studies, 'We didn't try to find them because we didn't want to know.'

PMH Atwater[16] was different, and was prepared to consider unpleasant NDEs. In 1989 she was running late for a flight when the following exchange took place:

> I had to run lengthy corridors at Dulles International Airport near Washington, D.C., to catch my next flight. As I ran, another woman scurrying in the opposite direction yelled, 'I know who you are; you're the woman I just saw on television. You're the gutsy one who talks about unpleasant near-death experiences. Keep doing it. Don't stop.'
>
> I was so startled by her comment, I momentarily slowed my pace and yelled back, 'Who are you? What do you mean by that?'
>
> Her answer surprised me. 'I'm a surgical nurse at a hospital in Phoenix, Arizona. We have lots of near-death cases there, and almost all of them are the unpleasant kind. You know what I mean – people who wind up in Hell!'
>
> Before I could respond further, she was out of sight.

At this point, Atwater had already found that 105 out of around 700 interviewees had described 'hellish' NDEs.

Group 3. Other NDE studies, done a while after the experience and more biased in their selection of accounts for analysis, suggest unpleasant NDEs to be as low as 1%, which would imply only 160000 or so Americans have had them. But for anyone who has one, the percentage is irrelevant – he or she has to deal with an unexpected and traumatic event.

50%? 18%? 1% or even less? This statistical variation is ridiculous and ought to be addressed. Let's look into the very low figures a little more deeply.

In 1982, Raymond Moody and Kenneth Ring[17], both pioneering researchers in the field, analysed several thousand NDEs and came up with only 0.3% of NDErs having 'hellish' experiences. However, both men leant towards *positive* paranormal explanations and this may have influenced their selection of data. For example, Nancy Evans Bush[18] was office manager of IANDS when it began in 1982 and Ring was President. It was soon flooded with visitors with pleasant stories. She noticed that reports of unpleasant NDEs became lost in the heady enthusiasm that reigned at IANDS. Having had an unpleasant NDE herself years earlier, she was alert to these reports. When she later became the President of IANDS and checked back through their earlier records of NDEs, Nancy quickly identified around 50 unpleasant NDEs that Ring had failed either to see during the giddy times, or had failed to report on when gathering his statistics. Whatever the reason, we can no longer give Ring's statistics regarding unpleasant NDEs any credibility – although the value of his overall research and his individual description of particular NDEs remains unchallenged.

Nancy Bush is now President Emerita of IANDS and retired, having written extensively about unpleasant NDEs to help desperate returnees who have had these. Some credit her with saving their lives from despair.

So what is the truth regarding the frequency of unpleasant NDEs? We don't know. Data collection methods must first improve, and a more reliable comprehensive sample base must be developed. I presume it will lie between 20% and 50%. Even if the figure is as low as 20%, more than 3 million living Americans will have had an unpleasant NDE and need support and guidance right now – not tomorrow – but right now.

And what about those who have died and not revived, who comprise the majority of people throughout history? Many of them, I suppose, will today be enjoying the garden idyll of Paradise, a supposition based on NDE reports of meeting many ancestors there, while others will be languishing in the Prison section; both groups awaiting the final Judgement.

Medical Investigations.

Around the world, the medical profession has taken an interest in NDEs and has begun conducting innovative research.

His interest piqued by NDE reports, Pim van Lommel[19] gathered a team in Holland to do an extensive study. 344 patients in a clinical setting who had been resuscitated, from 26 years to 92 years old, were interviewed shortly after resuscitation, then two years and subsequently eight years later. 62 patients (18%) reported NDEs, of whom 41 (12%) described a deep core experience that included features such as going through a tunnel, speaking with dead relatives and friends, and experiencing a bright light. It appeared that the experiences were unrelated to processes in the dying brain. In addition, most patients had excellent recall of the events, which undermines the theory that the memories were false. Furthermore, the NDErs reported marked changes in their personalities and lifestyles – having become more compassionate, loving and giving when compared with those patients who survived cardiac arrest without NDEs. They had in addition lost their fear of death.

Research on the Blind

Ring[20] and Cooper studied 31 blind people, many of whom reported vision during their NDEs. 21 of these people had had an NDE while the remaining 10 had had an OBE, but with no continuing NDE. It was found that in the NDE sample, 14 had been blind from birth. 9 of these 14 born blind reported visual sensations during their experiences!

Support For NDErs

At present, it is perhaps safest to disregard most statistics published regarding NDEs.

However, all NDErs still need a deep understanding of their experience and what their future holds. They also require loving help and guidance, which can perhaps be given best by fellow returnees in a support group situation. There is a need for sensitive debriefing in these support groups. Beverly Brodsky[21], a Jewish lady who has run IANDS support groups for fifteen years following her own NDE, advises that such groups should be 'loving and open' and 'empower people to own their own stories'. Her approach is essential in all attempts to debrief NDErs, whether on an individual level or in a group situation.

Even though no two NDEs are identical, just as no two lives lived on Earth have ever been identical, none-the-less there are sufficient similar elements between returnees that genuine friendship and fellowship can be built around their commonalities. Raymond Moody[22] wrote, 'What has amazed me since the beginning of my interest are the great similarities in the reports, despite the fact that they come from people of highly varied religious, social and educational backgrounds'.

This fundamental similarity is a reason why support groups for NDErs can be effective.

Group therapy can be helpful, but runs the risk of the leadership or strong individuals within the group driving it along their own religious or philosophical direction – which excludes some of those who attend. All group leaders would do well to read Atwater's[23] description of Robert Stefani's approach, which she personally found to be effective. Both she and Stefani are NDErs. Just as alcoholics may relate better with other alcoholics, because of mutual understanding, for example in Alcoholics Anonymous groups, NDE support groups can be especially helpful if conducted well by encouraging NDErs to openly discuss their experiences. Unfortunately, an inadequate number are operating compared to the need for them.

However, returnees should keep aware that support group leaders and participants have no consistent explanation for NDE experiences, and the variety of suggestions on offer should be held lightly as returnees make their own adjustments.

Finally, to repeat a suggestion to returnees made earlier – please never allow any counsellor, book or opinion, mine included, to confuse what you learnt during your NDE. God designed it personally for you, so ponder its lessons and meaning, holding it safe and close to your heart.

Acknowledgements

My magnificent wife Brenda continues to be my primary support. She is my editor, proof reader and harshest critic, and keeps my writing centred. Her suggestions and input into the text are invaluable.

Accounts of NDES abound, but the search for explanations of NDEs is both confused and confusing. Before publishing in such a difficult area, I decided to send out my original text to a number of friends to criticise it and offer further suggestions. Their input has been highly valued and appreciated. Theological input in particular was checked thoroughly by Father John D'Alton, Pastor Vic Onions and Doug Murray. Jenny Bishop helped with the theology and with modernising some of the text. My daughter Tamlyn slaughtered my initial bad attempt at an Author's Introduction and other aspects of my communication, and the final version is much to her credit. An old friend and atheist, Geoff Hughes, pointed out important weaknesses, and I commend him for being able to do so in a book overtly Christian. Another old friend, Paul Cruice, helped with precise editing and penetrating advice. Many other friends and family members have shown interest during my years of writing this book, and provided helpful bits of information on the subject.

Two well-known American NDErs with whom I have talked, Captain Dale Black and Angie Fenimore, added their important perspectives from the point of view of having 'been there, done that'. In difficult areas, it is so important to be able to discuss the text with those who have had personal experience.

Besides Brenda, the most thorough analysis was by a friend Dr Lyn D'Alton – a multi-skilled lady knowledgeable in medicine, psychology, counselling and Christian mission work. Thank you, Lyn.

If the book helps anyone, which is the purpose for which it has been written, it is due in no small part to all those mentioned above. This has been a team effort!

My heartfelt thanks to you all.

Endnotes

Chapter 1 – Surviving a Near-Death Experience (NDE)

1. Captain Dale Black and Ken Gire (2010), *Flight to Heaven*, Bethany House Publishers, division of Baker Publishing Group, used by permission.
2. George Gallup (1982), *Adventures in Immortality: A Look Beyond the Threshold of Death*.
3. Dr Pim van Lommel et al, Dec 15th 2001 edition of *Lancet*.
4. Dr Raymond Moody (1975), *Life after Life*.
5. Dr Mary Neal MD (2011), *To Heaven and Back*.
6. Dr Cherie Sutherland (1992), *Transformed By The Light*.
7. *I Survived – Beyond and Back* TV series on Bio channel. Usually, only first names are used to identify interviewees.
8. Todd Burpo (2010), *Heaven Is For Real*.
9. PMH Atwater (1994), *Beyond the Light*.
10. Professor Bruce Greyson (2007), *Consistency of Near-Death Experience Accounts Over Two Decades*.
11. Dr Pim van Lommel (2011), *Consciousness Beyond Life*.
12. Dr Pim van Lommel in Advances in Experimental Medicine and Biology (2004), *About the Continuity of Our Consciousness*.
13. Emmanuel Swedenborg (1758) (English translation by John C Ager 1900), *The Teachings of Emanuel Swedenborg, Volume 1*.
14. Professor Bruce Greyson (2000), *Near Death Experiences*.
15. J. Steve Miller (2013), *Near-Death Experiences*.
16. Howard Storm (2005), *My Descent Into Death*.
17. Cardiologist Dr Michael Sabom (1998), *Light and Death*.
18. Dr Michael Sabom (1981), *Recollections of Death*.
19. Discussed by Dr Peter Fenwick (2012), during interview with Michael E Tymn, ASCS website.
20. Dr Kenneth Ring (1985), *Heading Towards Omega*.
21. Professor Bruce Grayson (2010), *Science And The Near-Death Experience*.
22. Dr Kenneth Ring (1999), *Mindsight: Near Death and Out-of-Body Experiences in the Blind*.

Chapter 2 – What Happens at Death

1. Howard Storm (2005), *My Descent Into Death*.
2. Dr Mary Neal MD (2011), *To Heaven and Back*.

3   Dr Duncan MacDougall (1901), reported in peer-reviewed *American Medicine*.
4   Irenaeus (circa AD 177 – 200), *Against Heresies* and *The Demonstration of the Apostolic Preaching*.
5   Dr Kenneth Ring (1999), *Mindsight: Near Death and Out-of-Body Experiences in the Blind*.
6   *I Survived – Beyond and Back* TV series on Bio channel.
    Usually, only first names are used to identify interviewees.
7   Dr Maurice Rawlings MD (1978), *Beyond Death's Door*.
8   Dr William Serdahely (2007), *Full Rebuttal to Keith Augustine's Attack on NDEs* – IANDS Journal of Near Death Studies Vol 26.
9   J. Steve Miller (2013), *Near-Death Experiences*.
10 Bruce Greyson, Editor of the *Journal of Near-Death Studies* (2007), article titled, *Commentary on "Psychophysioloical and Cultural Correlates Undermining a Survivalist Interpretation of Near-Death Experiences"*.
11 Dr Michael Marsh (Nov 2011) in Christianity Magazine, *Light After Death?*
12 Dr Sam Parnia interviewed March 2013 by New Scientist magazine.
13 Dr Sam Parnia (2014), in journal *Resuscitation*.

Chapter 3 – Pre-NDEs

1   Dr Raymond Moody (1975), *Life after Life*.
2   Dr Maurice Rawlings MD (1978), *Beyond Death's Door*.
3   Dr Melvin Morse (1994), *Parting Visions*.
4   Dr Fred Schoonmaker (*1996*), *An Introductory Analysis of the NDE – Two Worlds*.
5   J. Steve Miller (2013), *Near-Death Experiences*.
6   Dr Jeffrey Long (2010), *Evidence of the Afterlife*.
7   Dr Diane Komp (1992), *A Window To Heaven* and Elizabeth Stalcup (2010), *Finding Faith in a Cancer Ward*.
8   *I Survived – Beyond and Back* TV series on Bio channel.
    Usually, only first names are used to identify interviewees.
9   Celestial Travellers website. First names only are often used to identify interviewees.
10 Kevin Williams (2002), *Nothing Better Than Death*.
11 John Myers (1968), *Voices From the Edge of Eternity*.
12 Dr Penny Sartori (2008), *The Near-Death Experiences of Hospitalized Intensive Care Patients: A Five-Year Clinical Study*.

Chapter 4 – Blast-Off! The NDE Begins

1. Dr Richard Kent (2000), Richard Wright features as one of twenty-seven accounts in *Beyond the Final Frontier.*
2. Dr Richard Kent (2000), the amazing life and NDE of the missionary Rev. Royston Fraser features as one of twenty-seven accounts in *Beyond the Final Frontier.*
3. Douglas Connelly (1995), *After Life.*
4. Dr Mary Neal MD (2011), *To Heaven and Back.*
5. Mike Perry (2010), *67 Not Out website March 2010.*
6. Near Death Experience Research Foundation (NDERF), *PJ's NDE*
7. Dr Richard Kent (2000), Darrel Young features as one of twenty-seven accounts in *Beyond the Final Frontier.*
8. *I Survived – Beyond and Back* TV series on Bio channel. Usually, only first names are used to identify interviewees.
9. PMH Atwater (2010), *I Died Three Times in 1976 – The Complete Story.*
10. Dr Richard Kent (1997), *The Final Frontier* – available as a book or a movie.
11. Wikipedia (2015), *Waterboarding.*
12. M.J. Cooper (2011) in PubMed, *Near-death experience and out of body phenomenon during torture – a case report.*
13. PMH Atwater (1999), *Children of the New Millennium.*
14. Celestial Travellers website. First names only are often used to identify interviewees.
15. Dr Cherie Sutherland (1992), *Transformed By The Light.*
16. RaNelle Wallace (1994), *The Burning Within.*
17. Crystal McVea and Alex Tresnlowski (2013), Howard Books of Simon and Schuster, by permission, *Waking Up in Heaven.*
18. Dr Raymond Moody (1975), *Life after Life.*
19. Dr Richard Kent (2015), *What is it Really Like to Die, and What Happens Next?*
20. Dr A S Wiltse (1889) in the *Saint Louis Medical and Surgical Journal*
21. PMH Atwater (1994), *Beyond the Light*
22. Janice Miner Holden, editor (2009), *The Handbook of Near-Death Experiences.*
23. Dr George C, Ritchie with Elizabeth Sherrill (1978), *Return From Tomorrow,* a division of Baker Publishing Group, used by permission.
24. Dr Jeffrey Long (2010), *Evidence of the Afterlife.*
25. Captain Dale Black and Ken Gire (2010), *Flight to Heaven,* Bethany House Publishers, division of Baker Publishing Group, used by permission.

Chapter 5 – Entering the Spirit World

1. PMH Atwater's website/blogspot (2014), *Q & A with PMH Atwater*.
2. Dr Mary Neal MD (2011), *To Heaven and Back*.
3. Crystal McVea and Alex Tresnlowski (2013), Howard Books of Simon and Schuster, by permission, *Waking Up in Heaven*.
4. RaNelle Wallace (1994), *The Burning Within*.
5. Dr Peter Fenwick and Elizabeth Fenwick (1997), *The Truth in the Light*.
6. Near Death Experience Research Foundation (NDERF), *Gary R's NDE*.
7. Celestial Travellers website.
8. Dr Raymond Moody (1975), *Life after Life*.
9. Dr Maurice Rawlings MD (1978), *Beyond Death's Door*.
10. *I Survived – Beyond and Back* TV series on Bio channel. Usually, only first names are used to identify interviewees.
11. Captain Dale Black and Ken Gire (2010), *Flight to Heaven*, Bethany House Publishers, division of Baker Publishing Group, used by permission.

Chapter 6 – Paradise and God

1. Don Piper (2004), *90 Minutes in Heaven*.
2. RaNelle Wallace (1994), *The Burning Within*.
3. Dr Richard Kent (1997), Jim Sepulveda features as one of twenty-seven accounts in *The Final Frontier*.
4. Captain Dale Black and Ken Gire (2010), *Flight to Heaven*, Bethany House Publishers, division of Baker Publishing Group, used by permission.
5. Crystal McVea and Alex Tresnlowski (2013), Howard Books of Simon and Schuster, by permission, *Waking Up in Heaven*.
6. Dr Mary Neal MD (2011), *To Heaven and Back*.
7. *I Survived – Beyond and Back* TV series on Bio channel. Usually, only first names are used to identify interviewees.
8. Dr Richard Kent (1997), *The Final Frontier*.
9. Dr Maurice Rawlings MD (1978), *Beyond Death's Door*.
10. Mike Perry (2010), *67 Not Out website March 2010*.
11. Dr Richard Kent (1997), Jim Sepulveda features as one of twenty-seven accounts in *The Final Frontier*.
12. Dr George C, Ritchie with Elizabeth Sherrill (1978), *Return From Tomorrow*, a division of Baker Publishing Group, used by permission.
13. Robert Thompson (1985), *Bill W*.
14. Ian McCormack with Jenny Sharkey (2010), *A Glimpse of Eternity*.
15. Dean Braxton (2014), *In Heaven*.
16. Howard Storm (Nov 2011) in Christianity Magazine, *Light After Death?*

100 John Ankerberg and John Weldon (2011), *The Facts On Near-Death Experiences.*

Chapter 7 – The Life Review

1. Dr Richard Kent (2000), Susan Finlay features as one of twenty-seven accounts in *Beyond the Final Frontier.*
2. Grace Bubulka (1994), *Beyond This Reality.*
3. Dr George C, Ritchie with Elizabeth Sherrill (1978), *Return From Tomorrow,* a division of Baker Publishing Group, used by permission.
4. RaNelle Wallace (1994), *The Burning Within.*
5. Near Death Experience Research Foundation (NDERF), *Mary Beth Willi's 1994 NDE.*
6. PMH Atwater (2010), *I Died Three Times in 1976 – The Complete Story.*
7. Dr George Ritchie, *Guideposts Magazine article of April 1963.*
8. *I Survived – Beyond and Back* TV series on Bio channel.
   Usually, only first names are used to identify interviewees.
9. Dr Raymond Moody (1975), *Life after Life.*
10. Celestial Travellers website. First names only are often used to identify interviewees.
11. Dr Peter Fenwick and Elizabeth Fenwick (1997), *The Truth in the Light.*
12. Dr Pim van Lommel et al, Dec 15th 2001 edition of *Lancet.*
13. Dr Kenneth Ring in interview with Jeffery Mishlove (2013), reported on *NHNE website.*
14. Howard Storm (2005), *My Descent Into Death.*
15. Dr Maurice Rawlings MD (1978), *Beyond Death's Door.*

Chapter 8 – Incidents and People in Paradise

1. *I Survived – Beyond and Back* TV series on Bio channel.
   Usually, only first names are used to identify interviewees.
2. Dr Maurice Rawlings MD (1978), *Beyond Death's Door.*
3. RaNelle Wallace (1994), *The Burning Within*
4. Don Piper (2004), *90 Minutes in Heaven.*
5. Dr Raymond Moody (1975), *Life after Life.*
6. Captain Dale Black and Ken Gire (2010), *Flight to Heaven,* Bethany House Publishers, division of Baker Publishing Group, used by permission.
7. Celestial Travellers website. First names only are often used to identify interviewees.
8. Al Gibson, author with Dr Des Sinclair (2009), *Life on the Line.*
9. Dr Petti Wagner (1984), *Murdered Heiress.*

[10] Dr Richard Kent (2000), Daniel Ekechukwu features as one of twenty-seven accounts in *Beyond the Final Frontier.*
[11] Investigation by Berean Publishers (2015*), Concerning the Resurrection of Daniel Ekechukwu.*
[12] Crystal McVea and Alex Tresnlowski (2013), Howard Books of Simon and Schuster, by permission, *Waking Up in Heaven.*
[13] Kevin Williams (2014), *Near Death Experiences and the Afterlife.*
[14] Todd Burpo (2010), *Heaven Is For Real.*
[15] Mike Perry (2010), *67 Not Out website March 2010.*
[16] Dr A S Wiltse (1889) in the *Saint Louis Medical and Surgical Journal.*

Chapter 9 – The Void

[1] PMH Atwater (2010), *I Died Three Times in 1976 – The Complete Story.*
[2] Emmanuel Swedenborg (1758) (English translation by John C Ager 1900), *The Teachings of Emanuel Swedenborg, Volume 1.*
[3] Phillip Berman (1998), *The Journey Home.*
[4] David A Smith (2014), *Insights of God.*
[5] Life After Death (2015), *BJ McKelvie's NDE In Hell After He Commits Suicide.*
[6] Howard Storm (2005), *My Descent Into Death.*
[7] Reverend Howard Pittman (1999), *Placebo.*
[8] Kevin Williams (2014), *The Void and the Near Death Experience.*
[9] Dr George C, Ritchie with Elizabeth Sherrill (1978), *Return From Tomorrow.*

Chapter 10 – Other Prison Sections of Hades

[1] Bryan Melvin (2005), *A Land Unknown: Hell's Dominion.*
[2] Dr Richard Kent (2000), Rita Chuter features as one of twenty-seven accounts in *Beyond the Final Frontier.*
[3] Reverend Kenneth Hagin (1972), *I Believe In Visions.*
[4] Dr Penny Sartori (Nov 2011) in Christianity Magazine, *Light After Death?*
[5] *I Survived – Beyond and Back* TV series on Bio channel.
Usually, only first names are used to identify interviewees.
[6] Jean-Baptiste Delacour (1973), *Glimpses of the Beyond.*
[7] Bill Wiese (2006), *23 Minutes in Hell.*
[8] Robert Thompson Perry on NDERF website (2015), *One Soldier's NDE.*
[9] Dr Raymond Moody (2011), *The Light Beyond.*
[10] Dr Maurice Rawlings MD (1978), *Beyond Death's Door.*
[11] Dr George C, Ritchie with Elizabeth Sherrill (1978), *Return From Tomorrow,* a division of Baker Publishing Group, used by permission.
[12] Howard Storm (2005), *My Descent Into Death.*

13 Dr Richard Kent (1997), *The Final Frontier* – available as a book or a movie.
14 Reverend Timothy LaFond (2000), *From Hell to the Glory of God*.
15 Reverend Howard Pittman (1999), *Placebo*.
16 Dr Elizabeth Hillstrom (1995), *Testing the Spirits*.
17 PMH Atwater (1992) in Journal of Near Death Studies vol 10, *Is There a Hell?*
18 Dr Margot Grey (1985), *Return From Death*.
19 Dr Maurice Rawlings (1993), *To Hell and Back*
20 Ian McCormack with Jenny Sharkey (2010), *A Glimpse of Eternity*.
21 PMH Atwater (1992) in Journal of Near Death Studies vol 10, *Is There a Hell?*
22 Dr Barbara Rommer (2000), *Blessing in Disguise*.
23 Nancy Bush (2002) in Journal of Near-Death Studies 21, Afterward: *Making Meaning After a Frightening Near Death Experience*.
24 Dr Michael Sabom, quoted from a TV program, I think titled, Life and Death.

Chapter 11 – Suicides: A Special Case?

1 Angie Fenimore (1996), *Beyond the Darkness*.
2 SAVE website (2015), *Suicide Facts*.
3 Befrienders Worldwide website (2015), *Suicide Statistics*.
4 Dr Maurice Rawlings MD (1978), *Beyond Death's Door*.
5 Thomas Aquinas and Fathers of the English Dominican Provinc (1981), *The Summa Theologica of St Thomas Aquinas*.
6 PMH Atwater (1994), *Beyond the Light*.
7 Tertullian (197 AD), *Apologeticus*.
8 Dr Raymond Moody (1978), *Reflections on Life after Life*.
9 Deborah Weiler (2007), *Dead is Just a Four Letter Word*.
10 Dr Richard Kent (1997), Henrietta features as one of twenty-seven accounts in *The Final Frontier*.
11 Dr Pim van Lommel in Advances in Experimental Medicine and Biology (2004), *About the Continuity of Our Consciousness*.
12 Dr George C, Ritchie with Elizabeth Sherrill (1978), *Return From Tomorrow*, a division of Baker Publishing Group, used by permission.
13 Tamara Laroux (2006), *Delivered*.
14 Annabel Chaplin (1977), *The Bright Light of Death*.
15 David Rosen in Psychology Today (September 2011), *The Jumpers*.

Chapter 12 – Tours: Heaven, Hell and the Cosmos

1 Todd Burpo (2010), *Heaven Is For Real*.

2. Captain Dale Black and Ken Gire (2010), *Flight to Heaven*, Bethany House Publishers, division of Baker Publishing Group, used by permission.
3. Dr Richard Kent (2000), Simon Mackrell features as one of twenty-seven accounts in *Beyond the Final Frontier*.
4. Dr Maurice Rawlings MD (1978), *Beyond Death's Door*.
5. Dr Maurice Rawlings (1993), *To Hell and Back*.
6. Dr George C, Ritchie with Elizabeth Sherrill (1978), *Return From Tomorrow*, a division of Baker Publishing Group, used by permission.
7. Don Piper (2004), *90 Minutes in Heaven*.
8. Dr Raymond Moody (2011), *The Light Beyond*.
9. PMH Atwater (1999), *Children of the New Millennium*.
10. Jim Hagerty, reporter for the Examiner (July 24, 2014), *Man Recalls Dying Three Times, Going To Heaven*.
11. Kevin Williams, newsletter *Near Death Experiences and the Afterlife (July 1 2005)*.
12. PMH Atwater, in Journal of Transpersonal Research (2012 vol.4), *Straight Talk About the Near Death Phenomenon*.
13. Richard Bonefant (2001), in Journal of Near Death Studies, *A Child's Encounter with the Devil*.
14. Bill Wiese (2006), *23 Minutes in Hell*.
15. PMH Atwater (1992) in Journal of Near Death Studies vol 10, *Is There a Hell?*
16. Thomas Welch (1924), *Oregon's Amazing Miracle* (available in full on the Internet).
17. Geo Godkin, The Main Issue magazine, Issue 4, *Heaven and Hell*.

Chapter 13 – The Return and Soon After

1. *I Survived – Beyond and Back* TV series on Bio channel. Usually, only first names are used to identify interviewees.
2. Dr George C, Ritchie with Elizabeth Sherrill (1978), *Return From Tomorrow*, a division of Baker Publishing Group, used by permission, and *Guideposts Magazine* article of April 1963.
3. Crystal McVea and Alex Tresnlowski (2013), Howard Books of Simon and Schuster, by permission, *Waking Up in Heaven*.
4. Dr Cherie Sutherland (1992), *Transformed By The Light*.
5. Raewyn Moore, private correspondence.
6. Ian McCormack with Jenny Sharkey (2010), *A Glimpse of Eternity*.
7. Dr Raymond Moody (1975), *Life after Life*.
8. Todd Burpo (2010), *Heaven Is For Real*.
9. Mike Perry (2010), *67 Not Out website March 2010*.

10. Celestial Travellers website. First names only are often used to identify interviewees.
11. Near Death Experience Research Foundation (NDERF), *PJ's NDE*.
12. Carol Zaleski (1988), *Other World Journeys*.
13. PMH Atwater (2010), *I Died Three Times in 1976 – The Complete Story*.
14. Mickey Robinson (2003), *Falling to Heaven*.
15. John Ankerberg and John Weldon (2011), *The Facts On Near-Death Experiences*.
16. Dr Mary Neal MD (2011), *To Heaven and Back*.
17. Professor Gabbard and Twemlow (1985), *With the Eyes of the Mind, An Empirical Analysis of Out-of-Body States*.
18. Janice Miner Holden, editor (2009), *The Handbook of Near-Death Experiences*
19. Don Piper (2004), *90 Minutes in Heaven*.
20. PMH Atwater (1998), *Back From The Light*.
21. Personal correspondence with Dr Lyn D'Alton, who resides in Melbourne, Australia.
22. Dr Kenneth Ring (2000), *Lessons From The Light*.
23. PMH Atwater's website/blogspot (2014), *Q & A with PMH Atwater*.
24. PMH Atwater (2008), *Near Death States: The Pattern of After-effects*.
25. Dr Peter Fenwick and Elizabeth Fenwick (1997), *The Truth in the Light*.
26. PMH Atwater (1988), *Coming Back To Life*.
27. Dr Raymond Moody (2011), *The Light Beyond*.

Chapter 14 – Succeeding as a Returnee

1. Dr Raymond Moody (1975), *Life after Life*.
2. Dr Maurice Rawlings MD (1978), *Beyond Death's Door*.
3. *I Survived – Beyond and Back* TV series on Bio channel. Usually, only first names are used to identify interviewees.
4. Crystal McVea and Alex Tresnlowski (2013), Howard Books of Simon and Schuster, by permission, *Waking Up in Heaven*.
5. Celestial Travellers website. First names only are often used to identify interviewees.
6. Howard Storm (2005), *My Descent Into Death*.
7. J Isamu Yamamoto (1992), *Christian Research Journal Spring 1992*.
8. Near Death Experience Research Foundation (NDERF), *Mary Jo R NDE*.
9. RaNelle Wallace (1994), *The Burning Within*.
10. Near Death Experience Research Foundation (NDERF), *Mary Beth Willi's 1994 NDE*.
11. Dr George C, Ritchie with Elizabeth Sherrill (1978), *Return From Tomorrow*, a division of Baker Publishing Group, used by permission.

12   Dr Raymond Moody (1978) writing in the Foreword of George Ritchie's book, *Return From Tomorrow.*

Chapter 15 – The Global NDE

1. Celestial Travellers website. First names only are often used to identify interviewees.
2. International Association for Near Death Studies (IANDS) 2011, *Key Facts About Near Death Experiences.*
3. J. Steve Miller (2013), *Near-Death Experiences.*
4. Dr David San Filippo (2012), *Religious Interpretations of NDEs.*
5. Janice Miner Holden, Editor (2009), *The Handbook of Near-Death Experiences.*
6. PMH Atwater's website/blogspot (2014), *Q & A with PMH Atwater.*
7. Near Death Experience Research Foundation (NDERF), *Padma's 2005 NDE.*
8. Mahesh Chavda (2006), *Other Food.*
9. Susan Onizuka, NHNE Near Death Experience Network.
10. Near Death Experience Research Foundation (NDERF), *Shibani NDE.*
11. Near Death Experience Research Foundation (NDERF), *Wan I NDE.*
12. Near Death Experience Research Foundation (NDERF), *Khadija H NDE.*
13. Near Death Experience Research Foundation (NDERF), *Sameer NDE.*
14. Near Death Experience Research Foundation (NDERF), *Muhammad F NDE.*
15. Nasir Siddiki (2011) on YouTube and video presentations on Sid Roth webpage.
16. Jack O'Sullivan (2001), *The Guardian Tuesday 9 October 2001.*
17. John Esposito and Ibrahim Kalin (2009), *The 500 Most Influential Muslims.*
18. Dr Kenneth Ring (2000), *Lessons From The Light.*
19. Kevin Williams (2002), *Nothing Better Than Death.*
20. Barbara Harris Whitfield (1995), *Spiritual Awakenings.*
21. David Sunfellow (2011) on his NHNE website, *Jesus and Near Death Experiences.*
22. NDERF (2015) on their home page, *About Us.*
23. PMH Atwater's website/blogspot (September 2007), *Q & A with PMH Atwater.*
24. Dr Mary Neal MD (2011), *To Heaven and Back.*
25. Kevin Williams (2014), *Near Death Experiences and the Afterlife.*
26. PMH Atwater (1999), *Children of the New Millennium.*
27. Rita Bennett (1997), *To Heaven and Back.*

[28] Dr Kenneth Ring (1999), *Mindsight: Near Death and Out-of-Body Experiences in the Blind.*
[29] Howard Storm (2005), *My Descent Into Death.*
[30] Glenn Miller at the Christian Thinktank website (2014), *What About Those Who Have Never Heard The Gospel?*

Appendix

[1] George Gallup (1982), *Adventures in Immortality: A Look Beyond the Threshold of Death.*
[2] M. Olson and P. Dulaney (1993), Pub Med Dec; 11(4).
[3] Benjamin Linzmeier (2001) on NDERF website, *Attitudes Towards Near Death Experiences.*
[4] H Knoblauch (2001) in Journal of Near Death Studies no.20, *A Report on a Survey of Near-Death Experiences in Germany.*
[5] IANDS website (2015), *Key Facts About Near Death Experiences.*
[6] M Perera (2005) in Journal of Near Death Studies no.24, *Prevalence of Near-Death Experiences in Australia.*
[7] Dr Kenneth Ring (2000), *Lessons From The Light.*
[8] Dr Raymond Moody (2012), *Paranormal, My Life In Pursuit of the Afterlife.*
[9] Dr Maurice Rawlings (1993), *To Hell and Back.*
[10] Dr Maurice Rawlings MD (1978), *Beyond Death's Door.*
[11] Ron Rhodes (2013), *The Big Book of Bible Answers.*
[12] Dr Barbara Rommer (2000), *Blessing in Disguise.*
[13] PMH Atwater (1994), *Beyond the Light.*
[14] Janice Miner Holden, editor (2009), *The Handbook of Near-Death Experiences.*
[15] Professor Bruce Greyson (1992), *Spring '92 Journal of Near-Death Studies Vol.10, No.3*
[16] PMH Atwater (1992) in Journal of Near Death Studies vol 10, *Is There a Hell?*
[17] Raymond Moody and Kenneth Ring (1982), *Evergreen Study.*
[18] Nancy Evans Bush (2014), *Dancing Past the Dark.*
[19] Dr Pim van Lommel et al, Dec 15th 2001 edition of *Lancet.*
[20] Dr Kenneth Ring (1999), *Mindsight: Near Death and Out-of-Body Experiences in the Blind.*
[21] Dr Kenneth Ring (2000), *Lessons From The Light.*
[22] Dr Raymond Moody (1975), *Life after Life.*
[23] PMH Atwater (2008), *Near Death States: The Pattern of Aftereffects.* Website

Website

Please visit my website. My web address is www.ivanrudolph.com

You will find there details of my next unique book which has the unusual title:

THE EVOLUTION

OF

CREATION

NEAR DEATH EXPERIENCES
ENTER THE DEBATE!

Made in the USA
San Bernardino, CA
22 May 2016